An Insider's Guide to Managing Sporting Events

Jerry Solomon
President and CEO, StarGames

Human Kinetics

Library of Congress Cataloging-in-Publication Data

Solomon, Jerry, 1954-
    An insider's guide to managing sporting events / Jerry Solomon.
      p. cm.
    Includes index.
    ISBN 0-7360-3108-1
    1. Sports administration.   I. Title.
    GV713 .S63 2001
    796'.06'9--dc21
                                              2001039261

ISBN-10: 0-7360-3108-1
ISBN-13: 978-0-7360-3108-0

Acquisitions Editor: Linda Anne Bump, PhD, and Amy N. Pickering
Developmental Editor: Joanna Hatzopoulos
Assistant Editor: Derek Campbell
Copyeditor: Patsy Fortney
Proofreader: Erin Cler
Indexer: Sharon Duffy
Permission Manager: Dalene Reeder
Graphic Designer: Fred Starbird
Graphic Artist: Kathleen Boudreau-Fuoss
Photo Manager: Les Woodrum
Cover Designer: Jack W. Davis
Photographer (cover): Tom Roberts
Photographer (interior): Les Woodrum
Art Managers: Craig Newsom and Carl Johnson
Illustrators: Kathleen Boudreau-Fuoss and Craig Newsom
Printer: Versa Press

Printed in the United States of America   10   9   8   7

The paper in this book is certified under a sustainable forestry program.

Human Kinetics
Web site: www.HumanKinetics.com

United States: Human Kinetics, P.O. Box 5076, Champaign, IL 61825-5076
800-747-4457
email: humank@hkusa.com

Canada: Human Kinetics, 475 Devonshire Road Unit 100, Windsor, ON N8Y 2L5
800-465-7301 (in Canada only)
email: info@hkcanada.com

Europe: Human Kinetics, 107 Bradford Road, Stanningley, Leeds LS28 6 AT, United Kingdom
+44 (0) 113 255 5665
email: hk@hkeurope.com

Australia: Human Kinetics, 57A Price Avenue, Lower Mitcham, South Australia 5062
08 8372 0999
e-mail: info@hkaustralia.com

New Zealand: Human Kinetics, P.O. Box 80, Torrens Park, South Australia 5062
0800 222 062
e-mail: info@hknewzealand.com

**To Clay and Matthew.
May all your dreams come true.**

Contents

(Chapter **SEVEN**) **Your Television Options**   **133**

(Chapter **EIGHT**) **Time to Play**   **165**

Preface

Sports have always played an important role in my life, so when I had the opportunity to work in the sports industry, I jumped at it.

Actually, to say that I had the opportunity is really not accurate. The fact is that I made the opportunity by walking into the Colgate-Palmolive Company when I was a first-year graduate student at Columbia University and asking to speak to David Foster, who just happened to be the chairman of the board. The receptionist, a white-haired man who was probably about 65, looked at me like I was crazy because I didn't have an appointment and, from the looks of my clothes and backpack, was either unemployed or had just come from school. Fortunately for me, he was kind enough to put me on the phone with the senior vice president of marketing for Colgate right then and there. Three weeks later we agreed that they would give me an internship position in Colgate's sports and recreation division working on the Colgate Series women's tennis tour, Colgate Grand Prix men's tennis tour, New York City Marathon, and anything else on which they needed help. In exchange, I received school credit.

This episode marked my first sports marketing learning experience and taught me something that still cannot go understated: To succeed in the sports business, you have to be aggressive. Sports marketing presents an opportunity for someone to say "no" to you every day, so you just have to learn to have thick skin, ask for the order while learning from the experience, and move on if you get turned down.

Among the other things that my days at Colgate taught me was the value of my un-dergraduate and graduate school education. Had I not been a Columbia grad student it is doubtful that I would have had the chance to work for Colgate-Palmolive. At the same time, had the company not been inclined to help out an aggressive student trying to break into the business world, I might not be in the sports marketing business today. I really wish I could find that receptionist to thank him for his help!

The convergence of Colgate and Columbia in my life has always left a strong impression on me and one that has given me a longtime desire to give something back to the system as well as to those people coming out of school, trying to break into our business or simply trying to run one of the many local or grassroots events that are so critical to our world of sports. Thus, the impetus for writing this book.

When I got into the sports business some 20 years ago, it was much smaller and a lot less complicated. There were fewer professional teams, fewer sports, and no such thing as 24-hour sports cable television; marketing decisions were generally made by people who just happened to like the idea of their company or product being associated with a particular sport or athlete.

Sporting events in those days could generally be supported by ticket sales, television revenue, concessions, parking, and other miscellaneous income (primarily because player compensation was so much lower). Sponsorships were just coming onto the scene as an accepted and necessary component of making an event financially viable.

In the last two decades, the economics of sporting events has changed dramatically, creating a need for more expertise and greater demands on revenue generation. Despite the complexities and major financial risks associated with promoting events, many people are introduced to our business on the event side either selling local sponsorships, selling box seats, working on the facility, or assisting in the promotions and public relations area. This is because event managers, as the date of their event nears, tend to add staff in an effort to make sure that every detail is covered. The result is that events are often staffed by quite a few people who have very little practical experience in what they are doing.

Again, this is part of the motivation for me to write this book. I have seen many eager and well-meaning people come into the business and fail because they only had theoretical training to draw from. I hope to provide you with practical examples of what goes on behind the scenes of an event so that if this becomes your entry into the sports business, you will have a guide of sorts to help you figure out what to do.

To accomplish this goal, we will study real examples from events that I have either created, worked on, sold sponsorships for, or otherwise participated in by virtue of the fact that our company was responsible for putting them on. Some of these will be events on the ATP tennis tour or LPGA golf tour. Others will be events that are below the radar of mainstream television and press coverage, such as the Janet Evans Invitational Swim Meet. Regardless, there are lessons to be learned from every event, all of which can apply to whatever project you choose to undertake.

Going back to my education in the sports business, I was lucky. There were no books like this back then, but because it was a much more intimate business, I was able to take part in virtually every side of the business at a very young age. As the manager of the Colgate and later the Volvo Grand Prix of tennis, I was exposed to promotions, public relations, operations, television negotiation and production, sponsorship sales, athlete management, and financial planning. Over time, as the business manager for a variety of superstar athletes,

including Ivan Lendl and Michael Chang in tennis, Janet Evans in swimming, Shannon Miller in gymnastics, Karch Kiraly in volleyball, and Nancy Kerrigan (now my wife) in figure skating, I was able to see these events from a totally different perspective—that of the participant. This book will get into the manner in which the participants view an event as well because, after all, at virtually every level of event production, it is the athletes, both professional and amateur, who make the show viable to begin with.

Today, it seems almost impossible to receive the well-rounded exposure to the sports business that I was able to get in such a short period of time. Most people specialize in one area of the business today. And, further, most people even specialize in a narrow piece of that particular area. For example, someone who manages a tennis tournament generally doesn't also organize a golf tournament. People who represent basketball players rarely represent Olympic athletes. It has been said that my practice of sports marketing has been rather eclectic. For better or worse, I have been able to cross a lot of lines, and I hope to be able to pass some of the experiences that I have had on to you so that you might get a running start in the business or in setting up your own event.

I can assure you that not everything I have been part of has been a success, and some of the failures have been both embarrassing and costly. For example, in 1986, while I was at ProServ, we created the Avis Grasscourt Championships, which were designed to take place on the grass courts at the GlenEagles Country Club in South Florida. The event was specifically created to give Ivan Lendl a tune-up on grass prior to the 1987 Australian Open. Everything was in place, including television, sponsors, and a great schedule for the players and fans. However, a few weeks prior to the event we learned that the grass hadn't grown in properly, so the courts would not be ready, thus causing us to cancel the whole thing!

On a more positive note, the King of the Beach Invitational volleyball event, which was literally sketched out on the back of a napkin at a restaurant in Chicago, is now in its ninth year at the Hard Rock Hotel in Las Vegas. There the sand is brought in a week prior to the tournament to make sure that nothing goes wrong with the court! I will use these and other examples, some financial successes and some money losers (we call these "artistic successes"), to give you a tour of sorts on how events come to fruition.

HOW THIS BOOK IS ORGANIZED

In order to take you through an event from beginning to end, I have set this book up in eight chapters, each of which deals with a different element of an event's organization. Within each chapter are sections which break down that particular topic further by specific subject. Although you can use in isolation what you learn from one chapter, I think you are best served if you try to understand the totality of the making of an event before you try to deal with any one aspect. Keeping the big picture in mind can be very beneficial and will, hopefully, help you to profit.

Having said that, I have tried to organize the book in an orderly sequence that takes you from the creation of an event through the various big-issue strategies and finally to the nitty gritty of implementation. Because so many elements of an event happen simultaneously, keeping things in a logical sequence is not always easy. So keep this in mind at all times, understanding that the role of the event manager requires juggling a lot of issues at the same time.

Thus, in the **introduction** I basically set the stage for the rest of the book by giving some background on the events that are used throughout the book and providing you with a detailed time line from one of the events (Skating Goes Country). In **chapter 1** I begin to get into the development of operating an event by characterizing the type of events that exist and the manner by which you might acquire one or get one started. Events come in many sizes and levels of importance, so being sure that your event is well conceived and

has all of the proper sanctions can make or break you before you even begin.

Chapter 2 may deal with the most detailed and tangible issues in the entire book. In this chapter I review budget categories and cash flow. Simply put, without an accurate and detailed budget you might as well be flying by the seat of your pants. And without some feel for cash flow, you might find yourself out of business before the event gets started!

Chapter 3 discusses the importance of the site, or venue, for the event. Just like in the real estate business, "location, location, location" is the battle cry. The site can become your greatest ally or can work against you if it is in the wrong place or if the people at the facility are not on the same wavelength as you regarding the positioning of your project. As you will find throughout the book, in this chapter we will look at some of the venue-related contractual language that you will come across and discuss how to deal with these issues.

Chapter 4 takes a look at one aspect of the all-important revenue side of an event by examining sponsorship sales and servicing. In today's market, sponsorship will most certainly be the difference between a financial success and failure, so I will also attempt to illustrate some creative ideas to attract sponsors.

Chapter 5 deals with ticket sales, advertising, promotion, and other ancillary revenue sources that put you in direct touch with the public. As a result, oversights in these areas can cause problems that are way out of proportion to the dollar value involved. Remember that in every aspect of the event, people are your greatest commodity, so make sure that you are set up to communicate with your customers.

In **chapter 6** we are going to try to understand the needs and desires of the participants in the event. No matter what type of event you have, from grassroots to professional, you have to be able to attract the athletes. To help you out in this area, I will introduce you to some of the contract language that you should become familiar with, particularly as it relates to the rights and obligations that you and the performers might have to each other.

For certain events, television is arguably the most important facet, so I have devoted **chapter 7** to this subject (conversely, for some events, television may not even be an issue because they are not of the size or scope to command dedicated television time). First I am going to trace a little bit of the history of sports television and discuss the range of television options that you might face. Then I will get more into the detail of what your television agreement might look like by providing some sample contract passages and explaining some of the terms of art.

Putting on an event, no matter what magnitude, is not a one-man or -woman show. To put on the Olympics takes thousands of people. To put on a local 10K could require a staff of five. I have been lucky to work with Ray Benton and Josh Ripple, who are two of the best team builders in the business. It takes a team to manage an event and only when this is assembled will you be fully ready to start the show. Thus, in **chapter 8** we will walk through the managing of the event itself from the organization of the staff, to the time you arrive on the scene, to having a drink when it is all over. While you have put in a lot of hard work up to this point, what everyone will remember is what happened on site, so you can't overlook the actual implementation of the event. The day or week of your event will no doubt be exhausting, but if all goes well, you will be proud to have been part of a big success.

There has been a proliferation of sports events over the last 15 years, much of which is due to the growth of television. The networks' need for programming has enabled a lot of events to come to fruition that have not been well planned or well executed. I hope that this book will enable you to steer clear of some of the traps and come away with an event that brings back spectators, sponsors, athletes, and television year after year. Good luck!

Acknowledgments

First of all, this project never would have come about were it not for Craig Tartasky and his annual International Sports Summit. I was supposed to speak there in January of 1999. When the weather forced me to change my schedule, I felt badly for Craig because I was leaving a hole in his program. To help him out of a jam, I wrote a seven-page treatment of what I would have spoken about had I been able to make the trip. He was able to use that as a handout, and I used it as the outline for this book. I don't know whether to thank Craig or not!

Once I started the process of trying to write, I could never have gotten through it were it not for the support of Lon Monk, Frank Smith, Josh Ripple, Carrie Hoffman, Ed Young, my mother and father, and of course, my wife, Nancy Kerrigan. I also want to thank Linda Bump and Joanna Hatzopoulos from Human Kinetics. Although we did not always see eye to eye on the format for this project, their insights were truly helpful.

Lon, Frank, Carrie, and my dad all read the book at various stages and helped me to for-

mulate structure and direction. In particular, Lon helped me out with some of the definitions and in accurately recounting some of the event details.

It was Nancy who had to put up with all of the I time spent at the computer, though. She had to keep Matthew and Clay busy while I was writing. She had to put up with the mess on the kitchen table for months. And she had to put up with my frustration when I was about to miss a deadline. There were times when we were traveling together to events that she had to try to sleep through my pounding away on the computer in the early morning and then she had to perform at night. I am sure it wasn't always fun, so an extra bit of thanks and love to her!

Last, I want to thank all of the athletes, sponsors, production crews, spectators, and reporters who have somehow touched the events mentioned in this book. Without all of them—and the Colgate-Palmolive receptionist—I would not have had anything to write about.

Introduction: Events and Time Line

Throughout this book I will refer to various events that I have been involved with and that serve as the primary examples for many of the discussion points. To familiarize you with these events, I will explain a bit about them here. Each event has its own story, personality, high points, and low points. You may have heard of or even been to some of them.

In addition, I have listed in chronological order the sequence of operational events from the initial discussion to the television broadcast of Skating Goes Country—in other words, from start to finish. This detailed outline will provide you with a glimpse of what it takes to go from creation to implementation to packing up and going home. I strongly encourage you to refer to this time line often. It is a practical reference section that will help you to better understand the flow of an event. Along with your budget, this time line should govern the managing of your event. It will become one of the most important tools that you will have, so become as familiar with the issues covered by this time line as you possibly can. Later on I will give you a more generic time line that will break down by month the type of planning and progress that should govern your project. The time line presented here, and the more general time line presented later in the text, will be an invaluable tool to you as you create a calendar and checklist for your own events.

EVENTS

Following are descriptions of and some background on the events discussed throughout this book. Read about these events and refer back to them if you need to refresh your memory.

King of the Beach Invitational

This beach volleyball event was designed to determine the single best player in the world. The event was created by Karch Kiraly and presented to us in 1990 during a dinner meeting in Chicago. We sketched the format out on the back of a napkin and started the tournament a year later at the Marriott Hotel in Daytona Beach, Florida. After three years in Daytona, the event moved to Walt Disney World for one year before it found its current home at the Hard Rock Hotel in Las Vegas. As far as I know, this was the first pro beach volleyball event to sell tickets throughout the stadium. It also set records for the most prize money ever paid to a beach volleyball player. In just a couple of years, the King of the Beach Invitational became one of the most important events in the sport. The event began as a joint venture between ProServ and Karch and then was taken over by StarGames when the company was formed in 1995. When we divested ourselves of our various volleyball properties, the event was absorbed into the Association of Volleyball Professionals (AVP) Tour.

Halloween on Ice

This figure skating event, in which some of the world's greatest skaters perform in costume to Halloween-themed music, was created in 1995 as a way for Nancy Kerrigan to have part ownership in a show that would be geared to her home audience in New England. The show began as a joint venture among Nancy, StarGames, and the FleetCenter, where it debuted during the building's opening week. Today the show is co-owned and produced by StarGames and NAK Productions, which is Nancy's production company. Last year we moved the show to Myrtle Beach, South Carolina, where it will play annually at the Ice Castle Theatre.

5K Racquet Run

This summertime event was created in the mid-1980s to take advantage of the running boom and build awareness for the Washington, D.C., men's tennis tournament. While the event still exists, it no longer has anything to do with the tennis tournament. The event took place among the monuments in Washington.

McCall's LPGA Classic

Now defunct, the McCall's Classic was a 54-hole, fully sanctioned event on the LPGA Tour. ProServ owned and operated this event at the Stowe Mountain Resort in Stowe, Vermont, for two years. The setting was perfect but the location was isolated, limiting attendance and sponsor interest. Because of the size of a golf course, organizing a golf event presents many unique challenges and issues not shared by events in self-contained arenas.

Lane's Skating Goes Country

This event, which took place in November of 1999, was created to take advantage of the popularity of and synergy between figure skating and country music. The event is owned by StarGames and was produced with the assistance of Paul Hendrickson, Mike Long, Michael Visconti, and Meg Streeter. Each skater was required to perform to one country music hit and one country music Christmas song. In addition, we invited four country music acts to perform one of their hits and one Christmas song as well. Lane's Skating Goes Country was used as the example for the time line that follows, as it was the most recent event that we produced.

Best of the Beach Invitational

The women's version of the King of the Beach Invitational, this tournament was held only once (in 1997 in Huntington Beach, California) because of the politics of the sport of beach volleyball and the demise of the women's pro tour. Again, through a round-robin format, this event determined the best individual player in women's pro beach volleyball. We hope to bring this event back to life someday.

Skills Challenge

Another beach volleyball special event, the Skills Challenge, was first conceived when we were managing the AVP Tour. The event breaks down the sport into various disciplines and, through a judged competition, determines the best player at each element of the game. Again, because of the politics surrounding the sport, this event was held only once (in 1997) at a great little site in Irvine, California.

One Enchanted Evening

This skating show was developed to exhibit the romantic side of the pairs and dance elements of figure skating. The show aired on the Romance Classics Network (now WE: Women's Entertainment Network) on Valentine's Day 1999, which we felt was the perfect outlet and date, considering the subject matter. This show was taped without an audience, which made it somewhat unique and limits its application to certain elements of this book. Nevertheless, several aspects of the show still provide some practical examples to learn from.

AT&T Challenge

This men's tennis tournament is still owned and operated by ProServ (now Clear Channel, which acquired ProServ in 2000). Although my direct involvement with this event was limited, it provides some good examples of various issues that will be discussed in this book. The AT&T Challenge is a fully sanctioned event on the Association of Tennis Professionals (ATP) Tour with a 32-team draw in singles and a 16-team draw in doubles. Today the event is played at the Atlanta Athletic Club and is no longer sponsored by AT&T.

KidSports Foundation

This charitable organization was created in 1986 to make sports and professional athletes available to underprivileged youth throughout the greater Washington, D.C., area. Each year the Foundation held a fund-raiser to create revenues to support clinics and trips to professional games, purchase equipment, and so on. Of all of the things that I have started (the Foundation went out of existence after I left ProServ to start StarGames), the KidSports Foundation was one of the most satisfying.

Janet Evans Invitational

Janet was the hardest-working athlete I ever managed. We felt that as part of her legacy there should be a major swim meet in her name, thus the creation of this event. Actually, we did not really start a new event. Rather, in the summer of 1992 we merged our idea with the swim meet that was already taking place at the University of Southern California where Mark Shubert, Janet's coach, ran the program. This was a win–win situation for everyone.

Nancy Kerrigan and Friends

After the now-famous attack on Nancy prior to the 1994 Olympics, we felt it was necessary to provide her with an opportunity to perform in public prior to the frenzy that was ahead of her in Lillehammer. Nancy Kerrigan and Friends was created with this in mind. This one-time event took place at Matthews Arena in Boston.

TIME LINE FOR SKATING GOES COUNTRY

The following time line provides a real-life example of the steps involved in planning an event. You may not be familiar with some of the segments now, but you will be once you have read the chapters in this book. Keep in mind that this event was created in a pretty short time frame. You would be best served to have longer lead times.

Ten months out

February 10, 1999	Meeting with Trisha Walker (local promoter) to discuss the concept for the show and the viability of Nashville as the site
February 11	Trisha confirms that Nashville Arena is available
February 13	Initial offer received from Nashville Arena
February 20	Initial budget for the event created and approved

Nine months out

March 15	Initial proposal made to TNN

Eight months out

April 7	Agreement in principle with TNN for the Christmas show
April 14	Contract signed with Trisha Walker to handle local promotion

Seven months out

May 7	Initial TV production budget received from producer
May 18	Rental agreement with arena finalized
May 19–20	JS (event director/producer) visits Nashville for various meetings with Arena, artist managers, other venues, TNN
May 20	Offers begin being made to skaters and music talent
May 21	Ticket pricing confirmed with Arena
May 25	First draft of Arena contract received

Six months out

June 1	Signed skater commitment letters begin to be received
	Name for show determined
June 10	Sound and light bids received
	Sponsorship proposal sent to Lane Furniture's advertising agency

June 13–14	JS (event director/producer) visits Nashville for various planning meetings, including the following:
	a) Arena issues: press conference, on-sale date, load-in/load-out timetable, postshow party, merchandise restrictions/opportunities, dressing room needs, catering regulations, sponsor conflicts, preliminary seat kills, music clearance issues, parking
	b) Hotels: first proposals
	c) TNN: PR plan, show format, production guidelines

Five months out

July 12	TV production budget revised
July 16	Signed TNN contract received
July 17	TNN announces show as part of fall lineup at Cable TV convention
	Skater publicity information received from agents
July 20	StarGames press release announcing event in Nashville
July 22	Details of hotel deal confirmed in writing
	Agreement in principle with Lane to become title sponsor

Four months out

August 1–5	Ticket order form designed and printed
August 3	First draft of show running order created and issued to staff
August 4	Title sponsorship contract sent to Lane's agency for review
August 7	Event logo approved
August 13	TV director confirmed
August 15	Ticket order form mailed to mailing list
	Artist hired to design print ads
August 19	Budget revisions approved
August 25	Responses to ticket order forms start to be received
	Ticket account opened at bank
August 31	First wave of print and radio commercials and promotion begins

Three months out

| September 1 | Skater contracts sent for signature |
| September 5 | Press advisory sent announcing 9/27 press conference |

September 7	Tickets go on sale to general public
	Name for television show approved by TNN
September 9	Title sponsorship contract signed
September 14	Hotel contract signed
September 22	Major ticket promotion at Wild Horse Saloon in conjunction with CMA Awards
	Plans for 9/27 press conference finalized
September 23	TV show logo approved
September 24	International television deals for Far East and South America confirmed
September 26–28	Trip to Nashville to hold press conference with Nancy Kerrigan and Billy Ray Cyrus; announce Lane as title sponsor; hold an all-staff meeting, which included review of entire event from time of arrival in Nashville through time of departure; survey the site for production and television personnel; review with TNN; meet with artist managers to review show; meet with hotel to review details; review music

---

Two months out

October 5	Show running order revised
	Copy for second wave of radio approved
October 6	Budget updated and revised
October 19	Radio spot produced
October 20	Second wave of radio and print advertising begins
October 24	PA announcer identified
	Music selections finalized
October 28	International television contract signed
	Radio spot revised
	Television commercial finished
	Poster finished

One month out

November 1	Television ad campaign begins
	Poster distribution begins
	Elvis Stojko added to cast
	Press release issued

November 2	Final revisions to TV production budget
	First draft of hotel room list
November 3	Running order revised based on music selections
November 4	Press list and VIP guest list submitted
November 9	Deal closed for presenting sponsorship with Opryland Mills
November 10	Banners ordered
	First draft of television show running order created
	Merchandising details determined with arena
	Merchandise ordered

Two weeks out

November 11	Budget review
	Bumper music and live show background music chosen
	Welcome and information letter sent to participants
November 12	Details confirmed with Mothers Against Drunk Driving (MADD)
	PA announcer hired
November 15	Revise television ad buy for remaining eight days
	Contractual language with artists' managers finalized
	First skater interviews booked with local radio and print media
	Various television issues reviewed with show director
November 16	Staff meeting held to review outstanding issues
	Review layout for rinkside banners
	Make sure we bring enough petty cash for last-minute items
November 19	Staff travels to Nashville
	Meeting with arena staff to review event details, including credentials, insurance, seat kills, pre-event press
November 20	Music for preshow and intermission reviewed
	PA announcer script written
November 21	Equipment load-in
November 22	Talent arrives
	Preshow interviews and charity appearance for MADD
	Pretape television interstitials
	Dress rehearsal

November 23	Production meeting
	Rehearsal for show finale
	Show
	Load-out immediately following show
	Postshow party
November 24	All staff and participants depart Nashville
	Promotional clips delivered to TNN and international distributors
	Meeting with Arena to finalize all accounting and contractual issues
	Meeting with TNN to discuss postproduction and promotional schedule for television show
November 29–December 5	Television show edited
December 6	Show delivered to TNN and international distributors
December 8	Show revisions made
December 9	Final show delivered to TNN
December 14	TNN show aired

Note: Invoicing, bill paying, and other activities required to close books and wrap up the event continued into February 2000—two months after the show aired.

As you can see, there is quite a bit that goes into producing an event. While this time line is not meant to be intimidating, it does reinforce the old saying that "the devil is in the details." If you plan and execute, you will have a great event.

Chapter ONE

Creating an Event

Suppose you gave an event and nobody came. Impossible, you say? Well, do you remember the McCall's LPGA Championships in Vermont? What about the Stakes Match? I'll bet you missed the Scottish Grasscourt Championships. How many people miss the Criterium Circuit of Cycling or skating's Legends Competition? And whatever happened to the Sunkist Invitational?

The list of events that have come and gone is endless. Some of this is by design. For example, when we put on Nancy Kerrigan and Friends in February of 1994, we knew that it was going to be a one-time event designed to give Nancy an opportunity to skate after she was senselessly attacked and almost crippled by a group associated with one of her competitors during the U.S. National Championships in Detroit. She had seven weeks to get ready for the Lillehammer Olympics, and we felt that it was important for her to get out on the ice in front of a crowd before the Games.

However, we did not know that the LPGA event we ran at Stratton Mountain, Vermont, was destined for a short life, nor did anyone plan for Too Hot to Skate, a summer skating show, to last only two years. In fact, we plan to bring Too Hot to Skate back next year!

Some events, such as the Sunkist Invitational track meet, are very successful but run their course. Some are just ill conceived.

Why do some events make it while others don't? Why do some last 5 years and others 105 years? In this book we will explore a myriad of reasons using actual situations from events I have been involved with. In many cases an event's success or failure can rest in the planning and preplanning stages that brought the event to life in the first place. In some cases the key to success might even be found in the type of event you are contemplating and whether there is a market for it to begin with.

THE JUGGLING ACT

Creating and operating an event, regardless of whether it is grassroots or professional, is a juggling act. Of the many issues you have to deal with, most of them, particularly in the planning stages, happen simultaneously. While I think this will all become clear during the course of this book, in the big picture, running an event is *not* "painting by the numbers." You don't simply go from step A to step B to step C, and so on. You have to be a juggler. I hope that some of what you get out of this book enables you to learn to juggle a few more balls a bit faster and more proficiently.

By way of illustration, just because sponsorship sales are discussed in chapter 4 does not mean that it is the fourth major issue you should attack during the organization of your event. In fact, if by some chance you can sell the concept for your event to a corporate sponsor before you have really figured out all of the details, you will be that much ahead of the game.

As a practical matter, you will be soliciting sponsors at the same time as you will be talking to prospective venues, participants, television distributors, and other vendors. You will probably also have tickets on sale. As you will find out, there is nothing wrong with all of this happening at the same time. In fact, it's normal. However, it does make life interesting when, for example, you have questions from potential sponsors (or others) that relate to some area of the event that you haven't fully worked out yet. This is one place in which your ability to juggle will be challenged.

At some point in the evolution of your event, you are going to be "winging it"—addressing a question that doesn't yet have a firm answer. In some cases the fact that you don't know the answer might cost you a deal. In other cases this process can serve to help you focus by requiring you to solve an issue right on the spot. Regardless, you have to be ready for all things at all times, so always be on your toes . . . in other words, get ready to juggle!

To some degree, the juggling is what makes the event business exciting. In every case your judgment will be a pivotal factor in determining the results. You will have to make judgments in many situations in which there is no right or wrong answer. You will have to gather as much information as possible in the time allowed, rely heavily on your colleagues, and go with your best and most solid instincts. Only time will tell if your judgment turned out to be correct.

You have to be ready for all things at all times, so always be on your toes.

Your ability to make judgments should improve over time. This will be one of the keys to your success as an event manager. And, while there certainly is no substitute for experience, I hope this book gives you at least a bit of a head start when you next come up against any of these potentially awkward and challenging moments.

DEFINING YOUR EVENT

The first step in creating an event is to define it. Most events are defined by a few of the very basic things I have outlined below. You will have to decide which of these factors apply to the event you are planning.

• **Participants.** *Is this an amateur or professional event; is it of major or minor importance?* On the professional side, there are major events such as the World Series or Super Bowl and minor events such as a satellite tennis tournament or a Florida circuit golf event. On the "amateur" level, there are major bowl games such as the Orange Bowl or Rose Bowl and what I would consider the next tier of events such as the U.S. National Figure Skating Championships. These are supported by several other tiers of events extending all the way down to your local Little League. These amateur events take place in communities all around the world on a daily and weekly basis and form the backbone of international sports.

• **Geographic reach.** *Does your event have local, regional, national, or international impact?* A 5K race may only affect the participants and their families; a state championship high school basketball game may only draw attention from people in the state where it is held. Our King of the Beach Invitational had regional significance from Las Vegas to Los Angeles and San Diego; the NCAA Swimming and Diving Championships have national significance, while Wimbledon has international impact.

Depending on press and television coverage, the *reach* of an event may be somewhat different from its impact. For example, Nancy Kerrigan and Friends was essentially a local event, but because of the press and television, it became an international event. The King of the Beach television coverage gives it national reach. The AT&T Challenge tennis tournament in Atlanta is essentially a local event. However, its international television agreements and press coverage give it worldwide reach. Golf's U.S. Open has become international by every measure.

• **Sanction.** *Is your event recognized by a governing body within the sport?* At the professional level, an event without a sanction is generally considered a special event for which there are no mandated rules and regulations. Our Best of the Beach Invitational volleyball event for women was not sanctioned because no organization had jurisdiction. As a result, we could make our own rules as long as the players agreed. The AT&T Challenge is a sanctioned event by the Association of Tennis Professionals (ATP); thus, it is governed by a very tight set of rules. The Scottish Grasscourt Championships was not sanctioned and thus was considered an exhibition, with the outcome having no bearing on rankings.

Generally, sanctioned events *for the pros* are more important and more recognized by the sporting public than are nonsanctioned events. If the event is for amateurs, the sanction is critical as it will dictate who is eligible to participate. Thus, if you wanted to create a summer basketball league for college players, you would need a sanction from the NCAA. We needed NCAA approval for the Janet Evans Invitational because collegiate swimmers participated. Virtually any event that is geared toward nonprofessionals will need a sanction from that sport's governing body so that the players maintain their eligibility. Unlike with the pros, the sanction won't necessarily make your event more important; it will just make it "legal" as determined by the group with jurisdiction over the athletes and promoters.

So, one of the first things to do when planning an event is to determine where, in the overall spectrum, your event is going to fall. In so doing, a major, if not *the* major, issue that you have to tackle is what your motivation is for putting on this event in the first place. It might be as basic as earning a profit. But, it might also be much more complex.

KNOWING YOUR MISSION

Understanding your motivation is key because that will, in some cases, give you a road map for the other questions you are going to face. When we created Nancy Kerrigan and

The focus of the annual 5K race shown here is to raise money for a local charity. The budget is low, and volunteers from the community do the bulk of the work.

Friends, for example, it had a specific purpose that was geared to a particular moment in time. It was an event created to give Nancy an opportunity to perform in public after the rehabilitation of her knee and before facing a live audience and worldwide media attention at the Olympics. Profit was not the issue. In fact, all of the proceeds (almost $200,000) went to various charities in the Boston area. Longevity was not important. As I mentioned before, no one had any intention of this event happening again (although, in retrospect, we might have been smart to make this an annual event). So, our parameters were very specific.

With this narrow focus we knew that we could create an exhibition that had strong participant support, was geared to a local market, and needed a sanction solely to ensure the skaters' (including Nancy's) Olympic eligibility. The fact that this event actually transcended the Boston market was a function of the unique circumstances surrounding the event, the media frenzy that accompanied Nancy at the time, and the interest and support of people such as Rick Gentile at CBS Sports, Steve Seigel at Dunkin Donuts, and Chris Clouser at Northwest Airlines, each of whom got their company involved to provide a bigger platform, all of which was beneficial to Nancy.

Conversely, the King of the Beach Invitational volleyball event was created with the vision of it becoming the biggest event in the history of professional beach volleyball. Profit was the motive, international media attention was the goal, and breaking new ground for the sport and our company was the objective.

With our motives understood, we were able to define clearly our objective for the King of the Beach, which was

to put on a profitable elite professional event that had national and international implications and functioned under the highest official sanction available.

This became our mission statement.

As we did when creating the mission statement for the King of the Beach Invitational,

you should strive to define your event by describing all of your motives. If you can capture your event in one sentence (which may be difficult), you will be off to a good start.

A defining statement will help you create a road map for your event and will become an important management tool if you or your staff ever feel you are losing sight of your priorities. The contrasting goals (as defined in the mission statements) behind Nancy Kerrigan and Friends and the King of the Beach Invitational dictated very different paths for establishing and *managing* these events. The King of the Beach tournament had to be an official Association of Volleyball Professionals (AVP) Tour event for it to have credibility in the minds of the players and public. Therefore, our first step had to be to contact the sport's governing body—in this case, the Association of Volleyball Professionals—to seek their approval. We knew that without their sanction, this event would never get off the ground.

With the event for Nancy, time was short (we had about four weeks to organize the whole thing), so we first had to find out if the event was logistically feasible. Without a venue, an available date for the skaters, and a sponsor or two, this event could not have happened even if we had sanctions from every group from the International Olympic Committee (IOC) to the United States Figure Skating Association (USFSA). In this case, our first calls were to arenas in the Boston area. Only after knowing that we had "a place to play" did we concern ourselves with sanctions and other regulatory issues.

On perhaps a more fundamental level, you might want to put on an event to raise money for your local Little League or create an event, such as a junior tennis tournament, that will serve as a stepping-stone for local and regional athletes to qualify for rankings in their sport on a national level. In the Little League case your mission statement might read something like this:

Create a fund-raising all-star game that showcases the talent of local kids, the proceeds of which will go

toward enabling the team to participate in statewide summer leagues for the purpose of gaining additional playing and educational experiences.

From this one sentence everyone, from participants to sponsors to spectators to staff members, will know exactly what this event is all about.

Profitability

On an even more basic level, your primary objective for being in the event management business may simply be to earn profits. For example:

We are currently trying to bring an LPGA Tour event to Boston. The motivation here is twofold: First, we see a void in the marketplace, as there is no women's professional golf in New England. Second, we see an opportunity to make a good profit on an event that can have longevity for our company.

The working mission statement for a Boston-based LPGA event might read something like this:

Create or acquire a ladies' professional golf tournament that will attract the top players in the world. The event must be profitable after two years. The location for the tournament must be within reasonable driving distance of downtown Boston to make it a "Boston event" with the goal of attracting major

corporate support for the tournament. The event must have television opportunities and be geared toward having a long-term life in the area.

While a bit longer than one sentence, this mission statement provides specific direction for what information is needed prior to making a decision to proceed with the event. In this case we would need to:

- See if there are any golf courses available within the geographic boundaries required.
- Find out if there are any available dates on the LPGA Tour.
- See if any television outlets would be interested in such an event.

As you can see from these very different examples, the motivation for promoting an event can vary as much as the sport and the participants. Thus, the first rule of event planning and management is to figure out why you are doing this event in the first place. This is why your mission statement becomes a must.

Personality

Your mission statement should also help you determine your event's personality, which admittedly is an intangible element that is difficult to define. While I am not looking to make it more complicated, the best characterization of an event's personality is found in the Supreme Court's definition of pornography: You will know it when you see it. So much for simplifying things!

Your event will be judged from every conceivable angle by everyone who comes in contact with it. They will be asking: Did people know about it? Were the tickets too expensive? Was parking adequate? Was the competition entertaining? How was the food? Were the rest rooms clean? Were

> ■ ■ ■ ■ ■ ■ ■ ■ ■ ■ ■
>
> **T**he first rule of event planning and management is to figure out why you are doing this event in the first place.
>
> ■ ■ ■ ■ ■ ■ ■ ■ ■ ■ ■

the souvenirs worth buying? Did it start on time? Did it end in a reasonable period of time? The list goes on and on.

As difficult as it may be to create a personality for your event, it will nonetheless be a very important aspect of your job and, along with some of the other issues that we will cover, will be a measure of your success. It will also become a symbol for how you are personally defined in the marketplace. Therefore, if your mission statement can allude to the personality that you want your event to have, you will again establish a direction for your event that will make your job of managing the event that much easier. While this adds to the task of defining your event (and makes it all the more difficult to capture in one sentence), the time spent at the beginning of the event's creation will be well worth it later on. Invest the time up front and you will be able to answer a lot of the questions that are sure to surface later.

After you have established the motivation for the event, written your mission statement, and estimated whether you can pay for it (we will examine budgets in chapter 2), then, and only then, should you begin the process of creating or designing the event. The first step in this process (and don't forget that many of these things will happen simultaneously) will be to determine if you are better off starting from scratch or taking over an existing property. Most of this book is written assuming you are starting from scratch. If you buy an existing event, many of these decisions and issues will have been predetermined or already dealt with.

■ ■ ■ ■ ■ ■ ■ ■ ■ ■

Invest the time up front and you will be able to answer a lot of the questions that are sure to surface later.

■ ■ ■ ■ ■ ■ ■ ■ ■ ■

ACQUISITION OR CREATION

Many benefits can be gained from buying an existing event, including the event's history or goodwill, sponsors, cash flow, participant lists, ticket buyer lists, a spot on the calendar, and so forth. If you can achieve your objectives *and* afford the up-front financial obligation required by the seller, the chances are good that you will be best served by buying an event. However, in the majority of situations, either you will determine that you can't meet your objectives, that no events are available, or that those that are available are too expensive. So, being entrepreneurial, you will choose to create your own event.

Acquisition

Someone recently asked my opinion on whether he should buy an existing dance event or create one himself. The question was prompted by the fact that, while the existing event was for sale, this potential buyer thought he could save quite a bit of money by putting the acquisition cost into establishing a new event that was bigger and better. In some cases that might be true. In this particular case, however, the event in question was in its 17th year of operation, had positive cash flow, and was a U.S. Championship in a specific genre of dance. I explained to the potential buyer that no matter how quickly he could build a new event, the chances were slim that he could re-create the history and tradition of the existing event, and he would be hard pressed to achieve the significance conveyed by a sanctioned event with "U.S. Open" in its title. If the numbers made sense, I told him, he should buy the event. He did.

The decision of whether to acquire or create a sporting event isn't always so black and white, however. A set of criteria can help you make this decision. I suggest you begin by going back to your mission statement.

We have been on the selling side of the event business a couple of times but have purchased only one event, the AVP Championships of New England, which we bought from the AVP and eventually sold back to them. When we bought the event, we did so because it assured us of a prime summer date on the calendar, which was critical in the short New England summer window. When I sold ProServ's Washington, D.C., women's indoor tennis event, it was because Ion Tiriac (at the time Boris Becker's manager) was willing to pay a considerable multiple to purchase our date to bring an event to Germany. The date on the calendar and the sanction from the Women's Tennis Association (WTA) were the driving factors.

Determining a fair price for the sale or purchase of an event is often the sticking point. As with the sale of any business or business unit, there are many ways to put a value on an event: the most common are based on multiples of earnings, cash flow, or gross revenue. All of these are acceptable, but none necessarily carries the day. Your particular situation may suggest that these models don't matter.

In the case of the D.C. women's event, Tiriac had a major sponsor, German television, and a venue that were all willing to do virtually whatever it took to bring women's tennis to Germany to take advantage of the boom begun by Becker and Steffi Graf. Thus, Tiriac was willing to pay us more than the 10 times earnings multiple that probably would have been reasonable at that time. In the earlier dance example, because this particular buyer was equally prepared to start his own event if he couldn't negotiate a favorable price for the existing one, he was unwilling to pay 15 to 20 times earnings, which probably would have been reasonable in the marketplace at the time of that transaction.

The point here is that to evaluate whether to buy an existing event, you need to study the event's financial results (say, from the three prior years) and determine what, if any,

relevance they have to your situation (our results in Washington, D.C., had virtually no bearing on what Tiriac would do in Germany because it was a completely different market). You should then try to understand the going rate (i.e., multiple of earnings) for sports and entertainment properties in the broader marketplace. Then, knowing your own financial wherewithal, make a decision on how to proceed.

You also have to consider the following nonfinancial issues:

- Date availability
- Sanction
- Player interest
- Site
- Sponsorship
- Television

These nonfinancial elements (such as the ability to hold a U.S Open titled event in the dance example) will often be the key factors in your decision-making process.

In any case, the decision to purchase or create an event is critical and potentially costly, so be sure to bring financial experts into this analysis.

Creation

Many of the issues that surface during an acquisition decision should be factored into your thought process when determining whether to create an event. Again, financial and marketplace conditions are the key.

From a financial standpoint, creating an event will not require the same up-front purchase price that acquiring a property carries with it. However, you will potentially have some pretty heavy cash needs, nevertheless. Thus, you need to be prepared to spend some significant dollars before seeing any revenue flowing your way.

■ ■ ■ ■ ■ ■ ■ ■ ■ ■ ■

The decision to purchase or create an event is critical and potentially costly, so be sure to bring financial experts into this analysis.

■ ■ ■ ■ ■ ■ ■ ■ ■ ■ ■

While we will cover some of the issues of creating an event later in the book, here we will address various start-up expenditures. Perhaps the biggest one is an item that may not take any money directly out of your pocket but could be the most expensive cost of all—opportunity cost.

Starting an event takes a major commitment of time and energy. This is time and energy that you could spend doing something else that might deliver immediate financial gain for you. Therefore, the first issue you need to deal with when thinking through the creation process is, do you have the resources to devote to this project without it generating any income for you? If you can't afford the time at the front end of the event, then you should not go this route. Unless you have a sponsor or other financial backer lined up (or simply have the money yourself), the reality is that you could go weeks or months without seeing any money coming in while spending heavily at the same time.

In this regard, one of the key financial issues is whether you have the seed capital to start an event. As with the purchase price in an acquisition, starting an event takes up-front capital for things such as the following:

• **Applications.** Many sporting organizations will require that you make a nonrefundable deposit along with your application to start an event. For example, we recently wanted to apply for a sanction on the ATP Tennis Tour. The application requires a $10,000 deposit. Most grassroots events won't have that big of an up-front price tag, but you have to be prepared for this.

• **Venue deposits.** Just as with a governing body, many venues will require that you give

them a down payment on the use of their facility. We had to give a golf course $1,500 and the hotel $1,000 eight months in advance of an upcoming pro–celebrity golf tournament we were planning. These are not big fees, but as you will see, these costs add up.

• **Marketing costs.** Because you will have to market your event, you will need to create logos, brochures, videos, and so on. Again, we will discuss all of this in detail later, but these too can add significantly to your start-up costs.

In addition to the financial issues, the creation of an event requires a thorough study of the marketplace conditions. You should go through the exercise of studying the market whether you create or acquire an event. However, when acquiring an event, there will be a history that will tell you what you can expect. If the results have been lousy, don't buy the event unless you plan to move it!

However, with a new event you are taking a risk that the public will accept your project and support it through sponsorship, ticket purchases, merchandise purchases, and so forth. This is a *risk,* and, as with any event, that is really the bottom line.

Whether you create or acquire an event, this is a risky business. Essentially, as an event organizer you are an entrepreneur with all of the risks, rewards, pressures, and potential victories that go along with that line of work. As long as you recognize this and have the financial stability to absorb the up-front costs and potential losses (don't ever expect to make money in your first year!), then you can be successful . . . but be sure you have analyzed the financial implications carefully before proceeding any further.

■ ■ ■ ■ ■ ■ ■ ■ ■ ■ ■

The first issue you need to deal with when thinking through the creation process is, do you have the resources to devote to this project without it generating any income for you?

■ ■ ■ ■ ■ ■ ■ ■ ■ ■ ■

THE SANCTION

After going through the "create versus acquire" analysis, and assuming that you decide to start your event from scratch (and again, this book is written from the perspective of creating an event), you will have to determine if it needs, or will be enhanced by having, a sanction.

What exactly is a sanction anyway; why is it so important, and how do you know if you need one?

Defining the Sanction

A sanction is an official approval for your event. Sanctions are granted by the regulatory body that oversees your sport.

Virtually every sport has a governing body or player's association that organizes the sport on either a professional or amateur basis, or both. These governing bodies grant the all-important sanctions. On the Olympic side of things, the sanctioning bodies usually feed into the International Olympic Committee (IOC), which governs the Olympic Games and all of their qualifying events. On the professional side, there are many different sanctioning bodies.

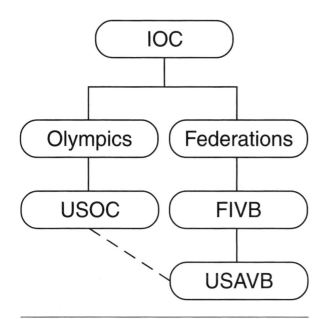

Figure 1.1 Diagram of Olympic sanctioning bodies.

The IOC, which is located in Lausanne, Switzerland, is made up of individual federations that govern each sport on a worldwide basis. Their governance runs to issues as varied as equipment specifications; athlete eligibility; international competition; scheduling; Olympic qualifying rules; rules and regulations of the sport; and the issuing of sanctions to organizers of world, international, and national competitions.

The Federation Internationale de Volleyball (FIVB), for example, is the IOC member that rules indoor and beach volleyball around the world. They govern the competitions that lead to Olympic qualification and determine what countries will hold international competitions, such as the World Championships, World Cup, and so on. Among other things, they also grant sanctions or approvals to organizers that want to put on special events.

Each federation is composed of national governing bodies (NGBs) that organize a sport in a particular country. In the United States, the NGB that governs volleyball is USA Volleyball (USAVB), which is a member of the FIVB. Each NGB (USAVB, for example) is also a member of its national federation. In the United States the national federation is the U.S. Olympic Committee (USOC), which represents the United States within the IOC. With multiple masters, this can all get very confusing, so let me try to clarify.

Importance of the Sanction

Back in 1986 we wanted to put on a series of men's indoor volleyball events that featured the United States against Brazil. To put on this series, we had to go to USAVB (the NGB) with the idea. They had to give it their blessing (or sanction) and then, on our behalf, go to the FIVB (the international federation) to get their approval. The sanctioning process allows the governing body (or bodies) to control the game around the world so that it is played under authorized rules with approved equipment. It also enables the federation to control the growth and flow of events, which is important to them for a variety of reasons. Without going through the sanctioning process, we could not have put on an event using official teams from the United States and Brazil.

By means of comparison, the situation in beach volleyball has been somewhat different. Again, this sport, which is a cousin to the indoor game and only adopted as an Olympic sport at the Atlanta Games in 1996, is governed internationally by the FIVB. However, in the United States the national governing bodies (USOC and USAVB) did not pay much attention to beach volleyball, so it was instead organized and developed by a group of players through an organization called the Association of Volleyball Professionals (AVP), which the players owned and controlled. The existence of the AVP, of which I was the chief executive officer for two years, made the creation and development of new beach volleyball events in the United States even more complicated.

During beach volleyball's developmental years, the AVP and FIVB were unable to see eye to eye on how the game should be organized. The AVP did not recognize the authority of the FIVB, and vice versa. As a result, if you wanted to start a beach volleyball event in the United States, as we did in 1991 with the King of the Beach Invitational, we had to make a decision on which body to go to for a sanction. At the time, since beach volleyball was not an Olympic sport, we went to the AVP for the sanction.

We entered into a long-term agreement in which the AVP guaranteed that the top players (virtually all Americans at that time) would participate in the King of the Beach event as long as we paid the organization a fee (10 percent of the total prize money) and agreed to operate the tournament according to the rules and regulations of the AVP Tour. The parameters set by the AVP's rules and regulations were potentially onerous.

For example, the AVP wanted to restrict the sponsors with whom we could do business based on product categories in which they had existing sponsorship deals. In the first couple of years of the event, we saw this as a serious problem since they had sponsors in some of the key areas, such as beer, sunglasses, balls, and cars. We were able to make a deal with the AVP that gave us a pro rata portion of the tour revenue from those sponsors in trade for our granting those companies the sponsorship rights to the King of the Beach event. Without that deal, the event would not have been affordable. Had we not understood the extent to which the AVP sanction reached, we could have ended up in a situation that was so restrictive that the financial viability of the event would have been threatened. If we had learned this *after* signing an agreement with the AVP, we would have had a real problem.

So, be sure you thoroughly understand the parameters of the sanction agreement *before* you enter into it, keeping in mind that in the King of the Beach example, without the sanction from the AVP, their members could not have played in our event, thus depriving us from having the best players in the world. Without these players, this new event, which we created from notes written on the back of a napkin during a meeting with Karch Kiraly (who came up with the idea in the first place), could not have come to life.

The need for the sanction for the King of the Beach Invitational applies to events in other sports and at every level. Let's say, for example, that the junior champion at your tennis club is an up-and-coming female tennis player to whom you would like to give the opportunity to play more competitive matches. You find out that in your geographic region there are only two events all summer long for junior tennis players. You decide that you want to put on an event that will give her practice in competitive situations and at the same time earn points toward her junior

> **B**e sure you thoroughly understand the parameters of the sanction agreement before you enter into it.

ranking with the U.S. Tennis Association (USTA).

To put on this event, you would have to apply to the governing body, the USTA, for a sanction that would make your junior tennis event a recognized tournament on the USTA schedule. In so doing, you would apply for a date on their calendar, which, if accepted, would come with stipulations regarding the size of the draw, the type of balls that you play with, the surface that you play on, the role of coaches, scoring formats, dress, sponsors, and so forth. Without this sanction the tournament could still be held, but your club champ would not gain any points toward her national ranking and could lose her eligibility.

At the junior level the restrictions put on you by the USTA are not particularly onerous and are intended to be helpful. In fact, I suspect that at every level the sanctioning rules are perceived by the governing body to be helpful. You might view them differently in some cases. Therefore, you will always have to grapple with this sanction decision.

Need for the Sanction

The need for a sanction can vary from sport to sport. In figure skating, for example, there are a variety of events and shows. Skating sanctions are primarily generated by the need for individual Olympic eligible skaters to receive permission to appear. Pros aren't regulated by any governing body and so can take part in any competition or show that they want. Likewise, a tennis player, as long as he or she is not in violation of any ATP or WTA rule, does not need a sanction to play in a nontour event or exhibition. As the event organizer, you should take the responsibility for obtaining a sanction or confirming that one is not necessary, but all of this will be triggered by the athlete's need for permission to participate. If the athletes don't need permission from some governing body, you may not care about gaining their sanction.

Using the 1998 version of our annual Halloween on Ice figure skating event as an example, because we had up-and-coming junior Jennifer Kirk in the show, we needed a sanction from the U.S. Figure Skating Association (USFSA). If Jennifer had appeared in the show without it being sanctioned, she could have lost her Olympic eligibility at the tender age of 13. Conversely, at our Skating Goes Country Christmas special produced for TNN, with the exception of the local figure skating club that provided the sanction, all of the skaters were professional, so there was no need to get a sanction from the USFSA. Again, the bottom line is that you need to know the rules and regulations for the particular sport and understand what role the governing body plays.

This becomes especially important in team sports events. If you wanted to put on a special event related to professional baseball, you would have to go through the Major League Baseball Players Association (MLBPA). During one of baseball's work stoppages we wanted to put on a special skills challenge involving some of the top baseball players. The MLBPA advised us that this would be in contradiction to the players' collective bargaining agreement and, further, in the opinion of the MLBPA, was contrary to the best interests of the sport. So there was no event!

If you want to put on a basketball exhibition using NBA players, you have to go to the NBA and the National Basketball Players Association (NBPA). As indicated earlier, when we wanted to put on a new beach volleyball event, we had to go through the AVP.

When we started the King of the Beach Invitational, the AVP controlled all the events in which their members participated. In 1990 we went to them and proposed what was then the biggest prize money event in the history of the sport—$200,000 for 14 players in a new and unique round-robin format to determine the best individual player. Jeff Dankworth, who was then running the AVP, had the foresight to understand that this was a great opportunity for his constituency, even though it meant giving up a modicum of control over the event itself. Over a period of time, we were able to strike the deal I referred to earlier, which enabled this new event to be brought to life. The King of the Beach event has since grown into one of the most prestigious titles in the sport and the showcase event for beach volleyball in the United States.

Could we have done the King of the Beach event without a sanction? Yes, but it would not have enabled us to meet our objectives as set out in our mission statement (i.e., put on an event with the best players in the world) because the top players would not have been allowed to play. Thus, as a practical matter, we could not have operated the King of the Beach Invitational without the AVP sanction.

This doesn't mean, however, that there aren't dozens of events that can't be done without going through this process. Virtually every professional figure skating event is done without a sanction. Ray Benton, who helped me so much early in my career, began the senior tennis tour without a sanction from anyone. At the local level, the 5K Racquet Run had no sanction, and none of our KidSports Foundation events were sanctioned by any governing body.

Remember, the mission statement for your event should help you make a decision as to whether you need a sanction.

Applying for the Sanction

If you decide that you need a sanction, the process for applying for a sanction for a new event is not particularly complicated (it depends on the sport), although it is not necessarily a rubber stamp either.

To apply for a sanction for a new event, begin by calling or writing the appropriate sanctioning body (see the list in appendix D) and tell them you want to start a new event that has their sanction. They will no doubt ask you a variety of questions and lead you through the process. Among other things, you will have to prove that you have the resources to follow through with your event, both financial and otherwise. This is not usually a complex process, but most organizations will be

thorough, particularly if large sums of money are involved.

If you are interested in applying to become the organizer of an existing major event on the national or world calendar (such as the U.S. Track and Field Championships or the World Gymnastics Championships), the process is much more lengthy and in many cases will include having to create a local organizing committee (LOC); having significant venues lined up; and in many instances, providing a financial guarantee. In this case you will be competing against other promoters and organizing committees from around the country or the world.

Unlike the application process for a newly created event, such as the King of the Beach Invitational or the junior tennis tournament discussed earlier, the sanctioning process for national and international events can take years. At one end of the spectrum is the Olympic Games themselves. These are awarded six years in advance and usually only after a process that takes several years (a process that has recently been the subject of a great deal of controversy for financial impropriety). A world championship or national championship will require a similar process. Therefore, if you decide that you want to promote an event of this magnitude, you must be organized well in advance and be able to prove that you can deliver everything from volunteers to hotel rooms to transportation to athlete lodging to sanction fees to prize money to sponsorship and local government support. Only those with significant experience and resources should undertake projects of this magnitude.

Regardless of the size and scope of your event, before making any decision on the sanction, contact the appropriate governing body and research your sport because each one is different. If you determine that you need or want a sanction, once you receive it from the proper federation, you will be on

Before making any decision on the sanction, contact the appropriate governing body and research your sport.

your way to establishing your event. This is when you can start the creative process of designing your property.

DESIGNING YOUR EVENT

Designing the event is where you have an opportunity to be creative and ultimately determines what will define the event. As discussed earlier, every event should have its own personality that will give it a place in the minds of the participants, spectators, sponsors, and others who will be instrumental to its success. In my opinion, one of the key elements to the personality of an event is its friendliness to the participants. I came to this conclusion early in my career.

When I worked on the Colgate Grand Prix men's professional tennis tour, certain events were known as "player-friendly" events, while others seemed to view the players as interchangeable pawns in the tournament committee's overall plan to make profits, entertain guests, create a platform for themselves, and so forth. There were successful tournaments on both ends of the spectrum. However, as you might imagine, the atmosphere at the player-friendly events was far more conducive to a positive experience than was the atmosphere at the tournaments that were not geared toward the players. Not surprisingly, the player-friendly events always seemed to have the stronger player fields, making for higher profits and greater spectator satisfaction.

Perhaps the most successful event in this respect was Jim Westhall's Volvo International in North Conway, New Hampshire. With its beautiful setting, player softball game, lobster feast, and helicopter transportation from the hotel to the site, the players made a point of putting this event on their calendars. One year, the final was rained out. Illustrative of the special feeling about this tournament, the players agreed to come back several weeks

Care of the athletes should always be at the top of the list for the organizer.

later to finish the match, indicating unprecedented cooperation. (Unfortunately, the event's management determined that the tournament outgrew the site and moved it to New Haven, Connecticut, where it eventually went out of business. There is a lesson to be learned from that evolution—or extinction—as well!)

Interestingly, Wimbledon, perhaps the most successful and certainly the oldest tennis tournament in the world, was during the mid-1980s the least player friendly of all. Steeped in tradition (and ignoring certain aspects of the 1973 player boycott), the All England Club management believed that the players would come no matter how they were treated because of the prestige associated with winning the Wimbledon title. After a while, the people in charge of the event started to see that certain players were not coming to the event and others were complaining and suggesting that perhaps tennis on grass had outlived its role in the game. Some players came right out and said that they could do without Wimbledon.

To their credit, the response from the Wimbledon Tournament Committee to this undercurrent of discontent among the players was relatively quick and dramatic. In a very short period of time, Wimbledon became among the friendliest to the players with its player lounges, restaurant, transportation desk, day care center for the players' children, and other amenities. (Unfortunately for the All England Club, before the 2000 championships, some of the old player issues began to surface again.) The point is that even the biggest and best events are judged by the participants, who ultimately are the people whom the spectators, sponsors, and television executives are most concerned about. Care of the athletes should always be at the top of the list for the organizer.

After you have determined your motives for putting on your event, making sure your event is geared toward the participants is a must.

We will get into more of this later, including some tips for making athletes comfortable at your event.

✔ Checklist for Creating an Event

Since you no doubt want to be known for being creative, well organized, player friendly, sponsor sensitive, and concerned about your customers, you had better make sure that you have covered the fundamentals thoroughly. Thus, during the initial stages of your event's creation, make sure you do the following:

✔ Understand why you want to do your event in the first place.

✔ Define your event with a short mission statement.

✔ Study the rules and regulations as they apply to the type of participants who will come to your event.

✔ Know the breadth of authority of the sport's governing body or bodies.

✔ Determine if you need a sanction for your event.

✔ Decide if you want to buy an existing event or start one from the ground floor.

✔ Put your event's organization (i.e., staff, finances, etc.) in the shape necessary to apply for a sanction.

✔ Start the application process.

✔ Think about how to gear your event to the participants.

✔ Think about the personality that you want your event to take on.

✔ *Most important,* develop a budget that enables you to analyze the event's probability for financial success. You can have a great concept, perfect date and location, and player support for your event, but if every calculation shows that the expenses will far outstrip the revenues, you should seriously think through the viability of your project.

Chapter 2 will give you the tools to develop an expense budget that allows for this most important analysis.

Working Model: Regional Tennis Tournament

To provide a framework to enable you to more easily understand the major points discussed throughout the book, I have created a working model—a hypothetical event that will illustrate in a practical manner the various elements involved in creating and operating an event.

The event I have created as the working model is an 18-and-under regional tennis tournament for boys and girls. The event will take place in your hometown. To get this event up and running, we would start with the following mission statement:

To create a sanctioned tennis event that will enable accomplished juniors (i.e., those with a state ranking) to participate in advanced-level competitive play on a regional level. The event will conform to USTA standards and be open to junior boys and girls from the surrounding four-state area. Any proceeds from the event, which must be fully funded by sponsors, television, or the site, will go to support junior tennis in the region through a grant process to be determined.

With the mission statement for this event in place, our next steps would be:

1. Determine the best location for the event.
2. Call the USTA to get an application to start the sanction process.
3. Having decided that the local tennis club is the best facility, talk to the club manager to determine dates for the event.
4. Get the USTA regional office involved to see if they can help support our efforts.
5. Find out the dates of any other junior tennis tournaments in the region to be sure that our event will not conflict with theirs.
6. Begin talking to the kids and their parents in the region to let them know what we are planning to be sure that there is support for the project.
7. Develop a preliminary budget.
8. Develop a preliminary time line so that we have some feel for what needs to be done and when.

Chapter TWO

Developing the Budget

After you decide to create an event, you *must* develop a budget. There simply is no next step that makes any sense, and frankly, the bulk of your decisions from this point forward will somehow hinge on your bible, the "almighty budget."

As the budget will point out, there are seemingly an infinite number of details to deal with when planning and organizing an event. For me, the details on the revenue side have always been a bit more interesting than the details on the expense side. Generally, I like creating revenue more than I like focusing on where the money is spent and how the implementation of the operation happens. This may be true for you as well, but keep in mind that you can get in trouble if you overlook the expense and operations side of the event. By paying particular attention to all of the points in this chapter, you can avoid many pitfalls.

Probably the best way to understand the purpose and structure of an event budget is to go through each item line by line, keeping in mind that the budget that you start with will not necessarily be the budget that you end up with. As your event takes shape, you will find that certain things that you expected are unnecessary, and others cost more or less than you thought; still other items that you didn't plan on needing for your event become a requirement. You have to remain flexible but still try to stay within the total expense parameters that you set up at the outset. Note that in the time line for Skating Goes Country the budget gets revised four or five times. Actually, it probably got reviewed 10 or 12 times, if not more. The point is that the budget is your bible, and it takes discipline to stay within it.

As an event producer you will often want to spend more for things that will enhance the look of the event. As a businessperson, you have to temper your creative side to maximize profits. The budget is where this dichotomy comes to a head, and if you learn nothing else from my experiences, learn to let the business side have more influence than the creative side. Flair for the creative is what will make your events great. Control over the budget is what will make them profitable. You decide where to draw the line!

With that in mind, on the following pages I will take you through a generic event budget, making introductory comments on each line item. Virtually any event in any sport can get started using this budget format as its underlying guide. From this basic starting point you

> **Y**ou can get in trouble if you overlook the expense and operations side of the event.

will be able to build something that fits the very specific needs of your particular event. When you combine this information with everything else we will discuss, you should have the tools to make the judgments necessary to manage a successful sports event.

LINE ITEMS

Every company or event manager will develop a unique format to his or her budget. Some managers even have their own terminology. At StarGames, our budgets break down along the lines outlined in the following section. Keep in mind that every item discussed in this chapter will appear again in different contexts throughout this book. This will not be the only reference to the budget.

The Budget

Revenues

Title sponsor	$_____
Presenting sponsor	$_____
Official sponsors	$_____
Ticket sales	$_____
Merchandising	$_____
Program	$_____
Domestic television	$_____
International television	$_____
Commercial sales	$_____
Ancillary events	$_____
Miscellaneous	$_____
Subtotal	$_____
Less fees to third parties	($_____)
Total revenues	$_____

Expenses

General and administrative (G & A)

Personnel	$_____
Office rent	$_____
Office supplies/equipment	$_____
Insurance	$_____
Travel/hotel	$_____
Entertainment	$_____
Trademark search	$_____
Total G & A	$_____

Talent

Compensation/prize money	$_____
Travel	$_____
Hotel	$_____
Food and beverage	$_____
Gifts/trophies/parties	$_____
Local transportation	$_____
Judges/officials	$_____
Physicians/trainers	$_____
Total talent	$_____

Production

Sound/lights	$_____
Site preparation	$_____
Crew	$_____
Travel	$_____
Hotel	$_____
Food and beverages	$_____
Music clearance	$_____
Practice facility	$_____
Local transportation	$_____
Props/decorations	$_____
Costumes/uniforms	$_____
Makeup	$_____
Total production	$_____

Facility

Rent	$_____
Stagehands/crew	$_____
Security	$_____
Box office	$_____
Stadium	$_____
Port-a-johns	$_____
Utilities	$_____
Total facility	$_____

Television production

(see appendix C for a complete breakdown)

Total television	$_____

Sales and marketing

Advertising	$_____
Media/public relations	$_____
Advertising production	$_____
Design fees	$_____
Collateral materials	$_____
Direct mail/ticket order forms	$_____
Sponsor costs	$_____
Entertainment	$_____
Postevent parties	$_____
Photographer	$_____
Merchandise—cost of goods	$_____
Program	$_____
Tents	$_____
Ancillary events	$_____
Total sales and marketing	$_____
Miscellaneous	$_____
Total expenses	$_____
Profit/(loss)	$_____

(We hope this last line will always show a profit!)

EXPENSES

The budget I just outlined lists revenues first, but I will begin this discussion with the expense side of the event because it is a bit more predictable and will give you a feel for how much revenue you will need. We will then come back to the revenue side.

General and Administrative

"G and A," as it is often called, is where I always try to start in creating the budget. This section covers all of the "must have" items, such as people, office space, and telephones, that are needed to run any business. This section can also be a catchall area for basic items you are not sure how to categorize. While some events may not have every budget category (your event may not be on television, for example), they all require the administrative elements that fall into this first section of the budget.

Personnel

For the most part, this category is pretty straightforward. It includes all of the office staff that you hire for the event. That number will vary widely from event to event based on size, complexity, and location. This figure should reflect not only your staff's salary but also all of their benefits (e.g., health insurance, vacation pay, and the like. We typically budget 20 percent of salary for benefits.). Some of these will be full-time people; others will be part-time. Some will be on a salary; others will be on a commission. You may not have to provide benefits to part-time employees whom you hire as independent contractors, so have your accountants review this thoroughly.

This line item does not include consultants, which I define as any outside firm or individual you hire to help you out in a specific area. These could include the television producer, head of operations, and so forth. We make these hires separate line items because their jobs are usually outside the scope of your day-to-day staff. The only time personnel gets at all tricky is when you or your company puts on several events. In that case you should allocate a portion of the cost for any of your staff that spend time on a particular event so that you can most accurately determine whether you made a profit. If you don't allocate these expenses, you have what I call hidden personnel costs, which can be a deceiving drain on event profitability. Make sure you include in this line item everyone who spends time on your event, no matter where they work from.

Office Rent

Again, this is not a complicated line item. It is simply the amount of money you pay for renting the office or offices that are specifically set up for your event. For example, for the King of the Beach event, we never held this tournament in the same city as we were based. So each year we had to open an office in Daytona Beach or Las Vegas for a couple of months before the event. The rental cost for that local office was a direct expense of the tournament and was charged to the King of the Beach budget. Similar to the personnel line item, if people who contribute to the event are working in other offices, you need to charge to the event a pro rata portion of the rent of those offices.

Office Supplies and Equipment

Office supplies include items such as pens, paper, copying machines, fax machines, telephones, paper clips, and rubber bands. In short, this line includes all the typical items that you need to operate the office and to support the event. If you want to be very detailed in your accounting, you could have a separate line for each item. To avoid driving ourselves crazy, however, we generally lump together the minor items and then have separate lines for major expenditures, such as telephone, fax machine, copying machine, and the like. Because these are the items that you will pay monthly rental for (unless you own them), they can easily be tracked. If you spend $1.19 on paper clips, it doesn't need its own line item!

Insurance

You will need a couple of different types of insurance—liability, television, errors and omissions, and so on. I will cover these in detail later. I bring it up here as the first of several reminders. *Don't forget insurance.* It may never come into play (we hope!), but it lets you sleep better at night.

Travel/Hotel

Travel refers to any expenses for trips, meals, local transportation, hotels, and so on that event staff incur while working on the event. As you will see, there are other travel line items in other categories of the budget that deal with talent, officials, production staff, and the like. You may want to set parameters (e.g., coach class travel, per diem spending, Satur-

day night stays, doubling up in rooms if more than one person is traveling) for staff expenses so that you can keep close tabs on everyone. Regardless, be sure to keep receipts for any expense over $25. This can be a nuisance, but make sure that you are a stickler about this policy because the IRS can ask to see them all. Travel expenses can add up in a hurry, so don't be bashful about requiring Saturday night stays, requesting corporate rates, and so on.

Entertainment

As with travel, a line item for entertainment shows up in various parts of the budget. In this section, entertainment refers to money spent trying to woo sponsors, site managers, television partners, athletes, and others to participate in your event. This might include dinner with a prospective sponsor, a gift for a potential participant, or tickets to a game for the site manager. Remember that much of what you will do is selling, and that requires more than just a good pitch. The sales process includes entertaining those you have targeted as potential partners, so make sure you budget for this as it very well could be the most effective, although least visible, money that you spend.

> ■ ■ ■ ■ ■ ■ ■ ■ ■ ■ ■
>
> **M**uch of what you will do is selling, and that requires more than just a good pitch.
>
> ■ ■ ■ ■ ■ ■ ■ ■ ■ ■ ■

Trademark Search

I am using this as a catchall phrase to include anything related to protecting your intellectual property rights, such as the name, logo, concept, or format of your event. As I will stress throughout, in today's marketplace the ownership of your trademark or copyright is very valuable. Spending a little money on protecting yourself in this area can go a long way. For example, we own the name Halloween on Ice. We *don't* own King of the Beach. Last year someone paid us to use the Halloween on Ice name and logo. We have annually paid someone else to use the King of the Beach title. *Big difference.* You may have to hire a law firm with expertise in this area, but the protection you buy will be worth the expense. If you don't think you can afford to hire someone, contact your state's patent and trademark office. The bottom line is that you should try to protect any unique creation that you conceive.

Talent

There is no event without the talent. While you may never want to admit this in your negotiations with them, it is a fact. Your budget should include a generous allocation for taking care of all of the needs of the talent, or as many as possible. If you take care of the talent well, you put yourself in a much better position to have a great event. But taking care of the talent can get pretty costly, so you have to figure out where to draw the line. I like to include anything and everything that is related to talent under this section of the budget, even though one could argue that items such as officials and judges could come under Production or some other heading. In my mind, however, the officials really are most closely associated with the athletes. As I stress throughout, try to make your event player friendly . . . and that starts with the budget.

Compensation and Prize Money

Another straightforward budget item, this is where you itemize the cost of paying the athletes to participate in your event. If you are paying appearance fees for an exhibition tennis event, they go here. If you are putting up $800,000 for an LPGA event, it would go here as well. If your event is a 10K in which the only "compensation" is a trophy, you can put that here or in the gift/trophy/parties line discussed later.

Travel

This is the second of three travel lines in the budget and represents the total cost of get-ting the talent (and their companions, if necessary) to the event. This includes airfare, taxis to the airport, limousines, and buses. As you can see, it does not include the hotel and local transportation costs once the athletes are in the city where the event is taking place. These are included on separate lines.

Hotel

You will find this line item a few times in the budget as well. Here it reflects the cost of housing the participants while they are in town for your event. Try to work out a trade or discount deal of some sort to keep these costs down. They can get expensive if you have a 32-team beach volleyball event (64 players) or a 144-field golf tournament and you are paying for everyone's hotel rooms!

Food and Beverages

Depending on the deal you make with your talent, this category can be related simply to the food provided to the players on site, or it can include on-site food and all other meals that you have to provide. If, in addition to providing food on site, you are paying the participants a per diem, I suggest you break this into two line items.

From my perspective, feeding the athletes is an important element of your event because it is very visible to them and certainly memorable. You don't want to have the participants complain of being unable to perform at peak levels because they were hungry, either because there wasn't enough food or because what was provided wasn't edible. I also think that the food and beverages that you supply are indicative of whether you are player friendly. As a tournament organizer, you don't want to get a bad rap, so spend a few extra bucks and make sure there is enough food.

In terms of drinks, remember this: Water, water, water. It is the simplest drink, but it is also the most likely to please everyone. Sure, you should have soft drinks, juices, energy replacement drinks, and the like, but

> *There is no event without the talent.*

you can never go wrong with water for a tired athlete.

Gifts, Trophies, and Parties

Let's start with the trophy. Most professional athletes I have been in contact with generally don't care that much about the trophy—unless it is their first one! In fact, for some, trophies are more of a pain than anything else. If the winner happens to live far away and is going on to another event before going home, he or she has the logistical issue of transporting it. You can choose to ship it, but unless it is something special that has a lot of tradition and history, it just might not be that meaningful. On the grassroots level, the feeling is probably just the opposite. The trophy will find an important spot in the winner's home.

Regardless, for the event and your sponsors—who are always looking for additional press coverage—a really nice trophy can mean some valuable extra ink. So, don't forget to order a trophy. During the first year of the King of the Beach Invitational I went to the tournament manager on the day of the final and out of simple curiosity asked to see the trophy. She looked at me as though I had two heads and only then did we realize that we didn't have one. She was pretty resourceful and ended up getting a sterling silver serving tray from the hotel restaurant. No one knew the difference. However, we didn't get much press coverage for our beautiful trophy.

Conversely, when we moved to the Hard Rock Hotel, someone had the idea of making the trophy an electric guitar, which has since become one of the trademarks of the event. Virtually all of the press coverage coming out of the last day of the tournament includes photos of that great trophy!

Participants may not care about the trophy, but for some reason the participants at every level of competition seem to find room to bring home their gifts from the event. Whether you give them a T-shirt, CD, or fleece jacket, everyone loves getting the event gift. Some of them are spoken about for years, and many of them serve as billboards for your event as participants wear them all over town or around the world. You don't need to spend a fortune on this item, but make sure that you put some thought into it and make it part of your event.

Parties fall somewhere between trophies and gifts. Depending on the time, place, food, invitees, and so forth, the participants can take them or leave them. If you are running a grassroots event, parties will be more appreciated than if you have a professional event in which a lot of money is on the line. At the professional level, parties can become almost more of a distraction.

Gifts, trophies, and parties come down to your budget and how you want the athletes to remember their stay at your event. You don't have to go crazy on these things, but make sure that what you do is tasteful and well scheduled.

> *Local transportation doesn't have to cost that much, but it is one of the areas that you just cannot skimp on.*

Local Transportation

Where gifts are a nice add-on, local transportation is a practical necessity. How would you explain to your audience that one of your star performers missed the event because he couldn't get a ride to the site? In chapter 1, I mentioned briefly the example of the Volvo International in North Conway, New Hampshire. In the middle of the summer in this small New England town, it could take 15 minutes to get from the hotel to the site . . . or two hours. That's right. There was a two-lane road that ran the five or so miles between the two. If the weather was good and the stadium sold out, the cars could back up for miles, so the tournament director had a helicopter on standby so that no one could ever say that the traffic caused them to miss the match. We

Developing the Budget 23

will talk later about our event in Antwerp, Belgium, where all of the players got a police escort to the stadium.

You don't necessarily need to go to these lengths, but you should make sure to provide plenty of transportation to and from the airport, hotel, and site so that none of the athletes have to wait too long to get a ride to where they are going. Yes, this will make them feel important and well taken care of, but it will also enable you to keep your mind on operating the event.

From a budget standpoint, you should be able to trade tickets and other exposure with local taxi, limousine, bus, rental car, or other agencies. You can usually get volunteer drivers for all of your cars. Local transportation doesn't have to cost that much, but it is one of the areas that you just cannot skimp on.

cials may be local and may even be volunteers, depending on the level of event. Whether they are paid or volunteers, you should still make sure that they have food, drinks, parking passes, access to transportation, and gifts. The outcome of your event may come down to an accurate call or judgment by the officials. Don't let a mistake happen because you did not take proper care of the judges, leaving them tired or short staffed.

Always remember that officials can make an event go more smoothly, so taking care of them is important.

Judges and Officials

This is another necessity of the event. You don't have to provide first-class transportation or accommodations for the officials, but at the same time, the event really can't go on without them. I have had the opportunity to work with three of the best officials—Dick Roberson and Frank Smith in tennis and Matt Gage in beach volleyball. These guys may be behind the scenes, but they make the event go smoothly. Find out the going rate for officials, give them the free reign to do their thing, and be prepared to pay them fairly while also providing their hotels, meals, and so forth. Fee information is available from the governing body that sanctions your event. Your offi-

Physicians or Trainers

Having a trainer on site might be a requirement by the sanctioning body, depending on the type of event that you are organizing. Regardless, having a trainer or doctor on site at all times is just a good idea. Remember, you are operating an event that involves intense physical performance, and people do get hurt, exhausted, and sick. You should have someone around who can attend to injuries and illness, and you should have access to a nearby hospital.

From an expense standpoint, depending on how well connected you or your event partners are, this aspect of the event should not cost a lot of money. There are usually doctors who are willing to donate their time in exchange for some tickets, parking passes, and the like, and while you may have to pay the trainers, you should be able to work out a good deal with them as well. Credits on TV and in the event program go a long way. In any case this is another of those areas in which cutting corners can come back to haunt you.

Production

Production involves all of the physical elements of setting up the event. This can be quite different for every project depending on the sport, site, and level of competition or exhibition (i.e., pro, amateur, grassroots). In skating you aren't going to bring in the same lighting rig for a club show as you are for a televised professional event. Similarly, in golf you won't use the same "stakes and rakes" for a club championship as you would for a PGA Tour event. As a result, it is hard to generalize here, so please keep that in mind. You will have to tailor your production budget to your specific event based on the overall production values you want to bring to your show.

Sound and Lights

If you are organizing an indoor event, most venues will have a sound and lighting system. The amount of additional equipment required to augment the facility's equipment will be a function of how big a show you want to put on and, of course, the nature of your event. The major arenas will probably have enough of a sound and light package to suit most of your needs. However, if you are indoors and on television, you may need to bring in more candlepower. If you are in an older building, you should expect to bring in some equipment to supplement what the facility has.

Outdoor events are a totally different situation. A golf tournament obviously won't need lights because it takes place only during the

Having a trainer or doctor on site at all times is just a good idea.

day. The site for a junior tennis event should also be pretty self-sufficient.

If your event is outdoors at night, you have to prepare very differently. When building your site from scratch, lights and sound have to be at the top of your list of crucial issues. And, if you are looking to entertain, whether indoors or out, you have to be prepared to spend some real money to accommodate your guests. For AVP (Association of Volleyball Professionals) events we carried an entire sound system because we were setting up, for the most part, at sites that needed to be built from the ground up.

At AVP events music was an important component of the entertainment, so we needed a sophisticated sound system. For Halloween on Ice we have used lasers, blue light, spotlights, and overhead lighting packages all at the same time. For Skating Goes Country we had to light not only the ice with theatrical lighting but also the stage for the musicians. As you might imagine, lighting can get *very* expensive, so don't be afraid to bid out the job to several organizations to get the best prices. Be prudent here, though. You don't want to sacrifice quality for a cheaper price if you don't have to. We almost always work with Paul Hendrickson out of Minneapolis because he understands our needs and delivers a great product. I know that we could find someone to do the work less expensively, but for reasons that I will explain later, the creative side of me never wants to sacrifice in this category. This is one of the many "push–pull" budget issues that you will face.

Site Preparation

Before moving into your facility, you may have to do a bit of face-lifting to put the site in shape for your particular event. We call this "site prep," and it needs to take place a day or two (or longer if you really need to do a lot of work) before your move-in. If you are going to an indoor arena, the site prep will be minimal. If you are going to a public place that is not really designed for events, then the site prep might be considerable. In terms of budgeting, this is primarily a manpower issue. If your site prep includes bringing in power, decorations, and the like, these should be covered in other line items.

Crew

Moving all this equipment around, installing it, operating it, and tearing it down can be a major undertaking depending on the amount of production value you are bringing to the project. While much of this equipment will be computerized, the transportation, load-in, and load-out will not be. It takes old-fashioned manpower. Some of these people will be the local stagehands that we will account for in the Facilities category. Others will be the people that come with the equipment package. Paul Hendrickson has a group of guys that he takes with him wherever he goes. You can try to keep the number of crew members down, but to some extent it is simply a function of how big a production you are planning. The bigger the package, the more people it will take. Most of the crew will have a day rate plus travel, hotel, and per diem if you bring them in from out of town.

Travel

This line item is pretty self-explanatory. From a production standpoint, you can avoid most of these costs if you can find a local crew and use local equipment. If not, bringing in people to your site from all over the country can be expensive, so make the reservations early to take advantage of every possible discount. Saturday night stays are a great innovation and are very useful here.

Hotel

With hotels you have the same issue as with travel. If you use local crews, they can sleep

■ ■ ■ ■ ■ ■ ■ ■ ■ ■ ■

Lighting can get very expensive, so don't be afraid to bid out the job to several organizations to get the best prices.

■ ■ ■ ■ ■ ■ ■ ■ ■ ■ ■

at home. If you bring people in from out of town, try to let them know in advance that they have to double up in the hotel. This can reduce hotel costs considerably.

Food and Beverages

Your production people work hard and have physical jobs. They need to be well fed. Also, in many cases you will be dealing with unions, so you will have prescribed meal and coffee break times. Find a caterer who can work within your budget, as you are going to have to feed these people several times during the event. If you are putting on a grassroots or charity event, don't hesitate to try to get food donated. You might even ask people to volunteer to cook. Sometimes the home-cooked stuff is better anyway. You may want to include the feeding of your volunteers within this line item. They are not paid, yet you could easily consider them part of your event crew.

Music Clearance

This line item is for live and television events. It is a tricky area because the rules and regulations are not as standardized as they could be nor are they policed uniformly. Nevertheless, it is important to ensure that you have cleared any music that you want to use at a live or televised event . . . or for any other reason, for that matter. The reason is simple: You are using someone else's product. They own it. If you want to play music by Elton John, you need to pay him. The clearance costs are paid to the artists through BMI, ASCAP, or the artists' record companies. If you don't pay, you are headed for trouble. My suggestion is that you hire an expert (they usually are not very expensive) to clear your music. Otherwise, you are sure to get lost in the maze that is music clearance. If you just need some generic music, there are libraries of music that are pre-cleared. I suggest this route for grassroots events. A radio station or television affiliate will probably be able to help you locate such a library if they don't have one of their own. Also, the cost of music can be great, so if you don't need it, it would be better to stay away from it. Remember that music adds tremendously to the ambience of your event. But you have to pay for it.

■ ■ ■ ■ ■ ■ ■ ■ ■ ■ ■

Music adds tremendously to the ambience of your event. But you have to pay for it.

■ ■ ■ ■ ■ ■ ■ ■ ■ ■ ■

Practice Facility

This line item could easily fall under the talent budget because, after all, it is only for the talent that you have practice courts, rinks, and driving ranges available. They are a *must,* and it is hard to offset these costs unless your venue has enough practice area. The nice thing is that it shouldn't cost you too much for the practice time (think trades here), but you *will* need it.

Local Transportation

You need to get your production people around town. Shuttle vans and rental cars work best. Your crew members need to be able to get to hardware stores, garages, and other places if anything goes wrong, so be sure that transportation is accessible. Volunteers can be helpful here. Even if volunteers aren't available, this should not be an expensive item. Again, trade if you can.

Props and Decorations

Similar to the lights and sound category, props or decorations may not be necessary at all—but it depends on the type of event you are putting on. However, in my experience, even the most modern facility can use a little color.

If you are producing a grassroots event, some inexpensive decorations can make a world of difference. This category really speaks to the impression you want to leave with the audience. For Halloween on Ice we have gone big and small with props. The crowd seems to like the show no matter what, but they definitely appreciate the extra effort when we bring out a full graveyard scene complete with spider webs. At the King of the Beach event, we have had a tendency to go overboard with decorating the site because we want to impress on people that this is a big-time event. You may not care about any of this, and more important, you may not be able to afford any of it. These are judgment calls that you will have to make. If you can find a way to afford props and decorations, you will not be sorry because they will really make your event or show stand out.

Costumes and Uniforms

Unless you are putting on an event that has some theatrical elements, you probably won't need costumes. This is one of our standard line items because we often promote themed skating shows. In those situations we feel that it is important to supplement the costumes that the talent brings with other items, such as masks for Halloween on Ice, sweaters and scarves for Skating Goes Country, and so forth. When you're putting on a competition, this element is usually not an issue unless you have an opening or closing ceremony in which you want all of the competitors to be dressed similarly. The pomp and circumstance is a nice touch, and I recommend it if it is appropriate and affordable.

Uniforms are another story. These need not be expensive or complicated, but I think it is nice to have the ushers dress in the same outfits, the security people identified by similar shirts or hats, and your staff wearing something that stands out. We have always done this at the King of the Beach, Best of the Beach, and other volleyball events, as well as at tennis events and golf events. I think uniforms are important for a few reasons, including the following:

- They make it easy to locate people in positions of authority.
- They give people stature in the eyes of the customer.
- They give your volunteers (or event-paid security and ushers) a usable gift and make them feel good about you, the event, and themselves. In fact, you can never do too much for your volunteers. You want them to come back year after year, and they are a great source of positive word of mouth for the event.
- From an economic standpoint, having all of these people wearing items that can be purchased at your souvenir stand might just be the impetus your customers need to go buy something.

From a budgeting standpoint, uniforms and costumes need not be expensive. In fact, if you have official clothing sponsors, they will usually be happy to outfit some or all of your staff at no cost as part of their deal. After all, what better exposure than to have 50 to 100 people at the event wearing their gear? If you have to purchase the uniforms, don't be afraid to negotiate. The exposure you are providing should be worth a sizable discount.

Makeup

Again, this is something that most likely will only come into play with certain sports (figure skating and gymnastics come immediately to mind), so in most cases you won't have to worry about makeup artists. However, if you do, try to get people who are experienced and really understand the demands of television and theatrical lighting. It doesn't do much good for you to bring specialists in if the talent doesn't think they know what they are doing. You should be able to find makeup artists locally in virtually any city or town.

Facility

As we will discuss in great detail in chapter 3, this part of the budget is where you will reflect all of the costs associated with doing business at your site. Try to get a handle on these costs as early as possible because, as we will see later, they might affect several of your other line items.

Rent

This line simply reflects whatever deal you make with the venue to operate from their site. It should include the base rent and any percentage of the ticket sales that you have to pay. In most cases your rent at an indoor facility will include all of your utilities, such as power, lights, electric, heat, air conditioning, and so on. Obviously, if you are at an outdoor facility, your rent structure is going to be completely different because you will have to bring in all of these items.

■ ■ ■ ■ ■ ■ ■ ■ ■ ■ ■

You can never do too much for your volunteers. You want them to come back year after year, and they are a great source of positive word of mouth for the event.

■ ■ ■ ■ ■ ■ ■ ■ ■ ■ ■

Stagehands or Crew

These are the people who supplement the production crew discussed earlier. It is a tough line item to gauge and often ends up costing you more than you anticipated because you get into overtime situations. This line appears in two categories because I differentiate between the basic production crew (i.e., sound and light experts) from the stagehands who simply provide additional manpower. If you are in a union building, make sure you completely understand their rules and regulations. If you are outdoors, be sure to hire enough personnel. In either case, don't forget to budget for overtime.

Security

If you are in an arena, this is not going to be something that you have to worry about too much. The cost of security should be included in your rent, and the building will make sure that the security staff arrives on time and does their job. If you are at an outside venue that you are creating (such as at the King of the Beach Invitational), however, security can become much more complex. You will have to determine the number of security people based on how much area you need to cover. Also, don't forget that if you are outside, you can't lock up as tightly at night, so you may need security around the clock. You should be able to make a good deal with a local security company, but remember to start this discussion early on so that you know they are available.

Box Office

The box office presents issues that are similar to security. If you are at an arena or stadium, it should have a box office and, for fees that will be incorporated into your rent or on a per-ticket basis, the venue will allow you to use their staff. When you are creating a site at a beach, park, or high school, you have to worry about setting up a box office. One of the best makeshift box offices is a portable trailer. You can rent these fairly inexpensively, and they can serve as an office for you as well. You can always set up tables under a tent if need be. Just make sure you have a convenient system for people to order tickets and an equally accessible place for people to pick up the tickets. Of similar importance is how you handle the cash that you take in. Your box office will need a lockbox or a relationship with a security company so that you never have too much cash around. You don't want your box office to be a target for a robbery!

> ■ ■ ■ ■ ■ ■ ■ ■ ■ ■ ■
>
> **M**ake sure you have a convenient system for people to order tickets and an equally accessible place for people to pick up the tickets.
>
> ■ ■ ■ ■ ■ ■ ■ ■ ■ ■ ■

Stadium

This line item refers to a situation in which you need to build your own site. If you are putting on an event that requires you to build bleacher seating and perhaps even the court or field of play (for example, at a three-on-three basketball tournament or street hockey event), all the costs go in this line item. If you are in this situation, you probably should have several subcategories that include bleachers, chairs if you have VIP seating, hospitality areas if you are building them, tents, ropes, and so on.

Port-a-Johns

This is my catchall line item for everything that you will need to handle the spectators.

Providing for Those With Disabilities

When you build a venue, don't forget to provide for those with disabilities. It is not only the nice thing to do, but it is also required by law under Title III of the Americans with Disabilities Act (ADA), which covers building codes. The ADA is governed by the U.S. Department of Justice. For more information about how this law applies to your stadium, you can either call the Department of Justice at 800-514-0301; write them at 950 Pennsylvania Ave., NW, Washington, D.C. 20530-0001; or visit their Web site at **www.usdoj.gov/crt/ada/adahom1.htm**.

Again, if you are in an established venue, they will have rest rooms, concession stands, souvenir stands, information booths, areas for product displays, and so forth. If you are outdoors, even in a stadium, you may have to build some of these items. If you are on a beach, you will have to build them all. This is where those costs go. I title this line "port-a-johns" because if you forget everything else, don't forget the rest rooms!

Utilities

Indoors this is normally covered in your rent expense. Outdoors you may need to bring in power, lights, phone lines, electrical generators, and the like. If so, they need their own line item in the budget, as you won't be able to do much without some form of power.

Television Production

See appendix C for a complete breakdown of the television production budget. I discuss television in some depth later, but television production is a separate book in and of itself, and I am sure that there have been several written. My best advice is to hire a producer who can take much of this off your plate. You can't be an expert in every area of event management, and unless you ultimately want to be in television (it seems everyone does!), this is an area best delegated to experts.

Frankly, I am not the best delegator that you will ever meet. However, even I have learned that television production is a very specialized area. I knew that I had learned my lesson about where to draw the line in this department when, before Skating Goes Country, the director (Meg Streeter) explained to me why she might not be ready during rehearsal. I told her that I was not even concerned, hadn't really thought about her being ready, and had every confidence that she would do the job when "the curtain came up." You have to have that kind of trust in the people around you or you are destined to do everything yourself,

which is a recipe for failure. Hire the best producer and director you can find and agree on a budget. Your job is to *manage* them so that they deliver the show within the numbers.

Sales and Marketing

Most sales and marketing expenses are tied into the plan to communicate and sell your event to sponsors, participants, fans, and the press. Sales and marketing expenses are largely discretionary dollars as opposed to some of the line items discussed previously, which are prerequisites for holding your event. Nevertheless, as we will learn later, these may be some of the most important dollars you spend. Many of these spending decisions will be tied to how much revenue you generate, leading to the old adage, You need to spend money to make money.

Advertising

You can take your advertising plan in many directions. Your decisions on which avenues to follow will no doubt be affected by how much money you have available. We generally break this particular line item into subcategories of print, radio, television, and "other" (which includes the Internet) so that we have a very specific road map for how to spend the dollars allocated to this category. This line item should reflect the amount you have to devote to the actual placement of the ads. As you will see, other elements of your advertising plan are included in some of the line items that follow.

Media or Public Relations

"PR," as it is referred to, is very important for a lot of reasons. PR can help spread the word about your event; act to build the stature of various performers who may not be that well known; and if positioned correctly, serve as a way to build your stature so that when you call on potential sponsors or other corporate partners, they know who *you* are. There is a

■ ■ ■ ■ ■ ■ ■ ■ ■ ■ ■ ■

If you forget everything else, don't forget the rest rooms!

■ ■ ■ ■ ■ ■ ■ ■ ■ ■ ■ ■

very good chance that a local public relations agency can do exactly what you need for very reasonable fees. They will need four to six months' lead time to get the job done. Don't overlook this line item. It can be quite important to the success of your event.

Advertising Production

Be careful here. You can spend $250,000 to produce a 30-second television commercial. Or you can spend under $10,000 to produce a commercial that delivers a similar message, although without the production value. If you spend a quarter of a million dollars, you'd better get a hell of a lot more return out of your commercial than if you spend $10,000. We typically spend a lot closer to the lower fees than the higher fees for our television spots; in fact, we've never spent anywhere near the $250,000 level. When you get to the higher numbers, you are probably shooting on film, which takes longer, requires a bigger crew and more union fees, and so forth, which of course will be more expensive. Remember, the look of your ad is only part of the issue. The message is most important. From my perspective, if you can shoot your spot on videotape with the correspondingly lower fees, do it. That is not to say that you should produce a cheesy spot. I get uncomfortable when I see a commercial that clearly was done on the cheap. But you can do good work—that is, creative and with production value—without spending a fortune.

In addition to television advertising, you will probably plan to use print or radio advertising. If your budget is tight, radio spots can almost always be produced at minimal cost by the radio stations with whom you are working. You can write the copy, and the station's on-air talent will usually provide the voice. If you want some music laid in, the station can help you get that as well. If you have a big budget, you can go into a studio and pay high-

priced talent to write music and ad copy, supply the voice, and do the production. For smaller events and those with limited budgets, the studio route won't be affordable.

The same is true of your print ads. You can use an ad agency or you can give the newspaper a basic idea of what you are looking for, and they will probably be able to design the ad for you. If you develop a good relationship with the radio and television stations as well as the local newspapers, you will save yourself money and get better placement and probably better pricing for your ads. Internet advertising is becoming increasingly effective, and that too does not have to involve expensive production to create an effective ad.

The bottom line: This line item is for production only. Since it represents only a part of your ad budget, keep your costs in line.

> ■ ■ ■ ■ ■ ■ ■ ■ ■ ■ ■ ■
>
> *The look of your ad is only part of the issue. The message is most important.*
>
> ■ ■ ■ ■ ■ ■ ■ ■ ■ ■ ■ ■

Design Fees

This is the cost of hiring an artist to design all of the communications pieces that we have been discussing. We have usually opted to find someone who is talented but trying to get a break. They are hungrier, cheaper, and willing to put in the time to get it right. While you are taking a chance to some degree by going this route (as opposed to hiring from an established design firm), you usually get good work at affordable prices.

Collateral Materials

These are all of the materials (brochures, posters, sales video, and the like) that you might use to sell your event to the public or to sponsors and television outlets. Collateral materials can become very expensive, so you have to plan carefully and try to figure out which ones will best support your sales effort. Do you really need a sales tape, and if so, can you make it just by editing existing footage either of past events or of similar-looking ones? Or do you need to create a script and storyboards, hire actors and a film crew, and start from scratch? Should you create a four-color brochure for sponsorship sales, or can you make do with something that you create on your computer? Do you need a poster, or after you produce 500 pieces, are they just going to sit in someone's office? All of these are financial issues, and since you have to stay within some overall budget, you won't get to do them all in most cases. Be prudent and try to determine which are the most important, and then find a way to produce them in the most cost-efficient manner.

Direct Mail and Ticket Order Forms

This is the cost of *producing and mailing* advance ticket order forms to your list of select fans. I emphasize this because, when figuring your budget, you must not forget the cost of sending the order form in the mail. Even at a mere 34 cents apiece, direct mail can get very expensive if you send out several thousand pieces. Make sure you calculate this into your costs. You will find that a bulk mail rate is not hard to get at your local post office, and the money that you save by obtaining that lower rate, even though the mail gets delivered a bit more slowly, is well worth the effort.

Sponsor Costs

Treat your sponsors well, but then again, I wouldn't go overboard unless you have a wildly successful event. You don't want the sponsors to think that they are giving you all that money for you to turn around and spend it on them. They could do that themselves. Nevertheless, a party and even some small gifts may be in order. We have done everything from a T-shirt to a goody bag complete with shirts, CDs, mousepads, party invitations, and items from other sponsors. The sponsors and their guests always appreciate the effort. But we generally control the costs in this line item pretty well.

Entertainment

You will have to entertain people throughout the event process. Some of this, such as taking a prospective sponsor to lunch or having breakfast with people from your site during the postevent wrap-up, might go in the G & A portion of the budget. We generally use this line to reflect entertainment costs *during* the event. Similar to many other items, this does not have to be extravagant, but it is going to happen, so plan accordingly.

Postevent Parties

As you will see after being involved with a couple of events, when it is all over, most people want to go home pretty quickly. However, if you have advertised a postevent party for ticket holders, this is the line item for those expenses. Also, as we will discuss later, don't overlook the morale of your staff; a postevent dinner celebrating your success is a nice touch. All of this can get expensive, so plan it in advance even if you want to make the dinner for your staff seem spontaneous! As for the bigger party for sponsors and ticket purchasers, this too can become a major expense if you let it get out of hand. We have generally limited these postevent bashes to beer, wine, soft drinks, and finger food or dessert because people do need to get home after the event. We don't go crazy, and I don't think you need to either. If you do, you may spend heavily and be left with a lot of untouched food.

Photographer

This doesn't have to cost you a lot of money, but I urge you to have a photographer on site.

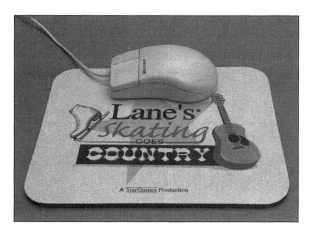

Treat your sponsors well by handing out small gifts, such as this mousepad.

You will want pictures of your event at some time in the future for a variety of reasons. From time to time you may want to use photos from your event as gifts to the participants. We had a great photographer at One Enchanted Evening, so I sent photos to each of the skaters. To get the most from your photographer, before the event you should give him or her a list of what you want shot. This will save everyone time, money, and aggravation.

Merchandise— Cost of Goods

While merchandise is going to show up as a line item in your revenues, you can't forget to include it as an expense as well. We will discuss the up-front cash needed to create the merchandise that you sell. This is where that figure will be plugged in. However, unlike many of your expenses that can be paid *after* the event, the merchandise is usually paid for *up front;* so you have to plan not only the expense but the cash flow as well.

hologram on the cover. We sold it for $10. That was in 1995. We still have some programs left!

Tents

If you are at an outdoor site that you are building from the ground up, you will need tents of all sizes. You can rent tents from a variety of sources, and again, you can negotiate by throwing in some benefits in addition to cash. Don't be afraid to try to barter to knock down these costs a bit.

This photograph would make an excellent gift for the winner of this race or an advertisement to promote next year's event.

Program

Keep in mind that you will not sell a program to everyone that walks through the gate, so you need to balance the value of the program against the desire to produce something that will leave a lasting impression. Consider this a business within itself. If you sell a lot of ads, go ahead and spend some extra money on your program. If not, either don't produce one or do it nicely—but cost effectively. The only time we really strayed from this policy was during the inaugural Halloween on Ice when we were playing the FleetCenter during its opening week. We created a high-gloss program and even considered putting a

Ancillary Events

You won't always have ancillary events around your tournament, but if you do, this is where you should list all of the expenses related to those activities. Whether it is tee times for a golf tournament, rental of a hall for a party, or hiring a band for a bash the way we have in Las Vegas, get into the details of these expenses and make sure that they are all covered here.

Miscellaneous

Frankly, if you have taken the time to get very detailed with your budget and the line items that make it up, you should have no need for a miscellaneous category. But you are bound to have missed something along the way, and at the time of the event, there is always something that comes up. This line item becomes a catchall for the things that you didn't take into account or that come up at the last minute because the lights blow, the food is late, there aren't as many props as you expected—the list goes on. With that in mind, don't let this become a sinkhole that blows your budget out of whack. You have to take responsibility for every line item and try to be as thorough as possible. Try not to spend anything against this line item (even though that is probably an unrealistic goal).

REVENUES

As I mentioned earlier, I am discussing revenues after expenses because they are *much* more difficult to predict. After all, you can pretty much decide that you are going to produce a certain number of posters for a particular dollar figure and, with the proper discipline, stay within that budget. I challenge you to take a new event and predict how many tickets you will sell or how much sponsorship revenue you will generate.

Nevertheless, the revenue budget is critical because it will let you determine whether you can cover the costs that you committed to on the expense side. With that in mind, the revenue side of your budget should include the following items (again, we will cover each of these line items in much greater detail later in the book).

Title Sponsor

The title sponsor is the lead sponsor of your event. In most cases this will be the company that pays you the most money. In terms of budgeting, you should include the gross fee paid by the sponsor in this line item and then incorporate any hard expenses paid out on their behalf (including staff and third-party commissions) in the appropriate expense line item. I would treat commissions paid out to employees or other third parties in the same

way: Add up the revenue and then include the commissions as an expense item (in the personnel line) or as a deduction from revenue as shown later.

Presenting Sponsor

The presenting sponsor will be your second-biggest sponsor. It is also the most difficult deal to make because you need to convince someone that the additional fees paid above an official sponsor category are worthwhile even though they will still be in a subsidiary position to the title sponsor. I separate this item out because of the potential magnitude of this particular sponsorship.

Official Sponsors

After separating out the title and presenting sponsor, we tend to lump the official sponsors together in one line item. You might break this down further in the backup pages to your basic budget.

Ticket Sales

This is pretty self-explanatory (the number of tickets you expect to sell multiplied by the price), but it is very difficult to judge, particularly in the first year of an event. Your initial budget will simply have a number that comes as a result of an educated guess (as will many of your opening revenue projections). You will definitely need to update this line item on a regular basis. Don't forget to deduct sales tax and credit card fees when calculating your *net* income from ticket sales.

Merchandising

Again, you can separate each individual item that you sell or use an all-encompassing number here while getting into the detail in the backup pages. I suggest the latter. I always want to get a good feel for where we stand on our revenues and expenses from a relatively quick glance, so the less paper, the better. In our budgets this line is a gross sales number, as we put the cost of these goods in the expense budget. I should warn you that a

Backup Pages

Sometimes the budget format outlined earlier will not allow for enough detail. In that case you might want to have the basic budget serve as a summary page (or pages) and then have a separate page for each line item. As your event grows, you are likely to have more sponsors, more advertising outlets, more vendors, and so on. You won't be able to keep everything in your head, so backup pages are a helpful tool. They simply reflect the detail of what is shown in a particular line item on your budget. A typical backup page for something like the official sponsor line item might look like this:

Official Sponsors (as of July 21)

Company	Gross fee	Invoice date	Date $ received
Official clothing	$10,000	July 1; Sept. 15	July 20; $5,000
Official drink	$10,000	June 25; Sept. 15	July 3; $5,000
Official car	$ 7,500	July 10; Sept. 15	outstanding

Update the backup pages on a regular basis so that they truly reflect the most current information on your event.

start-up event is not likely to make a lot of money from the sale of souvenirs. However, the offsetting PR value of having walking billboards may be worth the effort and expense.

Program

This line will have the revenues from ad sales and actual program sales. You will have accounted for the production costs in the expense budget. Some people like to use net numbers—revenue after expenses have been taken out. I suggest that you stay away from that type of accounting because it tends to hide the cost of production and thus can be misleading.

Domestic Television

The rights fee that you receive from a television network to air your show in the country where it is taking place will go in this line. Most of our events take place in the United States, so this line could say "U.S. television." A first-year or grassroots event is probably not going to earn much in the way of rights fees. In fact, for many events, if you can get on televi-

sion at all (and we will discuss the various television options later), you should consider it a big bonus.

International Television

The rights fees you earn from all other countries where your event is broadcast will go in this line. Again, unless you have an established event with international implications, you shouldn't count on much income from this line item; but you should be prepared for it nevertheless.

Commercial Sales

You might have the ability to earn revenue from selling commercial spots on the telecast of your event, depending on your television deal. You will list those revenues here. Remember when selling commercial time that most companies place their ads through an agency to whom they pay a commission. When you are making proposals to companies with regard to purchasing advertising time, remember to tell them the net amount you are looking for. If you are looking for $10,000 and forget to mention that this is the "net" amount, and you make the deal, you will end up with $8,300 (after the agency takes its 17 percent commission), which is better than nothing but not what you had in mind.

Ancillary Events

As we will discuss in some detail, many times you will have secondary events surrounding your main event to generate press coverage, to keep sponsors happy, or to entertain the athletes. Any revenue generated from these ancillary events should be listed in this line.

Miscellaneous

Any revenue that did not find a home in the previous lines should go here. I doubt that you will have much in this line because you should be able to classify every dollar that comes in under one of the previous categories.

Fees to Third Parties

You may at times have to make payments to third parties for commissions, commercial time that you have to buy for your sponsors, and any other fees that you pay out as a condition of a sponsorship or other deal. These expenses can be posted before coming to the final revenue calculation so that you have a net revenue number before deducting expenses. You can also put these items in the expense budget if you so desire, whatever is easiest for you and your accountants to interpret. If you have to pay fees to third parties—which is not necessarily a bad thing—make sure you have a line for this.

Profit/(Loss)

This is the difference between revenues and expenses. Your goal, of course, is profits!

CASH FLOW

Perhaps of equal importance to the budget itself is the timing of paying your bills and collecting your revenues. The coming and going of your cash is called cash flow. You need to be at least as detailed about cash flow as you are about your budget.

It is not enough to know how much revenue you are going to make. You also need to know when the money will be collected. Similarly, it is not enough to know how much you are going to spend on each line item. You also have to know when the invoices for those expenses will have to be paid.

■ ■ ■ ■ ■ ■ ■ ■ ■ ■ ■ ■

You need to be at least as detailed about cash flow as you are about your budget.

■ ■ ■ ■ ■ ■ ■ ■ ■ ■ ■ ■

We have always tried to time our cash flow so that bills are paid after third-party services are rendered, while sponsorship fees and other revenues are received, at least in part, before our delivering benefits. In that manner, we limit the amount of working capital that we need and can simply pay bills from cash we receive from the event. This ideal scenario—never go into your own pocket if you don't have to—is not always achievable, however.

Therefore, when it comes to cash flow and cash planning, make sure of a few things:

- Use a chart to graph the expected inflows and outflows of cash (see chart, next page).
- Know approximately how much cash you need to get your event started (seed capital).
- Try to delay the payment of expenses by contract, making sure that you don't pay for things until others have performed.
- Keep in mind that big companies are often slow to pay. This is something that always surprises me. You know they have the money, but often these behemoths have such involved payment procedures that they can rarely pay you on time. Don't

Sample Cash Flow Chart (assumes 10/1 event date and 10/15 TV air date)

	April	May	June	July	Aug	Sept	Oct	Nov	Dec
Revenue									
Title sponsor				✔			✔	✔	
Presenting sponsor						✔		✔	
Other sponsors		✔	✔		✔	✔	✔	✔	
Ticket sales				✔	✔	✔	✔		
TV commercial sales								✔	✔
Merchandise							✔		
Expenses									
Personnel	✔	✔	✔	✔	✔	✔	✔	✔	✔
Facility				✔			✔		
Printing		✔	✔			✔			
Travel	✔	✔	✔	✔	✔	✔	✔	✔	
Prize money							✔		
TV production					✔		✔	✔	
Labor (crew)						✔	✔		
Hotel	✔	✔	✔	✔	✔	✔	✔	✔	✔
Advertising					✔	✔	✔	✔	
PR		✔				✔		✔	
Parties							✔		
Promotion						✔	✔		
Merchandise						✔			

When planning your event, realize that expenses come prior to revenue being recieved, so plan accordingly.

take it personally. It happens all the time. Just make sure you plan for it.

- Treat cash flow as sacredly as you treat the budget itself.

As I said at the outset of this section, the budget should be your bible. You should develop it as soon as you possibly can and base many of your decisions on it. Review your budget often and be prepared to make the changes that are necessary as the event evolves. After the first couple of years of an event, the changes to the budget during the course of the event should be minimal because your familiarity with the property will make it more predictable. But in the early years of an event, the swings can catch you by surprise if you take your eye off this ball. *Don't*.

The budget and your mission statement form the foundation for your event. With these basic tools you are ready to launch into the various elements of event operations, all of which will be covered in the remaining chapters and require you and your staff to become jacks of all trades.

The first issue is where to play.

Working Model: Regional Tennis Tournament Budget

The initial budget for the regional tennis tournament in our working model would look something like this:

Working Model for Initial Budget

Revenue

Title sponsor	$ 25,000
Presenting sponsor	$ 7,500
Official sponsors (5@$4,000)	$ 20,000
Ticket sales (1,000@$10.00)	$ 10,000
Merchandising (250 T-shirts@$20)	$ 5,000
Program (10 ads@$250)	$ 2,500
TV (16 spots@$200)	$ 3,200
Miscellaneous (donations)	$ 3,000
Total revenue	$ 76,200

Expenses

G & A

Personnel	$ 2,500
Office rent	$ 1,000
Office supplies/equipment (paper, copies, mail, etc.)	$ 1,500
Insurance	$ 1,500
Travel	$ 2,000
Total G & A	$ 8,500

Talent

Compensation	N/A
Travel	$ 2,500
Hotel	$ 1,500
Food/beverages	$ 1,000
Gifts/trophies/parties	$ 2,000
Local transportation (rental vans)	$ 1,000
Judges/officials (food, gifts)	$ 1,000
Physicians/trainers	$ 500
Total talent	$ 9,500

Production

Sound/lights	N/A
Site preparation	N/A
Crew	N/A
Travel	N/A
Food/beverages	$ 500
Music clearance	N/A
Practice facility	N/A
Local transportation (rental car for runner)	$ 150
Props/decorations (decorations to spruce up the site)	$ 300
Costumes/uniforms (shirts for officials)	$ 300
Makeup	N/A
Total production	$ 1,250

Facility

Rent	$ 1,000
Stagehands/crew (you need a couple of people on hand)	$ 750
Security (perhaps unnecessary)	$ 500
Box office (10% of ticket sales)	$ 1,000
Stadium (400 seats@ $12.50/ seat; includes setup)	$ 5,000
Port-a-johns (port-a-johns and other facility needs)	$ 1,000
Total facility	$ 9,250

Television

Production (buy-on; production of a one-hour telecast)	$ 20,000

Sales and Marketing

Advertising (print, Internet)	$ 5,000
Media/publications (regional agency)	$ 2,500
Advertising production	N/A
Design fees (flyers, program, ads, etc.)	$ 1,000
Collateral materials (flyers, entry forms)	$ 1,000
Ticket order forms/ direct mail	$ 1,000

Sponsor costs (T-shirts, programs)	$ 2,000	Tents	Trade
		Ancillary events	N/A
Entertainment (lunches with sponsors, others)	$ 750	Total sales/marketing	$ 18,300
		Miscellaneous (includes cost of balls)	**$ 2,000**
Postevent parties	$ 750		
Photographer	$ 300		
Merchandise	$ 3,000	**Total expenses**	**$68,800**
Program	$ 1,000	**Profit/(loss)**	**$ 7,400**

According to this initial projection, this event would earn about a 9 percent return in its first year. Given that these are preliminary numbers and are based on a reasonably aggressive level of sponsorship sales, I would have liked to see a bit more of a cushion in case sponsorship sales fall short. Nevertheless, this is a first-year event, and you are prepared to break even or sustain a slight loss; so this projection is strong enough to warrant going forward with the event. With that in mind, it might be prudent to try to cut the budget a little further and give the sales staff some additional incentive to work out some trade deals that will add money directly to the bottom line.

Chapter THREE

Location, Location, Location

In order to solicit players and sponsors successfully, apply for sanctions, and if applicable, negotiate a television deal, you must be able to tell everyone where your event is taking place.

We have put on events in a variety of venues. Among these locations have been some of the most beautiful and talked about landmarks in the world, including Manhattan Beach, California; Las Vegas, Nevada; Scottsdale, Arizona; and New York's Madison Square Garden to name a few. With access to all of these world-class locations, you would think that we would never have a problem finding the perfect venue for an event. It isn't that easy, though.

THE PERFECT MARKET

Consider the pluses and minuses at the following sites:

• The beach setting in **Manhattan Beach, California,** is perfect for pro beach volleyball. However, unless you get a permit, the number of tickets you can sell at events that are actually held on the beach is restricted by the California Coastal Commission to 25 percent of the total. If you have 4,000 seats, you can sell 1,000. Everyone else must get in free, and that is true only if you get city approval; oth-

erwise, *all* spectators get in free. The application process for the permit is fraught with political problems. In 1997, while I was managing the AVP Tour, we had to cancel the Manhattan Beach Open because our effort to sell tickets resulted in picketing, lawsuits, and general hysteria . . . and no permit.

• In **Washington, D.C.,** after working with the parks department to build a beautiful state-of-the-art tennis facility, we were told by the local residents that they would only allow limited parking in the park where the stadium was located. This resulted in hundreds of ticket holders, many of whom had contributed considerable funds to help get the stadium built, having to walk substantial distances to get to their seats. They were not pleased.

• As I mentioned earlier, in **Del Ray Beach, Florida,** despite the fact that we were at a phenomenal new club, they couldn't get the grass to grow in time to hold our event. (My partner Lon Monk tells me now that he sneaked onto the courts anyway and got one of his rare grass-court wins against one of our colleagues!)

• In **Boston,** where the inaugural Halloween on Ice played to near sellout crowds during the opening week of the FleetCenter, we had a hard time selling sponsorships because the most likely corporate prospects had just spent their marketing dollars buying signage, suites, and other benefits for year-round exposure in the new building.

• At **Walt Disney World,** perhaps the finest theme park resort in the world, we had parking problems that stemmed from the standard procedures of the park. This affected overall attendance at our tournament. Also, because of the competing events going on within the various parks, some of the focus on our event was diluted.

• In **Providence, Rhode Island,** Halloween on Ice, which was supposed to benefit from being part of the Civic Center's 25th anniversary, actually suffered from lack of attention because the local staff was overwhelmed with the bigger anniversary celebration.

While I could list additional examples, the point is that it is difficult to find the perfect scenario; and just when you think you have figured out how to protect your event from any potential venue-related problems, you will no doubt find an issue that no one has anticipated. So, you have to pick your site carefully, understand the potential pitfalls, and be prepared to work around them or work through them with the venue management. If you are able to do this, you should be able to take advantage of the many benefits that your site can provide. We have had some wonderful experiences with our venues, including the following:

• When we taped One Enchanted Evening at the **Mullins Center at the University of Massachusetts in Amherst,** we needed complete security in the building for three days. They diverted all other activities for us so that we were able to tape the show completely free of any disturbances.

• The **FleetCenter** included us in their opening week advertising campaign and ticket sales mailings, thus saving us thousands of dollars that we otherwise would have had to spend for mailing lists, printing, and postage.

• The **City of Hermosa Beach** went to bat with the California Coastal Commission and granted us the right to hold two events in Hermosa within 60 days of each other when we had to cancel the Manhattan Beach Open.

• The **Hard Rock Hotel** worked with us so that we could essentially control all of the rooms at the hotel during the King of the Beach Invitational despite the fact that this meant turning away some of their regular customers.

• The **Tsongas Arena in Lowell, Massachusetts,** placed all of our ads for Halloween on Ice, thus providing us with access to their discounted advertising rates in the local papers. This saved us a considerable amount of money from our advertising and promotional budget because without the arena's help we would not have qualified for these discounted prices.

Again, you get the picture. If you work closely with a venue whose staff develops a vested interest in the success of your event, the partnership is invaluable. So, what is the trick to picking the right venue for your event, and how do you get them to feel a sense of partnership? There is no magic formula. Making your venue a partner in a legal sense is primarily dealt with in the contract negotiation, which I will discuss later. Giving them a sense of ownership and responsibility is going to have to come from you and the relationship you build. First, however, you have to pick the right market. In this regard, you should follow certain guidelines and watch out for some specific issues. But there is no guarantee that your site will work.

Determining Marketability

Before choosing the physical site, you have to judge whether the marketplace where you plan to hold the event can support a project of the nature that you have in mind. In other words,

• Is the sport popular?
• Are similar events happening at the same time?
• Will your target market of spectators be available?
• Is there a likelihood of success?

Establishing Tradition

One of the principles that I have always held high with respect to the location for any kind of event is the notion of tradition. The ultimate nonfinancial goal for any event is to become a tradition for that date and that particular site. Wimbledon would arguably be just another tennis tournament if it were not held at the All England Club. An event earns immediate respect if it is held at Madison Square Garden in New York. Our King of the Beach Invitational became bigger as its ties to the Hard Rock Hotel became more solidified, and Halloween on Ice was instantly on the radar screen in Boston because it was held at the new FleetCenter. You may want to take this into consideration when trying to determine where to hold your event.

It would probably be suicidal to try to hold an LPGA tournament within a five-mile radius and within three weeks of a PGA Tour event. Likewise, holding a charity 5K race a week after your neighboring town had a 10K run for a similar cause probably doesn't make sense. However, some ideas that may sound as though they may not work at first, might.

Putting on a figure skating event in the summer sounds crazy. Promoting beach volleyball in the winter appears unworkable. However, there is some merit to what is called "counterprogramming," or giving the public something you know they like when they least expect it. This is exactly what we had in mind when we helped develop the figure skating event Too Hot to Skate for Jefferson Pilot Sports in 1996.

Skating was in such great demand at the time that putting skating on television in prime time during the summer, when the audience was starved for some of a sport they had come to love (and tired of sitcom reruns), made sense. The show, which was held outdoors on a portable rink adjacent to the beach in Santa Cruz, California (which is packed with tourists during the summer), was a huge success for a couple of years.

■ ■ ■ ■ ■ ■ ■ ■ ■ ■ ■

The ultimate nonfinancial goal for any event is to become a tradition for that date and that particular site.

■ ■ ■ ■ ■ ■ ■ ■ ■ ■ ■

The same theory held true for beach volleyball. In the early 1990s Howard Freeman, a New York event promoter, had the idea of bringing beach volleyball indoors to Madison Square Garden right smack in the middle of the winter. By around February, people in the Northeast are so tired of the cold that they daydream about the summer. Holding an indoor "beach festival" with the best beach volleyball players in the world as the feature attraction was creative. While it may have seemed like an off-the-wall concept, major sponsors loved it, and 12,000 people showed up. The event continued for several years before it ran its course.

Determining the marketability of your event may require some considerable research on the local scene. In this regard, it is helpful to have a working knowledge of your market and is in part why most promoters tend to organize events in the vicinity of where they live and work every day. In the beach volleyball and skating examples discussed earlier (neither of which were our events, although we did come up with the concept for the skating show), the promoters knew their markets well. Madison Square Garden itself promoted the AVP (Association of Volleyball Professionals) indoor event.

Their staff, in theory, should know the New York audience as well or better than anyone. For Too Hot to Skate, JP Sports worked with Bill Graham Presents, the event management arm of the legendary rock 'n' roll promoter's company. Located in San Francisco, they were quite familiar with the Santa Cruz area, which is no more than 50 miles from their offices. Again, while there was no guarantee of success in either case, the fact that the promoters knew the market, how the sport was viewed there, the local schedule of events, and the availability of their target audience gave them a basis for determining the potential success for the project.

Local Knowledge

Whether you live and work in the place where you plan to hold your event or come into town from the outside (as we have done on several occasions), there are some very basic issues you must consider before choosing your ultimate venue. These include schedule, community leaders, and interest level.

Schedule

You have to know what competition you will face. In today's marketplace the options available to the public are numerous and ever expanding, so you need to try to learn about every possible event that you may come up against. These include everything from professional sports events to grassroots events to fund-raisers, theater openings, school plays, and museum functions. Whether you are running a grassroots event or a major spectator tournament, you probably will not want to try to sell sponsorships and tickets against the most popular charity event in the community. Not only will you have a hard time raising money, but also you won't get anyone's attention. One of your goals should be to become part of the local scene and a must-see

It is critical to try to make the event part of the fabric of the community.

(or -attend /-participate) event. In order to do so, you will need to schedule your event at a time when the community can accommodate it and give it the focus it will need.

When I was managing the AVP, I tried to stress to Allison Canfield, the tour's vice president of marketing, that it was critical to try to make the event part of the fabric of the community. With a tour whose schedule changes yearly, this is tough to do. However, with an annual event, if you can establish your date and site so that people know when your event is coming and where it will be held, they will put it on their social calendars and make their plans around it. If you can achieve that stature, you have a chance to be very successful. So research every potential competitive event using your local contacts, city magazines, newspapers, and visitor and tourist bureaus.

Also, don't forget to check the calendar for local holidays. If you are in New England, you may not want to schedule your event on Patriots Day, which is not only a holiday in the Commonwealth of Massachusetts but also the traditional day for the Boston Marathon. Talk about getting lost in the shuffle.

No matter how much research you do into the local schedule, you may come across some situations that no one knew about. In Nashville, after we had booked the arena, signed some of the talent, and generally let people in the community know that we were coming to town, we learned that another, albeit smaller, skating show was scheduled at a different building in Nashville just five days after ours. Ultimately, we joined forces with that promoter, but the point is, no matter how many people you talk to, you may not find out until a later date that something is planned that conflicts with your event. If that happens, and particularly if the events are going to draw from the same audience (as would have happened in Nashville), if it isn't too late, someone will probably need to adjust. The alternative could be a financial disaster for both projects.

Community Leaders

Often the most important people for your event's success are behind the scenes. Who pulls the strings at the local charities? Who can help you organize volunteers? If you need help at city hall, whose ear do you need? If you know all these people, great. However, if not, you had better get friendly with someone who does. If you are promoting in an area in which you are not well connected, finding the right local representative will be critical. They just might know who the key people are, where the skeletons are buried (meaning the local history; this is what I call "institutional knowledge"), and how to get you the ear of the local movers and shakers.

We decided that the perfect place for Skating Goes Country was Nashville. The only problem with that decision was that none of us had ever spent more than a day in the city and didn't know a thing about it. If we were going to have a chance to be successful, we were going to have to learn quickly as much as possible about "Music City." In order to shorten the learning curve, we decided to hire a local representative, someone who not only had experience operating events but also was well known and respected throughout Nashville and the country music industry. Through our StarGames Music partner Michael Visconti, we were able to work with Trisha Walker, who fit that description and just happened to have a real passion for this show. What Trisha knew instinctively about Nashville would have taken us time to research, which could have set us back weeks or even months.

With Trisha on our team (as well as Michael, who had relocated to Nashville for other reasons), we were able to cut through some of the initial red tape, such as getting quickly to the building manager for the Nashville Arena. Trisha was able to get an answer on arena availability within 15 minutes because she had known and worked with the arena manager for quite a while. As outsiders, if we had to get that information on our own, it could

have taken a couple of weeks to get our phone calls returned and receive an answer. That time lag might have killed the event because the network (TNN) needed to know quickly if we could deliver the edited show on a certain date. In order to accommodate the network, the live show was going to have to take place during a limited window of time. The local contact with the building was quite valuable as a result.

Trisha also knew what dates were likely to work given the fall Nashville social calendar. Perhaps more important, she introduced us to many of the people that we were going to depend on if the event was going to be a success. This included the managers for some of the country music artists and people from the Country Music Association, both of whom were critical since this event combined skating and country music. Finally, while it may seem trivial, Trisha also knew her way around town, which just saved us time.

Similarly, when we needed to get the City of Hermosa Beach involved in the AVP/Coastal Commission situation discussed earlier, it was certainly helpful to know that one of the AVP's senior executives had grown up with the head of the Hermosa Parks Department. He was able to get right to the city manager, who was able to make decisions and give quick answers to our questions.

If you stick to putting on events in your hometown, you may not have to worry about hiring someone with local or "institutional knowledge" because you might be aware of all of the issues and know many of the important people yourself. However, in either case, local knowledge will be critically important to your success; only by having local contacts will you be able to appropriately analyze certain important issues.

As the saying goes, sometimes it isn't what you know, but who you know that counts.

Interest Level

Perhaps the most important and possibly the most difficult issue that you will have to research and gauge is the interest level in the event that you are thinking about organizing. When putting on the AVP Championships of

New England, we had to determine if anyone in the Northeast would be interested in beach volleyball, a sport that is generally thought of as being important only in California. When organizing Skating Goes Country in Nashville, we had to try to find out if anyone would care. When establishing the KidSports Foundation and Gala, we had to be absolutely sure that there was enough interest to support the cause we were seeking to help. In each case we came to our conclusion somewhat differently.

In the Nashville example, we knew that country music was popular since the city is the home of the country music industry and bills itself as "Music City." However, figure skating is not always top of mind in Southern cities. I have seen a couple of skating events bomb in places such as Atlanta and Charlotte. So it was comforting to actually attend another skating event (Tom Collins' Champions on Ice) in Nashville, which drew an enthusiastic crowd of about 10,000. Knowing that there was a six-month gap between our event and Collins', we determined that there were enough skating fans to justify taking the risk that the market could support two events, particularly since ours was going to be quite different from anything that had preceded us. Had I gone to Champions on Ice and seen a lackluster crowd of 5,000, skating would never have "gone country," at least not in Nashville with StarGames as the promoter!

Since you won't always have the luxury of seeing firsthand an event that will be similar to yours, you may just have to do some old-fashioned research.

Local History

In the case of the AVP Championships of New England, there was no event to attend. How-

Local knowledge will be critically important to your success; only by having local contacts will you be able to appropriately analyze certain important issues.

ever, there was some history. Our friends at the FleetCenter had tried to organize an indoor beach volleyball festival of their own (similar to the one at Madison Square Garden) when they were still the Boston Garden. Despite an enormous snowstorm on the day of their event, they drew a crowd of about 3,000. While perhaps a disaster for an indoor arena, we were only planning a 2,800-seat stadium, so we were actually encouraged that so many had braved the weather and come out for the FleetCenter event.

Also, the AVP previously had held events in the region from time to time. Each of these had managed to attract reasonable crowds from what we were told. However, at those events there had been no admission fee, which there would be at our event. Further, the AVP had moved sites each time it had come to the Boston area so there was none of the continuity that I referred to earlier. Finally, the tour sponsor, Miller Lite beer, was not overly aggressive in the market. These facts were not particularly encouraging. Therefore, we had to dig a little deeper in our research, which we did by speaking with the Massachusetts Sports Partnership, senior management at New England Development and the Cape Cod Mall, local restaurateurs, and a few friends whose opinion we valued. We then carefully weighed what amounted to a lot of subjective opinion before we made our decision to move forward with the event.

In the KidSports Foundation example, we researched dates of other fund-raisers to be sure that the people we planned to invite (read "lean on") would not have a conflict. Otherwise, we went with our gut instinct, which said "go for it." Sometimes, that "gut check," if it is based on good input, can be the swing vote (although it can lead you pretty far astray too).

In order to base your gut instinct on some factual information, I strongly urge you to employ some more sophisticated research methods. This includes the compilation of more concrete information, such as hotel availability during the planned dates for your event and ticket prices and attendance for similarly situated events in the area. The local chamber of commerce can help here.

No matter how much research you do, when you put tickets on sale or announce that your event is taking place, there is no guarantee that anyone will show up. However, if you have done some research on the marketplace, you should at least have an idea of how your event will be received.

Regulations

Sometimes local knowledge is not enough. A couple of years ago we made a deal with the Trump Marina Hotel in Atlantic City, New Jersey, to bring the Best of the Beach Invitational there. Everyone was very excited about this event, which was going to bring together the best female beach volleyball players in a format similar to our men's King of the Beach event. After putting several things in motion, we learned some information about the local ordinances that even the hotel management was not fully aware of. For example, to build an outdoor stadium, we needed to have the city approve the structure. In and of itself, that was not unusual. What was unusual is that in Atlantic City they needed an architectural drawing of the stadium to determine whether they would grant the permit. This would have required hiring an architect to design what was going to be a very basic 2,000-seat stadium made of portable bleachers, something that we had had approved many times in the past for other events. We also had to go through a permitting process that, while also not unusual, was much more expensive than what we had ever experienced. When we added up all of the ad-

If you have done some research on the marketplace, you should at least have an idea of how your event will be received.

ditional expenses that resulted from the local regulations, the cost of putting on the event increased by about $20,000, making it less attractive financially. Because this event had small margins to begin with, we regrettably canceled it. Unless someone had tried to put on that specific event before, I don't think there was any way to anticipate all of these "hidden costs," which can add up pretty fast.

After deciding to take the AVP Championships of New England to Cape Cod, we learned that the local ordinances would limit our commercialization on the beach by outlawing sponsor inflatables and beer sales. This forced our hand and resulted in our building the site off the beach at the Cape Cod Mall. Conversely, despite the California Coastal Commission restrictions, we held the first Best of the Beach Invitational on the beach in Huntington Beach (without ticket sales!) because the setup costs off the beach were prohibitive and we didn't think Southern California fans would stand for the makeshift courts.

The moral of these stories is, again, get to know as much as you can about the area in which you want to hold your event because issues of this kind can crop up anywher and for any event, be it professional or grassroots!

THE PERFECT SITE

After doing as much research as possible, and assuming that you have determined that there is indeed a market for your event, that there is a place for it on the local schedule, and that you are comfortable with the fact that the community will embrace it, it is time to figure out the specific site for the project. Again, local knowledge becomes key since, if you have the choice of a number of possible locations, you should consider several important factors before making your final decision.

Research

While I strongly believe that at the end of the day the final decision on many issues is going to come down to gut instinct, there will be some people who are not comfortable with this as the ultimate in checks and balances for determining when and where to roll the dice with their money. If you are one of those people, then you may want to do some additional research. Keeping in mind that no amount of research will guarantee success, in addition to the research ideas discussed in this chapter, you might look for some supplemental data that support your conclusions. In this regard, you might try some of the following:

- **Other research.** If you have the budget, you can buy information from some of the organizations that do sports-related research. These include ESPN/Chilton polls; the National Sporting Goods Association (NSGA); the Sporting Goods Manufacturers Association (SGMA); EJ Krause, which organizes the annual sports summit in New York; and the Sports Marketing Report.
- **The Internet.** This is an amazing research tool, and it doesn't cost anything. If you have a Web site, you can do your own poll to ask the specific questions that you need answered. Otherwise, surf the Web and you can find almost anything that you need.
- **The chamber of commerce** in the area where you wish to hold your event will, in all likelihood, have reams of information that will be applicable to your event. They should have everything from weather patterns to tourist spending habits to calendars of events to lists of vendors. This is a great resource and will help you to establish some local relationships as well.
- **Local newspapers.** Virtually every town in the United States has its own local newspaper. These can be great research tools in that they will give you a flavor for everything that is going on locally from politics to school holidays to weddings. If you read these papers on a regular basis, you will definitely get a good feel for the goings-on in the area where you plan to hold your event.
- **Surveys.** These can be very sophisticated and costly or rather simplistic. Regardless of the budget, if you take the time to ask a few hundred people their opinion on your event, you will have a reasonable sampling of opinion. Whether done scientifically or not, this information can't hurt.

I don't think you can ever do enough research, but at some point you are going to have to make a decision. This is what management, risk taking, and entrepreneurship is all about. So gather your information and study it like crazy, but be prepared to go out on a limb and make a call—the research can help you choose the sturdiest limb, though!

Geography

If you are anything like me, getting your bearings, particularly in an unfamiliar setting, can be tough enough. Assuming that you have several options for the location of your event, you really need to understand the traffic flow, travel time, peak times of congestion, even things such as when religious services let out. All of these can affect where you might want to hold your event and when. While I know I am starting to sound repetitive, remember that local knowledge goes a long way.

When we organized the 5K Racquet Run, we could have put it near the tennis stadium or in downtown Washington, D.C. Knowing that most of our audience lived on the side of town opposite from the tennis stadium, we couldn't expect a lot of our patrons to travel a long distance to run at 8 A.M. We chose to hold the event downtown among the monuments.

In Atlanta, the AT&T Challenge could have been held at the Atlanta Athletic Club (in town) or at the tennis facility being built for the Olympics (on the outskirts of town). We concluded that while people will be inconvenienced for an event of the magnitude of the Olympics, few would drive an hour or more for this regular-series ATP event.

Similarly, when trying to figure out where to schedule our AVP Championships of New England, we had to determine if there would be enough people in downtown Boston on a summer weekend to justify keeping it in the city. Because so many people leave the area on weekends, we ultimately decided to move it to Cape Cod, where the bulk of our spectators spend their summers. As discussed earlier, once we decided to go to the Cape, we had to determine whether we should hold the event on the beach or off. We were criticized in the press for going to the Cape Cod Mall (where we had to build sand courts), but this actually got us (and the mall) a lot of press coverage for the tournament.

Another issue to contend with is the perception about the part of town in which your event takes place. Like it or not, some parts of town make people less comfortable than others. You don't want to be at a site to which people are reluctant to travel or don't want to frequent at night. This shouldn't be too tough to find out. But make sure you research this issue because if you have an option and

■ ■ ■ ■ ■ ■ ■ ■ ■ ■ ■ ■

***Y**our ability to set up a working shuttle system can determine if your ticket buyers are placated.*

■ ■ ■ ■ ■ ■ ■ ■ ■ ■ ■ ■

choose the wrong one, it can mean big problems for you.

Parking and Transportation

While it may not seem as though parking should be a make-or-break issue, think of your own experience as a spectator. How far are you willing to walk to get to your seats? How did you feel after taking the 25-minute shuttle bus ride with a driver who wasn't sure how to get to the stadium? (This actually happened to me at the Atlanta Olympics, of all places.)

When people pay to attend your event or donate money to fund your event, they should be treated well. Having the luxury of parking near the venue, and not at exorbitant rates, is very important in our planning. While in most cases, as the promoter, you will not control the parking concession (the arena or stadium, or in the case of events on public land, perhaps the municipal authority, will set the parking rates *and* keep the revenue), you can make sure that your spectators have the option to park close to the site by making this a priority in your venue selection. With a major arena this is probably not going to be a problem, as most buildings, and particularly all of the new ones being built, will have dealt with this issue adequately (although some of them charge an arm and a leg to park!).

Parking becomes more of an issue with sites that are, in effect, created. I have cited the Walt Disney World example previously. When we took the AT&T Challenge to the Atlanta Country Club, they clearly were not going to have parking for 7,000 people when they were used to having 1,000 people maximum on their busiest days. Even the City of Hermosa Beach, which on a given summer weekend might have several thousand people milling about the Strand, was challenged by the fact that our AVP event brought an additional 4,000 spectators. In cases such as these, your ability to work with the surrounding businesses, schools, and other places that control large parking facilities becomes key. Also, your ability to set up a *working* shuttle system can determine if your ticket buyers are placated. My favorite shuttle systems of all time were the helicopter in North Conway, New Hampshire, and the police escort service at the European Champions Championships in Antwerp, Belgium. Of course these were only for the players and people working at the event. You need to be a bit more practical for the spectators while also being efficient and making them comfortable. This is not easy and can be expensive, but it is a service worth going the extra mile on.

Included in the phrase "location, location, location," should be parking, which is certainly one of the factors that make a particular site work.

Facilities

Over the past 10 years or so, a movement has swept the country resulting in new arenas and stadiums being built in virtually every major market in the United States. Many of these have been built as a result of pressure from professional sports teams that threaten to relocate to new markets if their current market does not agree to build them a state-of-the-art arena or stadium replete with suites, jumbotrons (the big scoreboard with video capability), television lighting, and state-of-the-art technology from top to bottom. Others have been built under the guise that, without a new arena, a city cannot be "major league." Therefore, facilities get built without tenants and without a regular schedule of events to keep them busy. The cost to taxpayers is enormous, and to my shock, we then find that these "new" buildings become obsolete almost overnight. To say that the United States is overbuilt in the arena and stadium area is, in my opinion, a gross understatement (I read recently that over 50 new facilities have been built in the last 10 years!).

I believe that local governments often overreact to the threats from the teams. Likewise,

they overestimate the importance of a new arena or stadium to their city's or town's civic pride *and* its bottom line.

Having said that, this building glut can be a huge bonus for the promoter or event organizer who is not constrained by geography and date. With so many buildings wanting, in fact needing, events, you may find yourself in the driver's seat of a bidding situation among sites. While I don't recommend that you play this card too hard, it is something that you can and should use to your advantage when negotiating your site contract.

I suspect that this building boom will not last too much longer, so take advantage of it while you can.

Seating

Since your objective as a promoter is to fill all of the seats, you need to determine the right number of seats for your event (and this has to include your seat "kills"—those that you block out for the television cameras, electrical equipment, officials' stands, and the like). Oddly enough, particularly if you are trying to build an event for the long term, I would suggest you err on the side of having *too few* seats. To me, nothing looks worse or makes you feel worse than a half-empty stadium, which can happen even if your attendance is pretty good.

After holding Halloween on Ice at the FleetCenter for two years, we decided that the stadium was just too big for our show. While we averaged selling about 8,500 seats at the FleetCenter, the arena still looked empty because it held over 16,000 for figure skating. At the Hard Rock Hotel, where we built the stadium for volleyball, we know from our long history with this event that we will sell about 4,700 seats (not including the "holds," which are seats we don't sell but set aside for friends, VIPs, and special guests). The temptation each year is to build a bigger stadium in anticipation of the fact that maybe we are going to sell more tickets. However, having built the event up to the point at which there is an aura about it always being sold out, we didn't suddenly want to have empty seats, which would only hurt that image. You want to be sure that your site is the right size for your event.

At the FleetCenter, while we could have closed off a portion of the arena, it still would have felt as though we were "rattling around" in the building. Conversely, at the Hard Rock, we had to be sure that they had the space to expand the stadium if need be. You will want to judge your expected attendance and find an arena or build a stadium that fits your anticipated needs.

Again, I suggest that you go smaller rather than larger. As long as you accommodate a reasonable size crowd (meaning that you provide space that adequately meets the needs of the crowd, delivers reasonable numbers to your bottom line, and meets the expectations of the sponsors and vendors involved in the event), *let people clamor for tickets.* Be the most sought after ticket in town because your event is sold out. This will drive up the value of your event and help you in a variety of areas, including sponsorship sales. It will also give you negotiating leverage with your vendors. Remember, nothing will sound better to you and those involved in the event than the words *SOLD OUT!*

Be sure that your site is the right size for your event. This includes making sure you have the right number of seats for your anticipated audience size.

■ ■ ■ ■ ■ ■ ■ ■ ■ ■ ■ ■

Nothing will sound better to you and those involved in the event than the words SOLD OUT!

■ ■ ■ ■ ■ ■ ■ ■ ■ ■ ■ ■

Site Schedule

Promoting your event in advance is going to be quite important, so the more people you can expose to your event, the better. If your event is in a venue that has high traffic before your event, you will gain a lot of free advertising by virtue of the fact that most sites will promote their upcoming events. The Hard Rock Hotel is perfect from this standpoint because there is always something going on there and people are constantly coming through the hotel. Likewise, a big arena has events going on all the time. If your event takes place in the winter, when these arenas are most crowded, you are sure to get your event in front of a lot of potential customers. On the other hand, if you are running a grassroots event in a remote area of town or at a site that doesn't get much traffic, you will have to work that much harder to get the word out about your project. Given its Vermont resort setting, we had to work much harder to get out the message about the McCall's LPGA event than you would for an event taking place at a major sports arena during the basketball and hockey season.

Unlimited Capacity

If you are organizing an outdoor event that does not have a stadium—such as a marathon (or other long-distance run) or golf tournament—it is a lot tougher to achieve sold-out status since you have a lot more room. In these cases, the key will be the "prime seating" that you build. How many seats do you put at the finish line or on the 18th hole, and how do you make those available to the public? Again, "less is more" in these cases, so I suggest that you build bleacher seating that accommodates a reasonable number of fans, but not everyone. Make some of this priority seating for which you charge a premium. The balance can be general admission that gets filled on a first come, first served basis. Some people may be turned off by the fact that they couldn't get a seat. In all likelihood, though, many more will want to buy early for the following year so that they don't get shut out again.

Halloween on Ice, when at the FleetCenter, benefited from the promotion it received at the Boston Bruins and Celtics games. If applicable, you should take this into consideration when determining your venue.

NEGOTIATING THE SITE DEAL

Having used the preceding guidelines to narrow your choice of sites, you have to negotiate a deal that is going to enable you to operate your event within parameters that fit your budget and are suited to the magnitude of your project. The site management staff can be immensely supportive of your efforts; act passively and not contribute to the process; or in the worst case, place restrictions on you that hamper your every move. You (the "Lessee") have to carefully craft your agreement with the site operators (the "Lessor"—try not to get these two confused). To begin with, you might look for help in some of the following areas.

Advertising and Promotion

Perhaps the most important areas in which your venue can be of support to your event are those of advertising and promotion. At the outset of this book I asked if you could imagine giving an event and having no one come. If you don't handle your advertising and promotion right, that is exactly what might happen.

The venue can be key to your efforts to get the word out about your event because in most cases the site will be tapped into thousands of people through other events, mailing lists, VIP seats, club memberships, and the like. It also will in all likelihood have very close relationships with the local newspapers, magazines, and television and radio stations that provide them with insider advertising rates and favorable formulas for ticket promotions.

This is not always the case, however. The Janet Evans Invitational Swim Meet is held at the swim stadium at the University of Southern California. The stadium could offer very little in the way of advertising and promotional support other than some on-campus exposure. However, as I noted earlier, both the FleetCenter and Paul Tsongas Arena in Lowell, Massachusetts, were able to plug us into their advertising rates and schedules for Halloween on Ice.

Grassroots events and those run in public parks or other public spaces will probably not receive the same level of advertising support from their site as events held at a major stadium or arena (although parks and recreation department flyers and newsletters are a great way to get the word out about your event). A hotel or real estate project (where a number of golf and tennis events take place) will probably fall somewhere in between. The Hard Rock Hotel, which advertises heavily all over the country, has a lot of pull in the Las Vegas market. But it may not have as much influence in its market as the Nashville Arena (which advertises heavily and almost exclusively in Nashville) does in its market. If you can tap into these strengths, you will benefit greatly.

One way in which to force this issue is to work out a deal in which the venue actually has to pay for some of the event advertising (the glut of facilities gives you some leverage here). In all likelihood, you will have to give up some percentage of your ticket revenue in exchange (so the arena can recoup its expenses), but getting the arena to commit to the event financially is a huge asset to you. They may not agree to actually spend cash, choosing instead to barter for ad space (so factor that into your negotiating strategy). For you, the closer you can come to a scenario in which the venue has a financial stake and incentive to help you out, the better off you will be.

If you can get the venue to commit barter or hard dollars to advertising your event, it will prove very helpful. A typical trade-off in this situation would be for the venue to agree to spend a certain amount, say $20,000, to support the advertising budget of your event. In exchange, they might get 25 percent of the ticket sales until they have recouped their $20,000. There are many formulas that could apply in this situation. There's no problem with the site getting its money back quickly as long as they agree to spend some money on your behalf. Remember too that any ad placements that they make should be subject to your approval.

The same is true in the area of promotion. Most of your promotion will come in the form of ticket giveaways and contests. Again, the venue will probably be tied into several radio and television stations (cable and broadcast;

■ ■ ■ ■ ■ ■ ■ ■ ■ ■ ■

The closer you can come to a scenario in which the venue has a financial stake and incentive to help you out, the better off you will be.

■ ■ ■ ■ ■ ■ ■ ■ ■ ■ ■

AM and FM) that will be happy to take a number of your tickets and give them away over the air through sweepstakes, call-in contests, and the like. These promotions are, in a sense, free advertising for you because you are not paying any "hard dollars" for the airtime. Your site should be able to help you out with their connections in this area as well.

Box Office

Unless you are organizing an event in which the audience gets in for free, selling tickets is going to be one of the key measurements of your success. Obviously, if you are dependent on ticket sales for a large part of your revenue, then you had better have a well-oiled ticket sales campaign. While we will get into the strategy and tactics of ticket sales later, if your venue is in the business of selling tickets on a regular basis, they can help you cut through a lot of potential problems. If possible, you should make every effort to get their box office to handle the bulk of your ticket sales activity. In addition to taking advantage of their basic familiarity with the process and the ever-important area of customer relations, you can save on certain expenses by having the venue handle ticket sales. Also, they will in all likelihood be connected to Ticketmaster or another ticket vendor, so they can plug you right into their computerized system.

Imagine if you had to set up a phone system, hire operators, train them with regard to your specific ticket order issues, deal with credit card details, answer spectator questions, and so on. I remember vividly my first exposure to a big-time event. We had the box office for the Colgate Grand Prix Masters right in our suite of offices. While it was exciting to see all of the activity, I have since learned that it is far better to let this happen outside your regular office space, as it can also be distracting. A daily (or as some people on our staff will tell you, in my case, hourly) ticket sales report can keep you in the flow without the headache of the actual ticket operation. So, again, if you can get the site to manage this, you are better off. (Ticketmaster or another local ticketing service can provide all of these same functions for you if your venue is not so equipped.)

In the same vein, one of the key areas in which the venue's box office can be of assistance is in group sales. This is an area that is often given short shrift because it requires quite a bit of effort. However, the return is well worth it if you are successful.

The box office for your site should have a list of past ticket purchasers for events in the same genre as yours. They might also have a sophisticated breakdown of the demographic audience that tends to come to the arena. If you can tap into this customer database, you may be able to sell tickets in bulk, which, even though this will often be accompanied by a discount of up to 20 percent, is well worth it. Historically, groups do not buy the most expensive seats; so if you can sell large blocks of tickets to groups, you will be ahead of the game (you will find that the most expensive seats tend to sell first to the general public anyway). In your discussions with your site, irrespective of who ultimately handles the box office operation, at a minimum see if you can get them to make a commitment to a group ticket sales effort.

Labor

One of your biggest unknown expenses will be the local labor costs. If you are at an in-

■ ■ ■ ■ ■ ■ ■ ■ ■ ■ ■

In your discussions with your site, irrespective of who ultimately handles the box office operation, at a minimum see if you can get them to make a commitment to a group ticket sales effort.

■ ■ ■ ■ ■ ■ ■ ■ ■ ■ ■

door arena, you will have to work with their stagehands. If you play your event at a hotel property, you will have to interact with their staff. If you are in a public park, you will become partnered with the park service staff. Some of these sites may be union controlled. The sites that are not "union shops" will generally give you more flexibility with the pool of labor from which you can hire and thus the amount that you pay them. The unions, on the other hand, will have the authority to control your every move. I will never forget trying to relocate a courtside banner in Madison Square Garden at the Colgate Masters Tennis Tournament. Just as I was about to cut the plastic tie that held the banner, I was surrounded by three union workers who explained in no uncertain terms that nothing got moved in the Garden without their being involved. While on the surface that might have seemed nice since that meant I didn't have to do it myself, the reality is that this just cost the tournament money, time, and in some cases, efficiency as we had to work around their breaks, hours, overtime, and so forth. With a nonunion crew, while you will still have to give them breaks and pay overtime, you can make a deal that is specifically designed to suit your needs.

One of the problems with all of these labor costs is that it can be difficult to budget for them, in terms of both money and timing. If you are working in a union building, for example, you have to break for lunch at specific times, give the crew a break at a certain time, and end the day at a specific time. Otherwise, you go into overtime, which can be very expensive. After the taping of One Enchanted Evening, we got hit with an unbudgeted $4,000 labor bill. That did not make us very happy, but there was really not much we could have done about it (after all, the show must go on!). You may be able to get your venue partner to pay for a certain portion of the labor costs. Again, this is where giving the site a percentage of the gate might work to your advantage. So, make sure that you go through this issue thoroughly during the deal-making phase of your discussions, and try to be creative in coming up with a way to transfer some of the risk associated with these costs back to the site.

WRITING THE CONTRACT

Assuming that you have been able to come to an agreement on the various issues discussed thus far, it will be time to write the contract. This can be tricky, as much of this language might be peculiar to the venue that you are working with as opposed to being somewhat standard from site to site. Be careful and make sure that you (and your attorney) look for some of the points covered in this section.

■ ■ ■ ■ ■ ■ ■ ■ ■ ■ ■ ■

There are a lot of hidden costs of which you must be aware.

■ ■ ■ ■ ■ ■ ■ ■ ■ ■ ■ ■

General Financial

Naturally, you are going to pay particular attention to the big-picture financial issues. First and foremost in this category is the rental fee. Your decision on how to structure your deal should be influenced directly by your ability to take risk. If you have a big sponsor or television rights fees, expect sellout crowds at significant ticket prices, or just have a lot of money, you probably won't mind taking a big risk. If not, you are going to want to try to pass some of this onto the building. There are several options (too many to list here) to structuring this fee, including, but certainly not limited to, the following:

• **Most risky: straight rental.** In this scenario you pay a flat fee to rent the site. In ex-

change, the venue provides certain services that might range from security to box office to stagehands. You pay for everything else and keep 100 percent of the revenue.

• **Less risky: guaranteed fee against a percentage of ticket sales.** In this case you will pay less up front because of the potential upside to the arena. If a straight rental deal were $25,000, in this case you might pay $15,000 against 20 percent of your total ticket sales. You pay less up front but take the gamble that if your event is successful, you will end up paying more to your venue.

• **Even less risky: straight percentage of ticket sales.** This is one step farther down the risk chain. Keeping with the previous example, here you would pay no guarantee up front, but the site might receive 60 percent of your ticket sales. The amount of services that you get as part of your rental deal might shift as well, meaning that you may have some additional direct-billed costs such as security.

• **Least risky with a small upside: the building buys the show/event from you.** At the other end of the spectrum, you pay nothing to the site. They *pay you* a guaranteed fee for bringing the event into the building. The site pays for the advertising and building costs and keeps all of the ticket revenue.

Each of these scenarios has variations as well as upsides and downsides. In most cases the best direction for you will depend on your appetite for risk and your willingness to give up certain control over your event.

Hidden Costs

In addition to these big-picture financial issues that can be configured in any number of ways, there are a lot of hidden costs of which you *must* be aware. These include, in no particular order, insurance, lights, heat, electricity, water, PA system, jumbotron, spotlights, electricians and other personnel, television cables, dressing room furniture, security, box office, and catering. In each case there will be options to use or not use the site's people and equipment. Some arenas will include these items in the base rent. Others won't. Make sure that you understand the markup in each of these categories because there may be flexibility, and you may be able to negotiate a better deal by using outside vendors. You can and should get an estimate of all of these costs from the facility *before* you sign your agreement. They should be able to come pretty close to the actual figures unless, of course, you make radical changes to your program.

Settlement

Determining who is required to pay for each of the venue-related costs will become important when it comes time to make your settlement with the site. At the time of settlement (and you should do this sometime during your event so it is taken care of before you leave the site), you will go over everything that you owe the facility and that they owe you. Assuming that the venue has handled ticket sales and retained the money, using the contract as a guide, you will have to determine what should be deducted, what should be paid out, what should be withheld in the case of unexpected expenses after the fact, and so on. Remember, they do this every day. You don't. So make sure you know the ins and outs of your contract as thoroughly as possible. Don't be afraid to ask for a very specific accounting of all of the activities, and make sure you maintain a right to review all of the issues after the fact in case you missed something. This is *your money,* so don't be intimidated by the process.

*S*trive to get the biggest window possible on either side of the start and finish of your event.

Move-In and Move-Out

Whether you are indoors or out, whether your event is grassroots or pro, you are going to have to take control of your venue at some point so that you can actually produce your event. The timing of your "move-in" and "move-out" will affect a number of things, including how you prepare for the event; how much practice time the athletes have at the actual site; how much time your operations crew will have to set up the site and, equally important, tear it down; when your sponsors and television can set up, and so on. The venue management may or may not care how much time you take on either end of the event. For your sake, I strongly suggest that you negotiate the maximum time for both. In all likelihood, when the event is over, you are going to be tired and want to get out of there as quickly as possible. Nevertheless, strive to get the biggest window possible on either side of the start and finish of your event. You don't have to use the time, but it will be comforting to know that it is available.

Some facilities may not care too much about how much time you take. If you are holding an event at your local high school during the summer—when no one is in school and nothing is going on—you will have a lot more flexibility than you will if you are moving into a major arena in the middle of the winter and your event is sandwiched between a professional hockey game the night before and a professional basketball game the night after. In that case you are going to have the tightest schedule imaginable, so your crew will have to be sharp and your planning precise.

Country clubs will want the least amount of disturbance for their members, and hotels will want minimal interference for their customers. You should be able to anticipate some of this before your negotiations because you will know the facility's schedule.

Settlement Statement

When you go to settle the economics, you will be presented with a settlement statement. These can take different forms, but in general the settlement statement will look something like this.

Licensee (this will be you, your company, or the event): _____

Event (the name of the event): _____

Date (date of the settlement): _____

Terms (a brief synopsis of the financial elements of the contract): _____

Attendance: tickets paid for:

   comps: _____

   total: _____

Gross box office: _____

Usage fees: _____

Sales tax: _____

Net box office: _____

Facility rental: _____

Other charges: _____

Credit card: _____

Phones: _____

Runner: _____

Passes: _____

Television cable: _____

Dressing rooms: _____

Advertising: _____

Consignment tickets: _____

Merchandising sales: _____

Other contractual expenses incurred by the site: _____

Total charges: _____

Summary: _____

Net box office: _____

Less rent: _____

Less expenses: _____

Subtotal: _____

Advances (if any): _____

Amount due promoter: _____

You will (or should) get a backup sheet for each line item, all of which should tie into this summary page. If there are any discrepancies, you should get an explanation. Also, in anticipation of this settlement discussion, you should keep your own running total of all of these revenues and expenses. Depending on several factors, this is the statement that will show whether your event made a profit.

Also, in the case of the major arena, some of this will be somewhat standard. For example, no matter what is going on in the building, it would not be uncommon for them to expect you to "take possession" of the facility at midnight on the night before your event and to move out five to seven hours after the completion of your show. Assuming a one-night event with a 7:30 P.M. start time (such as a figure skating event), this will give you about 19 hours to move in and get ready. Assuming a 10:30 P.M. finish, you will need to be out of the building by about 3 A.M. After months of preparation, you will only be in the facility for 27 hours! So you have to be organized and ready to move.

On the other hand, if you have a weeklong event that requires a lot of setup, such as a beach volleyball event in which you have to bring in the sand and build the courts, you are going to need a lot more move-in time. In cases like this, such as our events at the Hard Rock Hotel or the AVP Championships of New England at the Cape Cod Mall, we might move in as much as 10 days before the event so that we can start building the courts and setting up tents, bleachers, rest room facilities, and so on. It might also take about four days to tear everything down, remove the sand, and ship everything out. This may seem like a more relaxed situation, but it really isn't because there is a lot more physical labor to manage. Your site may not look too favorably at giving you so much time. I can assure you that it is necessary, though, so fight for it.

Grassroots events often have the toughest situation of all. For many of these events you will be working with public parks, public streets, and local government officials who are trying to work you into their daily flow of normal activities. If you require streets to close and traffic patterns to be altered, you are going to have very tight windows so that the whole community is not turned upside down. This requires tremendous organization on the part of your event team.

Regardless of your situation, one of the keys to your event's operational success will be this move-in (or "load-in") and move-out (or "tear-down" or "load-out") window, so again, negotiate as long a time frame as possible so that you have some breathing room for yourself and your staff.

Liability

This is another of those legal issues that you probably didn't have in mind when you began creating your event. Nevertheless, liability (who is responsible financially and otherwise if something goes wrong) is a critical part of the agreement with your facility because you could be looking at major expenses and lawsuits if something serious were to happen.

Naturally, the venue that you are using is going to want anything and everything to be your risk and responsibility. You will be asked to return the site to "move-in" condition, meaning the same condition you found when you arrived on site. You will be asked to warrant that nothing was wrong with the site when you arrived to begin your setup, and the venue will not want any financial responsibility for your event if something should go wrong with the facility that forces you to cancel or postpone the show.

In some cases the boilerplate language in liability agreements is so one sided as to make you want to walk away from the deal right from the start. I can assure you that the thought has crossed my mind on more than one occasion. However, as with a lot of other things in the "standard" agreements that you will review, there is room for negotiation. Do not be intimidated into signing a document that doesn't protect you from situations over which you have no control. You should only be liable for the things that are in your control.

Conflicting Sponsors

Much of your revenue will depend on your sponsorship sales. Likewise, you may be moving into a site that is equally dependent on sponsors and advertisers (all of the new buildings are heavily sponsor supported). A typical example of this may be in the soft drink area where virtually every facility in the United States, whether public or private, new or old, big or small, has a "pouring rights" deal with Coke, Pepsi, or one of their competitors. You, on the other hand, might like to sell a soft drink sponsorship to a bottler that may or may not be involved in the site at which you are holding the event. You need to know what restrictions and potential conflicting corporate affiliations exist *before* you go out into the marketplace so that you are not embarrassed or find yourself in an unpleasant situation.

This issue of corporate sponsorship is not limited to the soft drink category. Virtually every new arena relies on advertising signage and other sponsorship to support their state-of-the-art architecture and technology. Increasingly, Little League fields, soccer fields, tennis courts, and now roadways are selling sponsorships and "naming rights." I even read recently that airports are thinking of getting into this business. The sponsorship issue is a deal point that you have to confront up front so that you do not find yourself in an uncomfortable conflict situation that ends up costing you valuable sponsorship dollars. Be aware too that the conflict issue is not limited to the site. As we will discuss later, if your event is on television, the network may have some advertiser exclusivities as well, which can complicate matters even further.

Since the examples for potential conflict are endless, you have to be very specific with your site and find out the exact nature of their relationships with their sponsors. For example, in working with Madison Square Garden, we found out that they had a deal in one of the major sponsorship categories that we wanted to sell. However, their deal allowed for a certain number of excluded events. They were willing to use the exclusion in the case of our event. This opened up an important sponsorship area for us. The Trump Marina Hotel had only the obligation to give their corporate partners the right of first negotiation for events coming onto the property. In the Trump Marina case we were able to turn one of their relationships into a benefit for ourselves and actually made a sponsorship deal with their soft drink partner (this was for the Best of the Beach event that we were eventually forced to cancel because of the permitting costs that I mentioned earlier). In some cases your facility may have no restrictions at all, as their advertisers may only have the right for their signage to be on the site but get absolutely no protection or exclusivity.

Whereas sponsor conflicts might seem at the outset to be a limiting factor (and in a public park situation in which the parks department may have a "no commercialization" rule, this can be very limiting and may force you to take your event to a different site), if you work with your site, you just might be able to create opportunities that benefit both of you. For example, you may find that one of the venue sponsors is looking to become involved with an event very similar to yours. If approached correctly, this might result in that sponsor becoming your title sponsor! One way to encourage such activity is to give your venue partner an incentive to bring sponsors into your event by paying them a commission (15–20 percent) for any sponsorship dollars they generate for your property.

Be sure to focus on this issue because it just might be one that directly affects your bottom line.

Boilerplate

This is not a category in and of itself. Rather, it is all of the standard issues that can get overlooked in the legalese. Therefore, pay attention to the following issues in any contract you are negotiating (again, in no particular order).

- **Merchandise sales.** If you are at an existing building or stadium, it will have its own vendors who will receive a piece of all of the revenue from the souvenirs that you sell on site. Pay particular attention to the revenue split (this should be anywhere from 75/25 to 60/40 in your favor), labor issues, inventory count (who does it and when, before *and* after the event), shipping (who pays), and receiving and storage procedures (where, extra charges, how long will they keep your items before and after the event). If you are building your venue, there will be a whole different set of considerations that will vary with the site. If you are at a public facility, government ordinances may restrict what you can sell, where you sell it, and what taxes you have to charge. If you are at a private club, there will be issues particular to the club (e.g., use of their logo, participation by the pro shop). Depending on your event, merchandise sales can be a large revenue item, so don't give away anything that you don't have to. However, as we will discuss later, merchandising can also be a big undertaking that may not be worthwhile.

• **Sampling.** As we will see later, this may be a key issue to your sponsors. Make sure you understand what sampling is allowed, what is not allowed, where the activity can take place, and who has the ultimate right to control this activity (in particular, can the venue veto any of your sponsor rights in this area?).

• **Broadcast rights.** You (or your television partner) should own all of the broadcast rights (including still photos) to the event, period. Be sure this is clearly reflected in the agreement because the venue may try to get in on the action here. It is important to obtain the rights from the venue to use its name and image in the telecast, advertising, promotion, home video, and any and all forms of media in which you may want to exploit the event. Be strong here to protect yourself and your rights. The venue management should understand your needs here and support your position because by doing so they will get the exposure from your event that they are probably seeking.

• **Television capability.** Speaking of broadcast rights, make sure that the site is television ready and if not, can accommodate the needs for a television broadcast if you are planning one. For events not being televised this will not be an issue. For others, if you can't produce a television show from the site, it may be the wrong venue for you. Things such as lighting, cable availability and access, power, and union issues all come to mind here. Assuming that producing a television show from your venue is feasible, you have to negotiate who pays for each of the items associated with the telecast. Most expenses will be yours, but if the facility requires extraordinary preparation to become television ready, you probably should pass some of these costs on to the site.

• **Program approval.** "Program" in this case refers to the content of your event—not the tournament program that you sell on site. While clauses like this are rarely invoked (I have never seen this one used), the site may try to maintain some element of control over your event. For example, if you are at a family

theme park, they may want to be sure that everything you do is appropriate for families. Probably reasonable but . . . who interprets what is appropriate? I try not to allow the site any control at all, although some input is probably reasonable. Try to write this clause in such a way that it is as favorable to you as possible. You don't want your venue management to be able to require last-minute changes in your event.

• **Evacuation of facility.** In this clause the venue will be looking to seek and demand your cooperation to vacate the premises if, in their judgment, there is a public safety issue. I have no problem with this in principle. Where I draw the line is that in such cases the site will often ask you to forfeit any arena charges and other costs that you have already incurred and waive your rights to any claims. Not fair! Therefore, you need to modify this language a bit if possible. At a minimum, don't waive the right to make claims in cases in which the site has been negligent.

• **Damages.** Here the site wants you to pay for any damages that it sustains as a result of you operating your event there. Again, I see no problem with this in principle. Just make sure that if this does come up, you are not being held liable for something that you didn't do. To mitigate these circumstances, take a good, long walk around the site during load-in and note any issues that might look to be a problem.

• **Cancellation.** This section of your agreement will primarily seek to hold you responsible for everything if you decide to cancel the event. I think this is as it should be unless the reason that you are canceling is as a result of a breach by the venue. For example, we weren't held liable in the Avis Grasscourts tennis event scenario when the club failed to grow the grass on the tennis courts in a timely manner. The only place I caution you here is to make sure that the site cannot cancel the event because something better comes along (they very well might prefer the Rolling Stones to a one-night tennis exhibition!).

• **Assignment.** While your venue will want the right to assign your agreement to another party, they will not want you to be able to do so. The fairest compromise is that neither party can assign the rights without written approval from the other. The reason for the concern both ways is that neither of you will want to suddenly be in an agreement with a new entity that you don't know. Such scenarios bring up issues of performance, intent of the agreement, and so on. This usually only comes into play if either the venue or your company are sold during the course of creating and operating your event. If that happens, there is every reason to expect that you will be able to work things out. Just protect yourself by making sure the contract gives you some room to maneuver here. Typically, you can deal with this issue by assuring each other that regardless of any assignment, the original parties will remain responsible for the event.

• **Interruptions.** This clause deals with the site's right to interrupt or terminate the event if there is an issue related to public safety. As with some of the other paragraphs of this nature, the primary concerns are liability and financial recovery.

• **Force majeure.** You will see this term quite often. It is also sometimes referred to as "acts of God." Basically, this paragraph says that if the event cannot go on because of damage by fire, weather, blackout, strike, national emergency, or *other cause beyond the reasonable control of the venue,* then the event will be canceled or postponed and you will have no recourse to recover any losses from the site. I don't think there will be much movement on this; it is pretty standard.

• **Indemnification.** This paragraph, another standard in virtually every agreement, simply says that if something happens that is your fault, you will protect the site from any losses. Make sure that it says that, likewise, if something happens that is the site's fault, they will protect you from any losses.

Your Working Relationship

The contract process may sound exhausting, but it is really important. Of equal or greater importance, though, will be your working relationship with the venue management.

Remember, in most cases your event will be one of many at a venue or in the alternative, be viewed as a nice advertising vehicle for a real estate development, club, city government, or hotel. The life of your venue goes on with or without your event and in most cases will not depend on your event for its ultimate success. (GlenEagles Country Club continued to sell fairway homes even though the Avis Grasscourt Championships were never held.)

On the other hand, you live and die by the success of your event, so what might be inconsequential issues to the site can be major hurdles for you. Certainly the Hard Rock Hotel does not rely on the King of the Beach event for their success. It is a nice event to have, but their year doesn't ride on what takes place that one weekend. For us, however, a $25,000 swing one way or the other could be important. Thus, their support and cooperation are always of utmost importance.

I can't encourage you enough to work hard to make the venue your partner since the real estate that they control is going to be your "home" for hopefully a very long time. With that in mind, as I indicated earlier, the development of a good working relationship with the site staff has got to be a primary objective.

✔ Venue Checklist

The decision of where to play your event is one of the most important decisions you will have to make. As you can see, there are a myriad of issues to take into consideration. Thus, make sure you do the following:

✔ Research the marketplace that you target for your event to be sure that it will support your project.

✔ If you don't have local knowledge of the area, try to hire someone who does. A lot can be gained from knowing the history of an area and similarly situated events.

✔ Survey the area to be sure that the site at which you would like to hold your event suits your needs from the number of seats to parking to schedule availability.

✔ Pick a venue whose size is compatible with that of your event. If anything, err on the side of going smaller rather than larger.

✔ Once you enter into discussions with the site, try to create a relationship that is mutually beneficial and encourages the site's management to play an active role in the advertising and promotion of your project.

✔ One of the areas in which your venue can be of greatest help is group ticket sales. Don't overlook this important revenue item.

✔ Negotiate a contract that provides for shared liability and protects each party equally.

Once you have done all of these things, remember that none of them will guarantee success!

Your site can be the focal point of many pleasant experiences—we have enjoyed many a fun week at the Hard Rock Hotel—and contribute greatly to your success if you handle the relationship with care. The site can also give your event immediate credibility and help you establish tradition. In tandem with the site management, strive to become part of the fabric of the community. If you can achieve that goal, you and your site partner will be in business together for a long time.

Working Model: Regional Tennis Tournament Venue

Given the relatively modest operating budget of this event, you really need to find a venue that has enough courts and other facilities so that there isn't a need to build much for the players, officials, and fans. In the perfect world, your local tennis club will be available and, understanding the benefits for its members, will make the club available for your event.

In this example, we are going to assume that the club is available on the summer dates that you desire and will agree to make the courts and clubhouse (which is modest but functional) available at a cost that is within the budget. Since you will need several days to complete the tournament (there will be 31 singles matches and 15 doubles matches) and a minimum of six courts on which to play, the club pro agrees to make 6 of the club's 10 courts available on Wednesday, Thursday, and Friday afternoons, then all day on Saturday and half the day on Sunday.

As long as it doesn't rain, this should be enough to get the event completed, although players will have to play more than one match on a couple of days. They are young, though, so it shouldn't be a problem.

With the previous elements in place, you will need a basic letter signed by the club that memorializes the understanding. It might read something like this:

Dear Club Manager:

The purpose of this letter agreement ("Agreement") is to reduce to writing the understanding between the Tennis Club ("Club") and Tennis Tournament, Inc. ("Promoter"), which is located at 123 Tennis Avenue, Anywhere, USA. It is my understanding that we have agreed to the following:

1. Promoter desires to organize, promote, and operate a junior tennis tournament ("Event") featuring top players from the four-state region playing a single elimination singles and doubles tournament.

2. Club agrees to make Club's facilities, including six (6) tennis courts, the clubhouse, locker rooms, restaurant, parking lot, security, and other Club services, available to Promoter during the five-day period beginning Wednesday, August 10 and concluding Sunday, August 14. Club's facilities shall be available to Promoter for the Event only from 1 P.M. until 8 P.M. on August 10 to 12; from 8 A.M. until 8 P.M. on August 13; and from 1 P.M. until 8 P.M. on Sunday, August 14.

3. In addition to the above usage, Promoter shall have the right to use an office in the Club beginning two (2) weeks prior to the Event. Promoter shall vacate the premises four (4) days following the conclusion of the Event.

4. Promoter shall have the right to use the name and logo of Club on all materials produced for the Event subject to reasonable approval by Club.

5. Club agrees to actively promote the Event with its members for a minimum of thirty (30) days prior to the Event. Such promotion shall include mention in the Club's newsletter.

6. Club agrees that Promoter shall have the right to televise the Event from Club's premises and maintain ownership of all rights to the Event in perpetuity for all media on a worldwide basis.

7. The parties agree to hold each other harmless from any and all claims resulting from the actions of the other party unless as a result of gross negligence of the other party.

8. For the rights granted herein, Promoter agrees to pay to Club a rental fee of one thousand dollars ($1,000) which shall be payable in two equal installments thirty (30) days prior to the start of the Event and thirty (30) days following the conclusion of the Event. In addition, Club shall receive ten percent (10%) of the revenue generated by ticket sales from the Event. Such percentage shall be payable thirty (30) days following the conclusion of the Event.

9. Club acknowledges that Promoter is dependent on sponsorship for the success of the Event and agrees that Promoter shall have the right to sell sponsorships that grant certain exposure and other benefits to Event sponsors. Club shall, subject to reasonable approval, cooperate with all such sponsorship needs and provide benefits where applicable. The only restriction with regard to sponsorship is that Club has an agreement with Wilson that their tennis balls be the exclusive ball played at the Club. Promoter agrees to comply with such exclusive relationship.

10. This Agreement shall be valid and binding upon the parties until such time as it is replaced by a long form agreement signed by the parties. It is the objective of the parties to enter into such an agreement within twenty (20) business days from the date of signature of this Agreement.

If you agree that the above accurately reflects the basic points of our understanding, please so indicate by signing in the space provided below.

On behalf of all of the players who will benefit from this event, I look forward to working with you.

Best regards,

Tennis Tournament, Inc.

ACCEPTED AND AGREED:

_____

Tennis Club

Chapter FOUR

Finding Your Sponsor

For better or worse, sponsorship support has become the lifeblood for events of every shape and size around the world, including local events such as the regional tennis tournament in our working model.

While some events have resisted taking on a title sponsor (Wimbledon, the Masters, and the Super Bowl come to mind), virtually every event counts on some form of sponsorship (either directly or indirectly through television advertising) to cover the ever-increasing costs of operation. Even events such as the Rose Bowl, which is steeped in tradition and has long resisted any form of sponsorship, have given in to the allure and perhaps the necessity of corporate sponsors or partners. While some purists might dream of an event with no corporate name in the title and no banners on the field of play, the economic reality dictates that sponsorship is a must.

In fact, without sponsors, it will be difficult to organize an event that makes any financial sense. This chapter defines sponsorship and discusses how to go about finding those all-important corporate partners.

WHAT IS SPONSORSHIP?

In its most simplistic definition, sponsorship is a situation in which a company pays a pro-moter a fee for the right to associate itself and its products with his or her event. Some companies sponsor events to entertain their customers or employees. Others become sponsors in an effort to advertise, promote, or sample their products and services to potential customers. Still other sponsorships are developed because a company wants to better its image through an association with a particular sport or charity.

Sponsorships come in all shapes and sizes, as companies look to achieve vastly different objectives from their sponsorship activity. Your job is to find the companies that are potential sponsors of your event, determine what they are looking to gain from an association with it, convince them that through your event they can reach their goals, close the deal to make them a sponsor, and then deliver the various benefits that you have promised and that they have paid for. No problem!

SPONSORSHIP PROPOSAL

Basically, soliciting sponsorships is a sales process. Rarely does a sponsor just happen to knock on your door and ask to be involved in your event.

The sponsorship sales process can be intimidating and discouraging. On the other hand, making a sponsorship deal can be exhilarating and electric. The people who really love the "high" of closing a deal are generally the best sponsorship salespeople. I have been there many times, and I still get excited about closing a deal, whether it is for $5,000 or $500,000.

Sponsorship solicitation usually begins with a written proposal that outlines the various benefits offered to a prospective corporate partner. I say "partner" because, as with your site, your goal should be to create a relationship with your sponsors that extends far beyond the four walls of your contract. If the relationship with your sponsor is defined solely by the language in your written agreement, I doubt that you will have a long-term arrangement with that company. But more on that later.

Our proposal for an official product sponsor for the 1998 King of the Beach Invitational (see figure 4.1) will serve as a good place to start the sponsorship discussion.

In some cases you might be well advised to create a sponsor fact sheet that accompanies or precedes the full-blown sponsorship proposal. Figure 4.2 is, in effect, a thumbnail version of the proposal itself and might even be referred to as an executive summary. The point of this shorter version of the proposal is simply length. Many people that you will contact are very busy. They will see a three- to five-page proposal and just not want to read something that long. A fact sheet can give them all of the relevant points in one or two pages, a length that people are comfortable with and willing to read. The fact sheet would look something like figure 4.2.

As you can see, this fact sheet basically mirrors the sponsorship proposal but reduces the length considerably by condensing all of the salient points. You may find that this format is far more productive for you in the long run.

A proposal of this nature is going to become your calling card during the solicitation process. It will be the first written material people see about your event. However, by itself it will not get you in the door, nor will it sell the deal. *You* have to do that. In order to have a chance to be successful you need to understand thoroughly your basic proposal and the offshoots available from it. To do so, let's go through the King of the Beach proposal point by point.

Presentation

Sometimes I think I am a bit of a dinosaur in the area of presentation. When I first got into the sports business, a sponsorship presentation was neatly typed out on your company or event stationary and sent with a cover letter to your contact at the prospective sponsor. Today, the three-page, plainly typed proposal is ancient history. It has been replaced by everything from computer presentations to nicely bound four-color booklets to videos. The competition for sponsors has become so tough that this presumably more sophisticated approach is deemed necessary to get the attention of your sponsor target. For me to disagree with this line of thinking would probably not be fair because it has become a way of life.

Having said that, a couple of things come to mind. First, be careful that the presentation doesn't outstrip the event. For example, if you are planning a junior tennis tournament and looking for modest amounts of money, spending a lot of money on a fancy presentation sends the wrong message. The same is true of a charity event. You don't want to give the impression (real or perceived) that the money being spent by a sponsor is, in the latter case, going to places other than the charity or, in the former

> ■ ■ ■ ■ ■ ■ ■ ■ ■ ■ ■ ■
>
> ***Your goal should be to create a relationship with your sponsors that extends far beyond the four walls of your contract.***
>
> ■ ■ ■ ■ ■ ■ ■ ■ ■ ■ ■ ■

King of the Beach Invitational Official Product Sponsor Package

EXCLUSIVITY
- XYZ receives product category exclusivity.

TELEVISION
- The event will be televised for a minimum of one (1) hour on ESPN in West Coast Prime Time with at least one (1) re-air on ESPN2 at a time to be determined by the network.
- XYZ will receive one (1) 00:00:30 commercial unit on each telecast.

SIGNAGE
- XYZ will receive on-court rotational signage on three (3) sides of the stadium court.
- XYZ's signage will be clearly visible for a minimum of 60 seconds on the television broadcast, provided XYZ purchases at least one (1) commercial unit.
- XYZ will be allowed four (4) 3' × 8' logo signs within the stadium (noncourtside).
- XYZ will be allowed four (4) 3' × 8' logo signs in high-traffic areas throughout the tournament grounds.
- XYZ will receive logo identification on the main corporate sponsor board.

ENTERTAINMENT
- XYZ will receive ten (10) sandbox seats for each session of the event (four sessions).
- XYZ will have use of the in-stadium hospitality platform (50 guests) for exclusive, private use during one (1) session of the event.
- XYZ will receive four (4) complimentary hotel room nights at the Hard Rock Hotel.
- XYZ will receive two (2) invitations to the King of the Beach Golf Outing (Thursday prior to the event).
- XYZ will receive eight (8) VIP invitations to "The Bash" player party.
- XYZ will receive four (4) VIP invitations to all ancillary hospitality functions.
- XYZ will receive twenty (20) general admission tickets to each session of the event for customer entertaining or ticket giveaway promotions.
  (Note to the reader: As discussed later, you will want to stress the sponsor's ability to promote your event independently in conjunction with their advertising and sales in the local market.)
  (All food, beverage, and decorating costs will be incurred by XYZ.)

DISPLAY/MERCHANDISE
- XYZ will have exclusive use of one (1) 10' × 10' display tent/area.
- XYZ will have the right to display and/or merchandise its product or services.
- XYZ will have the right to use the King of the Beach Invitational logo on products (except clothing).
  (Note to the reader: We had a separate clothing sponsor for this event [Speedo], so all clothing items related to the event had to be provided by that sponsor.)

PROMOTIONS/PUBLIC RELATIONS
- XYZ will have one (1) stadium court promotion each day of the event.
- XYZ will be allowed public address announcements throughout the event.
- XYZ will have the right to distribute publicity materials in the on-site public relations office.
- A national press release will be created and disseminated announcing XYZ's participation in the event.
- XYZ's logo will be included on press release and event letterhead.
- The right to have one (1) King of the Beach Invitational participant appear at on- and off-site event promotional activities subject to scheduling and noncompetitive endorsement relationships.
  (Note to the reader: This benefit is subject to your agreement with your participants in the event and has to be carefully coordinated so that you do not interfere with the player's event schedule both on and off the court.)
- XYZ will have the right to distribute a collateral piece in the King of the Beach Invitational welcome pack.
- XYZ will have the right to include an insert into each ticket mailing (i.e., coupon, product brochure, etc.).

ADVERTISING
- XYZ will receive ten (10) 00:00:30 radio units in the Las Vegas market during the two (2) weeks preceding the event.
- XYZ's logo will appear on all print advertisements produced by StarGames.
- XYZ's logo will appear in all television commercials produced by StarGames relating to this event.
- XYZ will be given one (1) full-page four-color advertisement in the official program.
- XYZ's logo will appear on the corporate sponsor page in the official program.
  Note: Approximately $100,000 will be spent in the local market advertising the event.

COST
In consideration of the above benefits, XYZ will pay to StarGames a cash fee of $25,000, which shall be payable in two (2) equal installments, with the first being due on signing an agreement and the second within five (5) days of the airing of the first ESPN telecast.

Figure 4.1 Sample sponsorship proposal.

KING OF THE BEACH INVITATIONAL FACT SHEET

EVENT: King of the Beach Invitational

DATE: March 10–13, 1999

LOCATION: Hard Rock Hotel and Casino, Las Vegas, Nevada

EVENT DESCRIPTION: The King of the Beach Invitational brings together the top 14 players from the AVP Tour to participate in a round-robin format over three days to determine the best individual player. Players rotate partners and earn points and prize money based on their results. The top four players advance to Sunday's final round, creating the most exciting event in the sport. Past champions include Karch Kiraly, Adam Johnson, Jose Loiola, and Eric Fonoimoana.

TELEVISION: The event will be televised on ESPN for one hour. The telecast date and time are still to be determined. There is one guaranteed re-air of the telecast on ESPN2.

SPONSOR BENEFITS: As an official product sponsor of the King of the Beach Invitational, XYZ will receive the following benefits:

- Product exclusivity
- One (1) 30-second commercial spot on the original and rebroadcast of the event on ESPN
- On-court signage in television camera range
- Tickets to each session of the event and access to the VIP hospitality area
- Four (4) complimentary room nights at the Hard Rock Hotel
- Invitations to all parties associated with the event
- The option to display and merchandise your product on site
- Daily on-court promotion
- A player appearance
- Name and logo on all materials produced for the event, including over $100,000 of in-market advertising
- Radio spots in the Las Vegas market featuring your product message
- An ad in the tournament program
- Additional benefits as determined for official product sponsors

COST: $25,000

Figure 4.2 Sample fact sheet.

case, not going to benefit the kids for whom you are trying to provide a place to play.

Also, keep in mind that you are soliciting busy people. The longer and fancier the presentation, in my experience, the less likely they are to read it with the immediacy that you had hoped for. I suspect that the high-gloss, state-of-the-art presentations get flipped through quickly and then get put into a reading file. They eventually get read because they look intriguing, but not with the same sense of urgency that you were looking for. While you should use the myriad of tools available to dress up your proposal so that it cuts through the clutter, simply be careful not to go overboard.

If you have a big event (e.g., a national championship), a more sophisticated look is probably in order. Four-color booklets, flip charts, video, graphs, and so on do make an impact. However, I believe that the event and the rights package are what sells, not the look of the presentation. So, while determining how best to "wrap" your proposal, make sure that the contents are substantial. Also, keep in mind that what you really hope is that someone calls you back and says, "We would like to discuss this with you." Your proposal should be the door opener. However, in all likelihood, your personal sales presentation will be what enables you to make the deal.

Sponsorship Levels

As you create your event, be thinking right from the start about how many sponsors you would like to have. Some part of this decision will be driven by how much money you need. If you can reach your financial goal with one corporate partner, in my opinion, so much the better. One sponsor avoids clutter and simplifies your life. You only have one company to deal with, and you can present a very clean-looking event. However, the reality is that sponsorship deals of the magnitude that are probably necessary to fund your entire event may be difficult to come by. As a result, you will most likely need to bring in multiple sponsors who all pay differing amounts.

That being the case, you need to determine how many sponsors in total you are prepared to have (the King of the Beach has averaged about 10 sponsors each year) and at what levels of participation and cost. There are many names for these sponsorship levels, but the most common ones include title sponsor, presenting sponsor, official product sponsor, associate, and partner. In general, these categories break down as follows:

■ ■ ■ ■ ■ ■ ■ ■ ■ ■ ■ ■

The event and the rights package are what sells, not the look of the presentation.

■ ■ ■ ■ ■ ■ ■ ■ ■ ■ ■ ■

- **Title sponsor.** This is the lead sponsor of the event (XYZ's King of the Beach Invitational). The title sponsor's corporate name and logo are featured in all communication regarding the event in the most prominent manner available while keeping with good taste. The title sponsor receives the most benefits of all the companies involved in your event.

- **Presenting sponsor.** Typically, this is the second biggest sponsor of your event. The presenting sponsor will most often have its name or logo come after the title of the event (XYZ's King of the Beach Invitational presented by ABC). The presenting sponsor receives benefits similar to those provided to the title sponsor but proportionate to what they pay. For example, the presenting sponsor's name and logo might be half the size of those of the title sponsor in your ads. They will receive proportionately fewer tickets, less signage, less television exposure, and so on. With some things, such as booth space

Urgency and Need

To some extent, your ability to close deals is directly proportional to your ability to create a sense of urgency . . . the need for someone to make a decision.

As much as I would like to say that urgency and need can be built into your proposal, the fact is that they cannot. The sense of need is what the sales process is all about—creating the market for your property. This can be illusive. The sense of urgency can be a bit more tangible in that you can use certain steps within the event process to try and force a decision from whomever you are working with. For example, if you are having a press conference to announce your event, you might use that to prod your potential sponsor into making a decision so *they* don't lose an opportunity. The start of your ad campaign or a major promotion can serve the same function. Sponsors will not want to miss these milestone moments in the countdown to your event. Use these occasions as sales techniques to close the deal.

and program ad pages, the differences will be minimal. If you are unable to find a title sponsor for the price you have in mind, you might negotiate to have your lead sponsor in the presenter role (the King of the Beach Invitational presented by XYZ).

• **Official product sponsor.** Normally, this will be the category with the most companies and is the area in which you have to be careful about corporate clutter. Too many sponsors might be a turnoff to certain companies and to the spectators. Official product sponsors typically receive in the neighborhood of one third of the benefits of your title sponsor. Their name is not in the title of the event. Their logo might be included in some ads, but not all. They receive fewer tickets, less promotion, and so on. All of this has to be calculated so that it is in proportion to what they pay. The dollars spent should directly affect the number of benefits you provide to the official product sponsors.

• **Associate, partner, and other levels.** I have found that any other classifications that you assign to your sponsors are simply offshoots of the three basic levels. These additional sponsor levels can be useful in expanding revenue streams. An associate sponsor might fall somewhere between the presenting sponsor and the official product sponsor. A corporate partner might receive half the benefits of an official product sponsor. In most cases, it takes a pretty big event to get to this depth of corporate participation. If your event is big enough (e.g., a major bowl game or national championship), you might have licensing partners too.

Finally, there might be other sponsorship options as well, depending on the type of

The number of sponsors you include in your event and their varying levels of sponsorship will largely depend on how much money you will need to fund your event.

event you have. A golf tournament might have hole and cart sponsors; a tennis tournament might have a clinic sponsor; a marathon might have a sponsor of the pre-race carbo-loading feast; and so forth. Here you have the opportunity to be very creative and add to your bottom line. (Remember, if you can do it without offending people, everything is sponsorable. We have had fashion show sponsors, hospitality area sponsors, changeover area sponsors, etc.) From an economic perspective, unless you have wrapped some of these options into the bigger packages, each of the sponsors of these ancillary elements will probably pay less for their participation in your event than those in the three basic categories. Therefore, you have to be careful about what benefits you provide and to whom. You don't want to find that you have given more or better benefits to your clinic sponsor than you gave to your official product sponsor, who paid four times as much money!

• **Licensing.** As I mentioned earlier, in some cases—and these will be the exceptions, not the rule—you might be able to license the name and logo of your event to companies that produce products that lend themselves to incorporating your logo. These are primarily going to be clothing, shoe, or other sporting equipment manufacturers. If you have a monster property such as the Super Bowl, you might make a deal with an automobile company or other major product manufacturer to put your event name on their product. These deals are usually royalty based, with your compensation dependent on sales. We have always insisted on some form of upfront guarantee against the royalty, and I think you should try to get that as well. To be perfectly clear, though, in most cases licensing will only be a factor for the really major events. We were able to license the King of the Beach logo on one or two occasions and tried to do so with a couple of other events, but this kind of thing is primarily left to the Wimbledons and Masters of the world.

With the above as background let's review in detail the various aspects of your sponsorship proposal using the King of the Beach proposal (figure 4.1) as our guide.

■ ■ ■ ■ ■ ■ ■ ■ ■ ■ ■

Product exclusivity should be a given in your proposals.

■ ■ ■ ■ ■ ■ ■ ■ ■ ■ ■

Exclusivity

XYZ receives product category exclusivity.

Except as it might relate to television advertising and preexisting venue signage, product exclusivity should be a given in your proposals. In virtually every case exclusivity is going to be expected by a prospective sponsor who will not want to share the stage at your event with another company in the same business. With that in mind, if your event is big enough, or if you are a good enough salesperson, certain categories that may seem to be geared to a single company might be able to be divided. It is not unusual to see an official domestic car and official imported car, or an automobile and truck. The drink category is sometimes broken down into carbonated, noncarbonated, energy, water, alcoholic (hard liquor), and beer. The telecommunications industry is another area in which you might have multiple sponsors. However, it is highly unlikely that you will see Coke and Pepsi, Ford and Chevrolet, or Merrill Lynch and Charles Schwab sponsoring the same event.

Again, creativity and salesmanship are the keys to exploiting this sometimes very fine line. Don't be surprised, however, if some sponsors become very definitive as to where they can live with the category divisions. I suggest that you not dig your heels in too deeply on this issue because in most cases the desire for product exclusivity is a pretty reasonable request.

Before leaving this discussion of exclusivity, you may recall that I referred earlier to potential venue sponsorship conflicts (this same issue will rear its head in your television negotiations). Suffice it to say, *before* sending out any proposals, be absolutely sure that you have covered this issue with your other event partners to be sure that you are not selling something you don't have the right to sell.

Television Package

The event will be televised for a minimum of one (1) hour on ESPN in West Coast Prime Time with at least one re-air on ESPN2 at a time to be determined by the network.

XYZ will receive one (1) 00:00:30 commercial unit on each telecast.

While we will cover most of the issues related to television in chapter 7, the type of television coverage and amount of on-air exposure that a company will receive from your event will be of great importance to most sponsors.

Perhaps the most delicate issue that you will face with regard to television exposure will be the amount of time a company's signage will appear on the air during the telecast. As you can see in the King of the Beach proposal, courtside signage exposure is, to some extent, a function of whether a company purchases commercial time on the telecast. In most of our events we stipulate that in order to have their signage *clearly* visible on television (there is always the chance that a camera will briefly pan the sponsor's logo), a sponsor must purchase commercial time. This is for a couple of reasons. First, if a company could gain logo exposure during the telecast without purchasing commercial time, they might always choose this option. As a result, much of the television time could go unsold, hurting both you and the broadcasting network. So, second, the network will probably insist on it anyway.

Consider the confusion if the network has paid you a rights fee and then you sell sponsorships that provide signage exposure without the purchase of commercial time. You and the network would be in a constant state of conflict. The only time this policy might become a problem (other than with any charity group whose signs should be visible to the cameras at no cost) is when one of your sponsors does not do any television advertising. We have had this situation with Speedo in conjunction with our volleyball events. Because they don't have a television commercial, we have allowed them, as the official clothing provider, to have courtside signage in television camera range. But this definitely should be the exception, not the rule.

Following are a couple of other issues in your sponsorship proposals that relate to television:

• **Billboards.** Typically, your telecast will have opening and closing billboards (e.g., "Today's telecast is brought to you by XYZ" along with the corporate logo) and perhaps some in the middle of the show. Note that there is no mention of these billboards in the King of the Beach official product sponsorship proposal. This is because they have been saved for the title and presenting sponsors, who should purchase more commercial time and pay more money in order to get this im-

portant additional benefit. (*Note:* In order to have their name in the title of the event on television, most networks will require that the title sponsor purchase at least three commercial spots per hour. This too is a policy that we have carried through to our proposals.)

• **Vignettes.** A vignette is basically a 60- or 90-second segment of your show that brings the viewer "up close" to a sponsor, charity, or other significant element of the event. These vignettes are essentially "in-program" ads that have a great deal of value because they are basically commercials with additional credibility since they are within the television show and thus appear as arms-length editorials. If your network partner has agreed to include one or more vignettes in your show, these should become a valuable part of your proposal. We tend to save these for the major sponsors or the site.

Signage

XYZ will receive on-court rotational signage on three (3) sides of the stadium court.

XYZ's signage will be clearly visible for a minimum of 60 seconds on the television broadcast, provided XYZ purchases at least one (1) commercial unit.

XYZ will be allowed four (4) 3' × 8' logo signs within the stadium (noncourtside).

XYZ will be allowed four (4) 3' × 8' logo signs in high-traffic areas throughout the tournament grounds.

XYZ will receive logo identification on the main corporate sponsor board.

While this may seem pretty self-explanatory, signage is perhaps the most visible benefit that you provide to a sponsor, so you have to be clear on the details. While you might think "a sign is a sign," the makeup of banners and other signage has changed quite a bit over the last 20 years.

When I first got into the sports business, most sponsors created their own signage, which basically replicated their corporate logo. As a result, you might have found yourself at a tennis tournament in which each banner was a different color: red, white, yellow, green, multicolored, two colors, and so on. In retrospect, some stadiums or courts just looked awful. Eventually, the Association of Tennis Professionals (ATP) and other professional tours and leagues started to require a coordinated color scheme both for look and playability. Imagine a tennis player trying to see a white or yellow ball against a multicolored background, particularly one that had white or yellow in it! So to begin with, you should make sure your signage doesn't impede play.

The whole signage area became a bit more complicated when DORNA, a Spanish company, introduced rotational signage in the mid-1980s. With this system a computer is programmed to rotate signs that take turns dominating the court, field, or rink. This allows you, the event organizer, to control the amount of time a sponsor's signage is visible both to the live audience and on television. Television was slow to allow this system because they felt it gave too much exposure over the air without the sponsor paying the network. Eventually, the economics of rotational signage was worked out so that now this system has become the norm in virtually every sport.

We have used rotational signage regularly at our volleyball events and even employed it at Halloween on Ice. The artwork options that it allows are tremendous and really enhance your event. However, rotational signage can be expensive for an event with a limited budget since there is shipping and artwork involved, so make sure you can afford it.

Recently, the signage issue has been moved to yet a new level by the introduction of "virtual signage," which enables a corporate logo to be inserted electronically during a television feed so that signage that is not visible to the live audience can appear on television. Many issues have surfaced as a result of this new technology (financial, exclusivity, and rights ownership, to name a few), but the options are tremendous. You can even insert different virtual signage in different countries. Since television has not yet fully accepted this new technology, it has not become much of a factor yet. However, it will (the U.S. Open tennis championships just signed a major international television deal in which virtual signage will play an important role), and you need to be prepared for it.

Signage is perhaps the most visible benefit that you provide to a sponsor, so you have to be clear on the details.

Entertainment

XYZ will receive ten (10) sandbox seats for each session of the event (four sessions).

XYZ will have use of the in-stadium hospitality platform (50 guests) for exclusive, private use during one (1) session of the event.

XYZ will receive four (4) complimentary hotel room nights at the Hard Rock Hotel.

XYZ will receive two (2) invitations to the King of the Beach Golf Outing (Thursday prior to the event).

XYZ will receive eight (8) VIP invitations to "The Bash" player party.

XYZ will receive four (4) VIP invitations to all ancillary hospitality functions.

XYZ will receive twenty (20) general admission tickets to each session of the event for customer entertaining or ticket giveaway promotions.

(All food, beverage, and decorating costs will be incurred by XYZ.)

This is one of the more tangible benefits that you can provide to a company, and depending on the sponsor or the event, hospitality can be one of the most used or the most underused elements of your event. In beach volleyball, for example, where the setting is perfect for entertaining customers and their families, sponsors rarely use the available hospitality options to their fullest extent. The King of the Beach Invitational, despite its seemingly ideal location at the Hard Rock Hotel, has never been a big draw for sponsor entertainment. At golf tournaments, regardless of the setting, corporate entertaining is almost more important than the exposure provided through television and other forms of media. Even at the McCall's LPGA Classic, which suffered from its isolated location in Vermont, McCall's entertained about 500 people over a three-day period. Over 50 corporations were involved at the 1999 Ryder Cup at the Country Club in Brookline, Massachusetts. The vast majority of them had no involvement in the television broadcast but brought in dozens of their top customers at a cost of hundreds of thousands of dollars.

My point is that you are best served by making your event a corporate hospitality paradise. Start out by making sure that your venue can handle your needs. Then, provide great seats, top-level catering, comfortable entertainment facilities that are either permanent or portable (most people will not object to tents), and access to some of the talent.

Access to the talent will depend of course on your contract with the athletes. Make sure that you can compel participants to appear at cocktail parties and the like because corporate sponsors and their guests love to rub shoulders with the talent. In this regard, if your sponsors will allow you to commingle their guests with the public, so much the better because then you can also sell tickets to an after-show party at premium prices. At Skating Goes Country, the top-tier tickets were sold for $125, which included a party with the cast afterwards. Guests of Lane Furniture, the title sponsor, attended as well.

To enhance the entertainment value of your event, I suggest that you develop secondary activities for your sponsors' guests. The golf tournament at the King of the Beach event was a big attraction, as are autograph sessions at figure skating shows and clinics at golf or tennis events. Again, *creativity is the key.* Most of these activities don't add much to your budget and are easily incorporated into the cost of the sponsorship.

You are best served by making your event a corporate hospitality paradise.

You can enhance your hospitality package by adding little things, such as hotel rooms at no cost, free programs for the sponsors' guests, goody bags with T-shirts, autographed pictures, and the like. The latter items make great souvenirs and are much appreciated by everyone—especially people who can bring them home to their kids and be a hero for a day! There may be no better sales tool than having the family of one of your sponsors love your event. While not many decision makers may admit it, the influence of spouses and kids is enormous in a subtle sort of way.

Encourage your sponsors to entertain at your event (you will want them to maximize every aspect of their sponsorship, but again, entertainment may be the most tangible). Sponsors who are emotionally involved are more likely to stay committed to the event for the long term. Also, there is no stronger statement about your event than having one of your sponsors close a big deal with a customer while at your event. You will have a partner and a fan for a long time!

Display/Merchandise

XYZ will have exclusive use of one (1) 10' × 10' display tent/area.

XYZ will have the right to display and/or merchandise its product or services.

XYZ will have the right to use the King of the Beach Invitational logo on products (except clothing).

For some companies, the ability to come in direct contact with the public (their customers and potential customers) is reason enough to become a sponsor of your event. It is not that often that a company has an opportunity to reach its desired demographic audience in a captive setting and either directly sample their product or demonstrate it in an atmosphere in which the customer has *paid* to attend. Sports events provide such a setting and thus can be very important to some of your prospective corporate partners. As a result, the display booth area that you might casually offer as part of the package can in some instances be the most important part of the deal. So don't treat it lightly.

As we discussed in the chapter on venue selection, because sampling can be so important, you have to be sure that it is allowed. During the 1998 Halloween on Ice tour sampling was of critical importance to both Nestle and Ocean Spray. Had they not been able to hand out products to everyone as they left the buildings, I doubt they would have agreed

to our deal no matter how much television coverage we were able to provide. This was particularly important to Nestle, which was introducing a new product; the opportunity to actually get it into the hands of the female consumer (the primary market for skating events and their new product, Nestle's Treasures) was key. Fortunately, none of the buildings tried to block this activity.

From an operations standpoint, a company's desire to sample or otherwise directly communicate with the consumer suggests that, when designing your site, you should provide for an area that attracts your spectators because it is visually or otherwise enticing. If nothing else goes according to plan, at least make sure that your sponsors are able to reach their objective of directly and personally interacting with the customer. Nothing will be more meaningful to a sponsor than a report to headquarters from the field that someone either bought their display item or went right out and purchased their product as a result of the display.

Amazingly, this has happened to us most frequently with one of the more expensive display products—automobiles. During Volvo's sponsorship of the men's tennis tour, there were several occasions when we would hear stories of people buying the car in which a ball-guessing contest was held. When Honda sponsored the AVP Tour, I remember two events at which people saw a CRV at the event, asked where the closest dealer was, and went right from the tournament to buy the car. As a tournament organizer, you can't beat that for proving the validity of sponsoring your event!

Promotions/Public Relations

XYZ will have one (1) stadium court promotion each day of the event.

> ■ ■ ■ ■ ■ ■ ■ ■ ■ ■
>
> **Y**ou will want your sponsors to maximize every aspect of their sponsorship, but again, entertainment may be the most tangible.
>
> ■ ■ ■ ■ ■ ■ ■ ■ ■ ■

XYZ will be allowed public address announcements throughout the event.

XYZ will have the right to distribute publicity materials in the on-site public relations office.

A national press release will be created and disseminated announcing XYZ's participation in the event.

XYZ's logo will be included on press release and event letterhead.

The right to have one (1) King of the Beach Invitational participant appear at on- and off-site event promotional activities subject to scheduling and noncompetitive endorsement relationships. (Note to the reader: This benefit is subject to your agreement with your participants in the event and has to be carefully coordinated so that you do not interfere with the player's event schedule both on and off the court.)

XYZ will have the right to distribute a collateral piece in the King of the Beach Invitational welcome pack.

XYZ will have the right to include an insert into each ticket mailing (i.e., coupon, product brochure, etc.).

This category really has to be considered in two very distinct manners. First, there is the promotion that you employ to make people aware of the event as a means of coaxing them

to attend. The second is promotion that your sponsor does to reinforce their product or service and its affiliation with the event. The first you control. The second you don't.

Your promotion is critical in that it helps you sell tickets and attract an audience. It also provides your sponsors with tremendous exposure that they would otherwise have to buy through different channels. Your sponsor's promotional efforts can be equally as effective. They provide additional advertising for you at no cost and, just as important, serve to further involve your sponsor in the event. The more your sponsors participate in the event, the better off you will be (unless they have a miserable experience) because they will then be in a position to evaluate their benefits of the event from more angles than simply whether the television commercials ran and the show delivered an acceptable rating (their active participation becomes even more important if you don't have television coverage).

So, encourage your corporate partners to exploit your event past the four walls of the contract.

It has been said that to properly take advantage of a sponsorship buy, a company should spend *at least* as much on or around the event as they do for the sponsorship itself. A $10,000 official product sponsor should spend no less than $10,000 on sampling, entertaining, and promotions. A $100,000 title sponsor should spend, at a minimum, another $100,000, and so on. Part of your job is to give sponsors a platform from which to make these expenditures and thus receive additional benefits. In order to do so, you have to provide them with as many options as possible. This is where introductions to local radio or television stations, access to athletes, ancillary events, and the like can be very valuable.

Your promotions are another story. As opposed to straight advertising, promotion is a

> ■ ■ ■ ■ ■ ■ ■ ■ ■ ■ ■
>
> **M**ake sure
> that your sponsors are able
> to reach their objective
> of directly and personally
> interacting with the customer.
>
> ■ ■ ■ ■ ■ ■ ■ ■ ■ ■ ■

way to make noise about your event in areas outside of radio, television, and print. We will discuss some of these ideas later, but suffice it to say, things, such as ticket giveaways, sweepstakes, coupons, and so on, are important to getting your message out. They also can provide a way for your sponsors to engage in promotion through two-for-one ticket offers, discounts with the purchase of sponsor products, and the like. This is truly an area in which there are few boundaries, many traditional promotions, and tremendous room to be creative both for the event and for your sponsors.

Advertising

XYZ will receive ten (10) 00:00:30 radio units in the Las Vegas market during the two (2) weeks preceding the event.

XYZ's logo will appear on all print advertisements produced by StarGames.

XYZ's logo will appear in all television commercials produced by StarGames relating to this event.

XYZ will be given one (1) full-page four-color advertisement in the official program.

XYZ's logo will appear on the corporate sponsor page in the official program.

Note: Approximately $100,000 will be spent in the local market advertising the event.

As with promotion, advertising has two benefits. The first is obviously the sales message: "Our event is coming on such and such a date and you should not miss it, so buy tickets now." We will discuss this in more detail later. From a sponsor's point of view (and especially that of the title and presenting sponsor), your advertising budget is important because their name and logo will be seen every time

you run an ad. This gives a prospective sponsor something tangible to measure when evaluating your proposal and its price.

Companies try to value your event according to many different formulas, but most come back to the same measurements by which they analyze their traditional advertising. The most accepted valuation is based on what is called "cost per thousand," in which companies try to determine the cost of reaching a thousand people. Over time, most companies and their advertising agencies will have worked out a cost-per-thousand range that is acceptable to them, with a lower ratio (say, $8 per thousand) being better than a higher ratio (say, $40 per thousand). The more advertising that you are planning to do, all of which will include your sponsor's identification, the more quantifiable your sponsorship package will be and the lower the company's cost per thousand for sponsoring your event. Whether your advertising is paid for in cash or trade, you should count it all and make sure that you emphasize this in your sales presentation. When we calculate our advertising expenditure, we include straight advertising buys (i.e., television, radio, newspaper), ticket brochure mailings, posters, and so forth. Every dollar that you spend (or trade) to get your message out should be made known to your prospective sponsor.

Your advertising package is also an area for creativity. In our King of the Beach proposal we provide the sponsor radio spots for their own product message in the local market. You won't see this in every deal, but it was a very popular idea. Add the unexpected. It is sure to create some sizzle to your proposal.

Cost

In consideration of the above benefits, XYZ will pay to StarGames a cash fee of $25,000, which shall be payable in two (2) equal installments, with the first being due on signing an agreement and the second within five (5) days of the airing of the first ESPN telecast.

Obviously, for most everyone concerned, this is the bottom line. You need to come up with a cost for your various sponsorship levels that you can justify when pressed by those to whom you are soliciting. Every potential sponsor will understand that the price you set is intended to help cover the cost of your event, including the cost of implementing their sponsorship deal. What might raise some eyebrows is the premium you build in. With that in mind, there are a number of elements to factor in when determining your pricing, including the following:

• **The cost of your event and the percentage of those costs you anticipate covering from sponsorship.** We have tried to use a formula that pegs the title sponsorship to 125 percent of the cost of the talent. Thus, if you have an event with prize money of $100,000, the title sponsorship would be priced at a minimum of $125,000 and the benefits provided geared to that level of spending. If you are paying appearance fees only, then you would set the price at 125 percent of the total being paid to the athletes. This formula has evolved over time (at one point we started with the title sponsorship being equal to the player compensation), and frankly, we don't always achieve this ratio, but it gives us a place to start. The presenting sponsorship is usually priced at about 50 to 60 percent of the title sponsorship. (We have always found this to be the toughest level to sell because it is a lot more expensive than the official product sponsorship but clearly secondary to the title sponsorship. It is a tricky deal to make.) Official product sponsors can range anywhere from 10 to 25 percent of the title sponsorship price.

• **The cost of servicing the sponsorship that you sell.** For example, if you are giving a sponsor 75 tickets that have an average price of $15, then the cost to you for that part of the deal is $1,075. I call this the "soft cost" because there is no cash out of your pocket. It is more an opportunity cost, as you will no longer have those seats to sell. On the other hand, if it costs you $1,000 to rent and install a tent for a display area specifically for that sponsor, that has to be calculated into your price. That is a

"hard cost" because you actually go out of pocket. The more you can point to actual costs (hard or soft), the better off you will be when having to justify your price structure.

• **The "value for value" that you will provide and the premium on that for the "value added."** In plain English this means going back to the cost-per-thousand formula. Determine how many people you will expose the company to and how much publicity they will receive in all forms of media. You should put a value on everything from 30-second commercials (their cost) to articles about the event that mention the sponsor name (base this on the cost of buying an ad the size of the article. If you have some historical examples of this, it can help a lot), and contrast this to the amount that they would otherwise have to pay to generate this type of exposure to determine the sponsorship cost. This is a more sophisticated approach and may require some help from an ad agency.

• **What you think the market will bear.** This requires some feel, probably some experience, and some knowledge about your competition and the marketplace in which you are promoting. If a similar event (not necessarily in the same sport but the same level of event) is priced much higher or lower than yours, this will give you some sense of the marketplace.

With all of this cost analysis and price justification, you won't always be able to make a deal even if a company is genuinely interested in your event. In Nashville we had a company with a major local presence that wanted to be part of the event. However, for a fee that was less than our lowest official product sponsorship was priced, they wanted to have three separate banners at rinkside, all in television camera range. As much as we would have liked to have them involved in the event, we had to say no because we could not justify giving them so much exposure.

SALES PROCESS

Now that you have your sponsorship proposal written, you can begin the task of

Working Model: Tournament Sponsorship Proposal

In an effort to support our working model event, we are going to need a few good local sponsors. What follows is the title sponsorship proposal that could be sent to local banks, supermarkets, and other local/regional businesses that might see value in becoming the sponsor of this event and helping out kids in the area.

REGIONAL TENNIS CHAMPIONSHIPS TITLE SPONSORSHIP PROPOSAL

EXCLUSIVITY
- The event will be referred to as the XYZ Cup (or other name to be mutually agreed on) in all forms of advertising, promotion, public relations, etc.
- XYZ will receive product category exclusivity.

TELEVISION
- The event will be televised on a regional cable television outlet a minimum of two (2) times, the original broadcast and one (1) re-air.
- XYZ will receive an opening and closing billboard in the show.
- XYZ will receive two (2) 30-second commercials during each telecast.
- XYZ will have its banners within television camera range.
- XYZ will have the opportunity to make an on-air presentation to the winner.
- The telecast will have a minimum 60-second vignette talking about XYZ's support of junior tennis.

SIGNAGE
- XYZ will receive eight (8) 3' × 8' product banners on the center court.
- XYZ's name and logo will be incorporated into four (4) tournament banners on the center court (XYZ Cup).
- Four (4) other 3' × 8' product banners will be visible in high-traffic areas throughout the tournament grounds.
- One (1) additional 3' × 8' sponsor banner will be on each other court used for tournament play.
- One (1) additional event banner using XYZ's name will be on each court used for tournament play.
  Note: The cost of banner production for product-specific banners will be borne by XYZ.

ENTERTAINMENT
- The center court will have a seating area specifically reserved for up to 20 of XYZ's guests at all times.

DISPLAY/MERCHANDISE
- XYZ will have the right to display merchandise in a high-traffic area on site.
- XYZ will have the right to sample its product to spectators and players during the event.

PROMOTIONS/PUBLIC RELATIONS
- XYZ will receive a minimum of three (3) public address announcements each day of the event.
- A press release will be created and disseminated on a regional basis announcing XYZ's participation in the event.
- XYZ will be named in all other press releases and materials produced for the event.
- XYZ will have the right to invite the players to its offices and/or store for a photo opportunity.

ADVERTISING
- XYZ's name and logo will appear on all flyers produced to invite players to participate in the event.
- XYZ will be the sponsor of the tournament drawsheet, which will be produced for the event.

COST
The cost to XYZ for the above benefits, including the right to use the event's name and logo in XYZ's advertising and promotion, is $25,000, which will be payable in two (2) equal installments, with the first being due upon signing the agreement and the second within five (5) days of the conclusion of the event.

trying to make a deal. This process usually starts by making cold calls and sending out pitch letters in an effort to get yourself in front of prospective buyers. However, since there are literally hundreds, if not thousands, of prospects, where do you start? Do you take the "shotgun" approach, in which you send out dozens of proposals, or the "rifle" approach, in which you target companies that you think best match up to what you have to offer. And whom do you call to start the discussion?

I prefer the more targeted rifle approach. The broader shotgun approach, for me, seems to waste too much time and energy. I want to pick companies to go after with whom I think the success rate will be pretty high. Regardless of the direction you choose to take, I suggest that you narrow down the choices of where to send your information. But how do you even start that process?

Fortunately, a number of resources allow you to follow the advertising and promotional plans of major companies. Magazines, such as *Adweek, The SportsBusinessJournal, Advertising Age, The Sports Marketing Newsletter, IEG Reports, SportsSponsor Fact Book, Brandweek,* and *Crain's New York Business Review,* are all great places to begin your sponsorship journey (as is the Internet, where you can learn a lot about most companies from their Web sites, including the names of various contacts). In these periodicals you will learn about corporate plans, ad agency hirings and firings, personnel movement, and just about everything else you might need to get started. The relevant articles will usually give you contact names. If they don't, call the company. The receptionist will usually know who is in charge of sports sponsorships. If the company doesn't have someone specifically assigned

■ ■ ■ ■ ■ ■ ■ ■ ■ ■ ■ ■

What separates the "haves" from the "have nots" in the sponsorship game is aggressiveness, a stick-to-it attitude, passion, salesmanship, and the ability to "close."

■ ■ ■ ■ ■ ■ ■ ■ ■ ■ ■ ■

to that job, ask for the vice president of marketing, who, if you get through to him or her, can at least point you in the right direction.

It is up to you to cull from all of the available information the items that are applicable to your event. While this may be difficult, you can *never* say that there is a lack of information. If the above list doesn't supply enough material for you, just keep reading. Whether it is *Sports Illustrated, Time, Newsweek, Fast Company, Wired,* or the many magazines that are geared to each and every sport, information on companies, contacts, and corporate strategies is plentiful. I have a goal of finding a minimum of three work-related items in every magazine I read. Whether this means tearing out the ad of a potential sponsor or an article on a company or executive, there is always something in these magazines that relates somehow to the selling of your event.

With all of this information around and hundreds of promoters seeking sponsors, what separates the "haves" from the "have nots" in the sponsorship game is aggressiveness, a stick-to-it attitude, passion, salesmanship, and the ability to "close." You have to *want* to sell. You have to *believe* in your property. You have to have the imagination to *create the marketplace* for your event. You have to *ask for the order* and convince someone to say *yes.*

Arguably, no company that markets its products or services (other than sporting goods companies perhaps) *needs* sports sponsorship. The product manager for virtually every product or service can easily rationalize that traditional advertising and promotion—from print to television to couponing to sweepstakes—work just fine and never expose him or her to the questions from upper management that are certain to come from something as difficult to measure as a sports sponsorship. The president of a major packaged goods company once told me that product managers are, both by training and by the nature of the corporate structure, risk averse and not very creative. They can never be taken to task for implementing a couponing program that delivers a 2 percent return. This is a standard practice in the industry, and upper management will rarely call them on the carpet for such a strategy. However, a sponsorship that delivers a lot of intangible benefits but little in the way of measurable results, regardless of its creativity or exposure and positioning benefits, can always be second guessed.

Your job is to convince the product manager and perhaps their senior management that your event will deliver both tangible results that fare well against standard promotions (end aisle space in supermarkets and additional case purchases, for example) and advertising (reaching the target market at an acceptable cost per thousand), while at the same time delivering the intangibles that enable the product message to rise above the clutter. This is not an easy task but certainly doable if you are enthusiastic, aggressive, and *well prepared.*

Preparing Yourself

Everyone will prepare for the sales effort in his or her own way. In most cases that preparation should center on your ability to create the market. As we discussed earlier, it is only by creating the market in the mind of your potential buyer that you have a real chance at success.

For me, preparing to explain the marketplace and create the need for a company to be in that space has not been a big problem. Rather, my preparation is more geared to getting myself in the right state of mind to ask for the order. I have always known my product well, and I am pretty creative in developing packages that deliver benefits beyond the expected. However, I am not always up to the task of delivering a hard sales pitch. I have to be in the right frame of mind. I have to prepare myself mentally to make the call knowing that parts of the discussion will not necessarily be that comfortable, and at the end, I have to ask the other person to spend money that he or she was not planning to spend.

My preparation is basically geared to readying myself to ask for the order because I have found that to be the toughest part of the sales process. It is easy to talk about the event, the participants, the site, and so on. It is not too difficult to come up with the "behind the scenes" insight that some people like to hear because it gives them confidence that you are for real and can deliver the goods. After all that is said, though, you have to give them the news of how much this is all going to cost. If there is going to be a time in the conversation when I am going to hesitate, it is going to be when I have to say, ". . . and the price for all that is X," particularly if it is a big number. To ask for $5,000 is no big deal, but to ask for $500,000 or a million dollars is quite another story.

So for me, preparation is really geared to this one issue. You will have to find out where your internal pressure point is. That will determine how you prepare. Listen to yourself carefully in this area because it could be the make-or-break element for you as a salesperson.

Cold Calling

For someone new to the business, your preparation will probably be most necessary before making that ever-intimidating "cold call."

Sponsorship sales is an art in and of itself that frankly some people never master. Sponsorship sales often begin with a call to a person at a company that you have identified as a potential partner for your event . . . but never met. All I can say is that many an entry-level sports marketing executive has crashed and burned when it came to sponsorship sales and cold calls. I have personally never been a big fan of making these calls; they are awkward and just plain not that much fun. But I have made hundreds of them and credit Ray Benton with at least giving me the tools and the gumption to pick up the phone and try to sell. Those who can't sell, for the most part, don't make it in our business. Those who can't make cold calls rarely get a chance to sell. A cold call requires the following types of preparation:

• **Know your product and your parameters.** Memorize your proposals. You have to be able to deliver your pitch with passion. If you are not familiar with your property or the variations on the sponsorship package, the listener will sense that. You must ooze confidence and knowledge.

• **Know their product.** Research the company before you call. Put yourself in a position to talk from strength by knowing as much as possible about a particular product or company. If the prospective sponsor senses that you are really winging it, they might lose interest. Make them feel that they are the most important person and product in the world to you by knowing as much about them as you can.

• **Practice your speech.** Give your opening speech several times before trying it for real. You want to be comfortable when you are making your pitch. The more times you practice, the less nervous you will be. Find a colleague who will practice with you.

• **Exercise perseverance.** You will have many more turndowns and unanswered calls than you ever imagined. This is just a fact of life when it comes to selling. Don't take it personally.

• **Exhibit personality.** This has to do with *you*. What you say and how you say it have to be intriguing. The best sellers are great "schmoozers" and enjoy that part of the process as much as anything. This is where being a people person is a real strength.

• **Ask for a meeting.** Your goal is to get in front of people so you can try to sell. You will get your message across far better in person than over the phone. It is tough to get in front of people, and many a young salesperson too readily accepts "no" over the phone. There is nothing like a face-to-face meeting. You may not make the sale the first time, but the meeting will be the basis for forming a relationship that may come in handy down the road. When selling, you have to think of the property at hand as well as the ones in the future. Think of the first meeting as the start of a long-term relationship.

Closing the Deal

After you get in the door and create some interest in your event, you have to close the deal. That is where real salesmanship comes in.

Sponsorship sales is selling at its most basic. It requires a sales mentality from the outset. A good seller believes in the product, is *dying* to make the sale, and is well organized and creative. Keep in mind that selling is the same for a grassroots event as it is for a major championship. The principles are identical, even though it may seem easier to sell the Super Bowl than your local 10K.

> ■ ■ ■ ■ ■ ■ ■ ■ ■ ■
>
> **A** *good seller believes in the product, is dying to make the sale, and is well organized and creative.*
>
> ■ ■ ■ ■ ■ ■ ■ ■ ■ ■

The similarities inherent in selling events of all levels are unlike virtually anything that we have discussed or will discuss. Clearly there is a major difference between operating the U.S. Open Golf Championships and a one-day golf outing to raise money for your favorite charity. The disparity in selling these two events, though (once you get in the door), is not nearly as great. At every level, sponsorship sales are hard; they require strong nerves, a "don't take no for an answer" attitude, and the ability to close the deal.

The most important part of the sales process is closing the deal. We have talked about this earlier, but it is worth repeating. It is what the sales process is all about, and it is what will give you the warm and fuzzy feeling you get when you have accomplished a major goal.

Again, as discussed earlier, one thing that helps to close the deal is to create a sense of urgency. Make the prospective sponsor feel that this is something they need and that they need *now*. Find reasons within the planning cycle of your event to move them closer to finalizing the deal so they don't miss a press conference, ad placement, major promotion, or the like.

Closing the sponsorship deal is the payoff for your whole event. It is what will fund your activity, so it has to be the ultimate goal.

Timing Your Sponsorship Search

In a perfect world, you will give yourself about 18 months to find your sponsor partners. While that might seem like a lot of lead time, the reality is that companies work in budget cycles. If you miss their window, it can be difficult to sell them anything because all their money will already be committed. Thus, if you can get to your prospects at least six months in front of their annual planning cycle—and if you are looking for a lot of money, even longer lead times are helpful—you will at least have a chance to be incorporated into the following year's budget.

If you miss a company's annual budgeting plan, then you are fighting an uphill battle which may require them to dip into their "discretionary funds." These are marketing dollars that are approved for spending but not allocated to a specific project. Generally, the amount of discretionary money is limited, so it will be tough to generate a lot of money in this scenario. These discretionary funds are also the first to get cut when budgets are tightened . . . a practice that is commonplace and inevitable.

Obviously, getting to a company before its budget is set is pretty important, and every company works on different schedules. Since there is no magic way of knowing when a company sets its budget, you might as well ask. In any case, long lead times for sponsorship sales are very helpful. As a result, don't think that you are going to find a sponsor quickly. Unless you get lucky, that probably won't happen.

Corporate Relationships

I am skipping ahead here because, although I could go on about the sales process, this is not a book on how to sell. Nevertheless, selling just may be the most important element in bringing your event to life, so don't *you* skip over it!

If you have either made a sponsorship deal yourself or had one brought to you by an outside third party, you will of course enter into a formal agreement with the sponsoring company. As with the other agreements that we have discussed, the language for these contracts is unique and deserves some special attention. However, before we get into details on the construction of the written agreement, it is worthwhile to discuss the underlying relationship that you develop with your sponsors.

No matter how airtight the language and how well written the contract, nothing will replace a solid relationship with your sponsors. This is certainly as important as any of the relationships that you will build throughout the process of operating your event. In my opinion, the key to your relationship with your sponsors is communication. In most cases, your television and venue partners will be in the sports business on a daily basis. They understand the ups and downs and rhythms of the industry. Your sponsors, however, are usually not in the sports or entertainment business at all. They are in the business of selling a certain product or service that is enhanced by having an involvement with

■ ■ ■ ■ ■ ■ ■ ■ ■ ■ ■

The most important part of the sales process is closing the deal.

■ ■ ■ ■ ■ ■ ■ ■ ■ ■ ■

sports. They will not be able to anticipate the flows of the sports business and will need to have it explained to them on a regular basis.

For example, while you hope never to have to change your date or venue once you have determined those basic elements, the reality is that issues come up periodically that may require a change of plans. The last thing you want is to have to spring a major surprise on your sponsors. Remembering the GlenEagles Country Club fiasco in which the grass on the courts didn't grow in time, had we not kept Avis, Tiffany, Ray Ban, and the other sponsors in the loop, they would not have been in a position to make alternate plans when the event was canceled. Likewise, our Halloween on Ice show at the Providence Civic Center did not sell well. Because of close communication with Ocean Spray's ad agency, we knew that they had targeted the Providence show as one at which they were going to do their heaviest entertaining. We did not want the decision makers to be embarrassed when they arrived at a building that holds 12,000 people and had only 4,000 in the stands. We kept them abreast of this issue, and they moved some of their entertaining to the show in Lowell, Massachusetts, where we had a sellout.

Examples of this type of communication are endless. And they are not all related to bad news, either. Steady communication builds relationships that can outlast the company's participation in a particular event and may help you out somewhere down the road.

Keep in mind that your sponsors are not always in the sports or entertainment industry, so you need to communicate effectively with them at all stages.

Remember a few basic things related to sponsorships:

* corporate relationships are with people;
* marketing strategies change; and
* people move on to new companies.

You too will have changes in your career and other events that you will create or work on. By building a relationship through communication and trust, you will start to develop a bank of contacts that you may be able to bring into other projects at a later date. In 1994 Northwest Airlines sponsored our Christmas on Ice tour. They also were the title sponsor of the inaugural Halloween on Ice show in 1995. They were part of the event again in 1996. In 1997 their advertising strategy shifted, and figure skating did not fit their consumer profile. Nevertheless, we had developed a close enough relationship with the decision makers at Northwest that we are still in contact today, and no doubt they will be part of another one of our projects at some

■ ■ ■ ■ ■ ■ ■ ■ ■ ■ ■

__N__o matter how airtight the language and how well written the contract, nothing will replace a solid relationship with your sponsors.

■ ■ ■ ■ ■ ■ ■ ■ ■ ■ ■

point in the future (in fact, at the time of this writing they are about to be a sponsor of a new golf tournament that we are producing).

The point of all this is that corporate relationships are basically people-to-people relationships. Build these and you will have the underpinnings for great sponsorships that will only enhance your properties. If your relationships are based on communication, trust, and performance, then the contract will just be a formality.

SPONSORSHIP CONTRACT

No matter how strong your corporate relationships become, you should still have a contract and know what that contract means. Some of the most important elements of your sponsorship agreement include term, event definition, sponsor benefits, sponsor obligations, indemnity, insurance, confidentiality, and governing law. You may want to refer regularly to the working model contract at the end of this chapter while reading this contract analysis.

Term

This is the length of your agreement. In my opinion, longer is not always better. One of the issues that is certain to affect the length of your sponsorship deal is the financial commitment that the company is willing to make. However, that is not the only, and sometimes not even the most important, factor that will drive this decision. To begin to make a judgment on the value of a long-term deal, you must first understand the sponsor's objectives and decide how they mesh with yours.

Every sponsor of a sports event has a different set of goals. Some of these goals can be achieved in one year. Others might take ten. For example, if a sponsor is focused on short-term sales in the specific market in which an event takes place, they probably are not going to be concerned with the long-term brand building and recognition that can be gained through the continual association with an event. Conversely, if a company is looking to tie its name to an event and reap the benefits from the goodwill attached to that event,

then a short-term deal will make no sense for them because they will not earn that type of recognition in one or two years.

For you, there are upsides and downsides to each of the disparate positions. In the short-term example, if it is year one of your event and the potential sponsor is willing to spend heavily to promote their tie-in to the event as a means of gaining market share, this might be the best way to put your event on the map and penetrate the market. In the longer-term example, the company may not be willing to spend funds over and above their sponsorship fee, expecting you to do all the advertising and promotion. So you have to know what you want as well. Your mission statement might help you determine your position on the term.

There are obviously many permutations to the two extremes. If you have some options when considering how long a deal you want to make with a sponsor, make sure you factor in product category, objectives, compatibility, promotional plans, and fees.

We have had sponsors that fall into every category. Swatch, in a one-year deal for title sponsorship of King of the Beach, paid us reasonably well but did little or no additional advertising or promotion. Lane Furniture, again in a one-year deal, paid us less than we were looking for at Skating Goes Country but aggressively advertised the telecast, which helped us and TNN. Miller Lite, as a long-term sponsor of the King of the Beach Invitational, gave us a lot of local support in the Las Vegas market.

There are sponsorship examples of every shape, kind, and result. The length of the contract term often will be a clue as to the company's commitment to the event, so take all of these factors into consideration during this aspect of your negotiations.

Event Definition

While this may not be the most important clause in your agreement, in some respects it sets the tone for what your corporate partner will expect. In our agreements this paragraph usually comes right at the outset and spells out what will happen in the event itself. For example, in the King of the Beach contract the event is defined as a "three-day round-robin event featuring the top players in the world." It further explains the format of the event in broad terms so that everyone knows that this is not the regular double-elimination format that most pro beach volleyball tournaments follow. Similarly, for something like Halloween on Ice we would use this paragraph to explain that this is "an exhibition-style event with skating performed in costume to Halloween themed music." In this manner, no one will have false expectations about what is going to be presented. You should make it a point to include a paragraph of this nature. You might find that your initial mission statement will be helpful in crafting this language.

Sponsor Benefits

This will be one of the key paragraphs of the contract in that it will (or should) very specifically outline everything that you are granting to the sponsor. This paragraph should include all the details of what your sponsor has bought from you, including number of tickets, size of banners, VIP hospitality passes, television commercials, and the like. This should not be a hard paragraph to write because in most cases it will be a pretty straight regurgitation of what was in your initial proposal, with modifications based on your negotiations (so take careful notes during those discussions!). Most important, this is the paragraph on which you will eventually be judged by your corporate partners. They will point to this part of the contract if you promise athlete appearances and fail to live up to that obligation, or if you were supposed to give the sponsor 50 tickets and only came up with 40. In this regard, at the end of the day the key to your event and your personal credibility will be determined by your ability to deliver on the promises spelled out in this portion of the contract.

Sponsor Obligations

While the benefits clause will be the scorecard for your sponsors, the obligations paragraph will be where your benefits are listed. This part of the agreement should detail sponsorship fees due, promotional obligations to which your sponsor has committed, and any other products or services that they agree to provide. You should try to be very precise here, particularly as it relates to the less measurable elements of the deal. For example, in our agreement with Coca-Cola for the Best of the Beach Invitational (the one that never took place), we could have written that they would "provide beverages for the event." This would have been pretty open ended and subject to wild swings in interpretation. We could have tightened the language to say that they would "provide drinks for the player's lounge, courtside, the media tent, and the VIP hospitality area." While this would have been more specific, it still would have been vague enough so that different people could read it different ways. Under this definition, would they have had to provide one can to each area? Ten cans a day? A hundred cans in total? So, we wrote an agreement that was detailed down to the number of cans, the time of day that they would be delivered, how much we would be charged if we used more than the allotted amount, and what products they had to provide. In this manner, there could be little debate if we didn't have enough product for ev-

> *The key to your event and your personal credibility will be determined by your ability to deliver on the promises spelled out in this portion of the contract.*

eryone or if we needed more than anticipated.

Specificity in every paragraph of each of your contracts will be helpful. Since the sponsor obligations clause outlines *your* benefits, I suggest that you be a little extra thorough here so that you get everything you bargained for.

Indemnity

This is one of my old favorites and should make its way into every one of your agreements for the event. While the indemnity language in your sponsorship contract will be similar to that of the indemnity language in other contracts (athlete, venue, television), I draw specific attention to it here because you often will be involved with big companies that get sued for minor product failures and other issues on a fairly regular basis. Making sure that you are indemnified by your sponsors for things that might go wrong with their product during your event or at times otherwise related to your event is critical. When major companies get sued for nonperformance or product failings, the fees can get big in a hurry. You should not have to be a part of a dispute that has nothing to do with your event. Make sure that you are protected . . . and get your attorneys to review this paragraph!

Insurance

The insurance clause falls into the same category as the indemnity paragraph in that it stands for one thing: protection. It will not be a big deal for a sponsor to add you in a very limited way to their umbrella insurance coverage so that if anything goes wrong with their product or service during your event or in any way related to your event, you will be covered by *their* insurance. This will mean that, in the case of any recoupment by a spectator, participant, worker, or volunteer as a result of an issue related to the sponsor, you won't have to pay. Your sponsor will likely ask you to add them to your policy as well. This should not be a problem for you either since you should be sure to arrange for ample in-

surance to cover just about any situation (you can even get rain insurance if you so desire). Again, insurance protection will not offend a sponsor once they have made the decision to become involved with your tournament, so don't be bashful about asking for this relatively standard coverage.

Confidentiality

For the sake of both you and your sponsor, confidentiality is an important part of your sponsorship agreement. Regardless of whether it is spelled out in writing, both parties have to be able to keep their mouths shut about sensitive issues!

No major company, be it public or private, will want you to have the right to let the public know how much they paid for the rights to your event. If they want to make that public, they should ask for your permission, but I doubt they will want you to have the unilateral right to make this information known. Think of the embarrassment a major corporation might face if they are spending a lot of money with you and at the same time laying off some of their staff or announcing quarterly losses. This can and does happen, so you should be prepared to respect their need for nondisclosure.

Conversely, you will be out trying to sell sponsorships to quite a few companies. As much as you might like to think that every company at every sponsorship level will pay the same amount, the reality is that they won't. Some official product sponsors will receive slightly more benefits and pay a bit more. Others might pay less in cash and more in goods and services. Still others might be getting a better deal on one event because they do a lot of business with you at other events. Irrespective of the rationale behind a certain deal or deals, you don't want to have this information bandied about in public because it can create headaches for you with each of the companies involved in your event, not to mention potential fallout with athletes, the public, and other partners in your event. You don't want to have to explain to company A why they paid more than company B, nor are you going to want to explain to a vendor (a caterer, for example) who knows you have major sponsorship support why you are negotiating so hard on a particular expense item. So, make sure that your sponsors are as sensitive to your confidentiality needs as they want you to be to theirs.

Governing Law

This is another of those paragraphs that is important primarily for your protection. Let's continue with the assumption that you will be working with companies that are bigger than yours and have much deeper pockets. The venue (court) for settling any disputes with those companies can be important. Of course, your goal should be to avoid any litigation with your sponsors. However, the reality is that from time to time sponsors and promoters do have differences of opinion that require court settlements. These can get very expensive, and one of the things that can make them expensive is the state in which the contract is governed.

Take StarGames, for example. We are based in Massachusetts, which is also where our outside counsel is based. We would prefer that any lawsuit be fought in the Commonwealth of Massachusetts. For illustration purposes, if we were to have to defend a suit in Illinois, we would probably have to hire an additional law firm located in that state, travel there often, and spend a lot of money on phone calls, Federal Express, and the like. Also, it is just a lot more comfortable to defend yourself in your home state—not quite a "home court advantage," but similar!

Anyway, you will not always win this one in your negotiations, and it may seem like a small thing that will never come into play. However, if you can have the contract governed under the rules of your home state, you will have a small advantage down the road if you ever find yourself in a lawsuit.

IMPORTANCE OF RELATIONSHIPS

You will notice that many of the contractual issues that I have discussed are defensive in nature and designed to give you a leg up if you ever have problems. Naturally you will never go into an agreement expecting legal issues; however, you do have to plan for them in the contract. As I mentioned before, while the contract is indeed important, the key to the success of your sponsorships and any potential litigation is going to be the relationships you are able to build with your corporate partners. Let me emphasize the word *partners* because if you can get your sponsors to feel that they have a real stake in your event, most of the contractual issues will take care of themselves.

Perhaps our greatest corporate partner has been Bob Pincus of what was then D.C. National Bank. As the president of the title sponsoring company, Bob took a personal interest in the D.C. National Bank tennis tournament to the point where his ego and reputation were on the line with his customers. As a result, he got involved in aspects of the event that many corporate executives probably wouldn't deal with. In turn, I don't remember the contract ever being invoked except as it related to renewals of the agreement. While this isn't always the case, it should be the goal.

Other close corporate friends have been the people at Northwest Airlines with whom we have developed a relationship in which, while we have no obligation to do so, we essentially give them a right of first negotiation for all of our properties. This is based solely on the relationship we have developed with Craig Braasch. Northwest has sponsored several of our events, and we feel a closeness with Craig that transcends any contract, which simply reinforces the fact that you make deals with people, not companies.

You make deals with people, not companies.

The contract, no matter how well written, pales in comparison to the relationships that you build with the people behind the companies, words, and numbers. I have seen numerous people succeed in our business because they were personable and, instinctively or otherwise, knew how to make relationships work. On the other hand, I have seen some very smart and capable people not reach their potential because they lacked people skills.

If you are new to the business, you probably will not have many, if any, key corporate contacts. You will develop these relationships over time by *delivering what you promise.* These relationships don't just grow because you are a nice person. Deliver the goods, and you will be on your way!

✔ Sponsorship Checklist

When all is said and done, sponsorship is a sales and servicing exercise that, in many cases, will determine whether your event will succeed or fail financially. We have had several artistic successes—great events that everyone loved—that did not meet our financial projections because we were unable to generate enough sponsorship dollars. Don't underestimate the power of good sponsors. Make them equally as much your focus as everything else related to your event. In order to do this:

✔ Recognize that sponsors are a critical part of your event.

✔ Develop an easy-to-read and creative sponsorship proposal.

✔ Make sure there are no conflicts between your sponsorship proposals and your other agreements.

✔ Remember that this is a sales exercise and requires a sales mentality.

✔ Create a sense of urgency during the sales process.

✔ Know the competition so you can price your sponsor levels appropriately.

✔ Determine how many sponsors you think your event can handle.

✔ Make sure your site can handle your corporate hospitality needs.

✔ Plan promotions that add value to your sponsor's participation in your event.

✔ Determine quantifiable values for your advertising and promotional campaigns.

✔ Research potential sponsors with an eye toward understanding their needs before making your pitch.

✔ Concentrate on relationship building.

✔ *Ask for the order.*

✔ Make sure your contract protects you in every way possible.

✔ Remember that sponsorship deals are made with *people.*

Now that you have solicited sponsors and generated enough revenue to secure your event, it will be time to focus on the other revenue streams, such as tickets, merchandise, and any ancillary areas. Because these are the areas in which you come into direct contact with the spectators, they require a whole different approach. This will be discussed in the next chapter.

Working Model: Tennis Tournament Letter Agreement

The following is a sample letter agreement for the Regional Junior Tennis Tournament.

Dear Product Manager,

The purpose of this letter agreement ("Agreement") is to reduce to writing the understanding between Tennis Tournament, Inc. ("TTI") and XYZ Corporation ("XYZ" or "Sponsor") with respect to XYZ's sponsorship of the Regional Tennis Tournament ("Event").

The specific terms and conditions to which the parties have agreed are as follows:

1. <u>Term</u>. The Term of this Agreement shall commence upon execution of the Agreement and conclude the day following the Event or at such time as all obligations of the parties are performed, unless terminated or extended by the parties as set forth herein.

2. <u>Event</u>. The Event is a USTA-sanctioned tennis tournament for boys and girls aged 16 to 18. Participants shall come from the four-state area and must be ranked in their state.

3. <u>Site/Date</u>. The Event shall:
   a) be held August 10-14, 2001; and
   b) be held at the Tennis Club ("Club") in Any Town, USA.

4. <u>Sponsor Benefits</u>. TTI agrees that it shall be responsible for the management, marketing, and operational needs in order to conduct the Event and provide the following sponsorship benefits to XYZ throughout the Term and in connection with the Event:

   a) XYZ will be recognized as the title sponsor of the Event. In this connection, the Event will be referred to as "XYZ Cup" (or another name to be mutually agreed upon) in all forms of sales, marketing, and promotional materials produced in connection with the Event, including press releases, posters, flyers, etc. TTI reserves the right to include a presenting sponsor in the name of the Event. XYZ shall have the right to use the Event name and logo in advertising and promotional materials with TTI's prior written approval of the manner and location, such approval not to be unreasonably withheld. If said use is not disapproved within forty-eight (48) hours of receipt by TTI, said logo and its use shall be deemed approved.

   b) XYZ shall be the exclusive sponsor in its product category, which shall be defined as fast food restaurants. TTI agrees that it will not solicit or confirm any other fast food restaurant as a sponsor of the Event.

   c) Banner signage on site will be as follows:
   • Eight (8) 3' × 8' signs on center court of which no fewer than four shall be in TV camera range
   • Four (4) 3' × 8' signs on court #1
   • Two (2) 3' × 8' signs on all other courts
   • Four (4) signs on the grounds of the site

   The cost of all banners and signage shall be borne by XYZ.

   d) XYZ shall have the right to host the participants at one of XYZ's restaurants for publicity and photo purposes provided that XYZ receives USTA approval for such activity such that the amateur status of each of the participants is protected.

   e) XYZ will receive twenty (20) courtside seats at center court at each session of the event.

   f) Periodic public address announcements will be made during the Event on site to promote XYZ's restaurants. XYZ shall provide the copy for such announcements.

   g) XYZ has the right to have a representative of XYZ participate in any and all press conferences and awards presentations in conjunction with the Event.

   h) XYZ has the right to conduct in-store promotions and contests in connection with the Event subject to reasonable approval by TTI.

   i) XYZ has the right to distribute, sample, display, and/or sell product on site during the Event. The cost of such activity will be borne by XYZ.

5. <u>Obligations of XYZ.</u> In consideration for the rights and benefits granted above, XYZ agrees that it shall:

   a) Use its best efforts to market and promote the Event through its restaurants in the Any Town area by way of in-store posters, collateral materials, promotions, etc. All such materials shall be consistent with the standards set by the Event and subject to reasonable approval by TTI.

   b) Pay to TTI a fee of Twenty-Five Thousand Dollars ($25,000) according to the following schedule:
   • $12,500 upon execution of this Agreement
   • $12,500 within ten (10) days of the conclusion of the Event

   In the event the Event is not conducted for any reason other than those set forth herein below, TTI agrees to refund any money paid pursuant to this paragraph. Said payments shall be made by check payable to TTI and sent to Regional Junior Tennis Tournament, 100 Tennis Way, Any Town, USA.

c) Provide food and beverage for the Event participants each day of the event as follows:

On August 10-12: 100 sandwiches and drinks to be delivered at 5 P.M.

On August 13 and 14: 75 sandwiches and drinks to be delivered at noon and 5 P.M. each day

d) Pay TTI ten percent (10%) of the revenue received from the sale of product on site during the Event.

e) Add TTI and the Club as additional insureds on any and all insurance policies in connection with any promotion of the event.

6. Warranties. XYZ and TTI warrant that they are free to enter into this Agreement and that the rights granted hereunder will not infringe upon the rights of any third party.

7. Indemnity. The parties herein agree to protect, defend (at the indemnified parties' option), indemnify, and save harmless each other and their officers, agents, and employees from and against any and all expenses, damages, claims, lawsuits, actions, judgments, and costs whatsoever, including reasonable attorney's fees, arising out of, or in any way connected with, any claim or action arising out of or caused by any facilities, products, or services supplied by the indemnifying party in conjunction with this Agreement, or any other claims related to the indemnifying party, or any other facilities, products, or services of parties, unless such claims arise from the gross negligence or willful misconduct of the indemnified party, its agents, or employees. Without limiting the preceding, XYZ agrees to indemnify TTI for any claims or actions brought against TTI by vendors or customers of XYZ or other third parties for damages that are a result of any false representations made by XYZ or its vendors about the Event or the participants unless the claims are a result of TTI gross negligence. TTI agrees to indemnify XYZ for any claims or actions brought against XYZ for damages by participants, venues, or others involved in the Event unless the claims are a result of XYZ's negligence.

8. Insurance. TTI agrees to obtain, at its expense, comprehensive general liability insurance for a minimum of One Million U.S. Dollars ($1,000,000) combined bodily injury and property damage in a single occurrence, and excess (umbrella) liability coverage for a minimum of Three Million U.S. Dollars ($3,000,000). Such insurance shall be issued by a major insurance carrier authorized to do business in the state of _____, shall be maintained until the performance of the Event is completed, and shall specifically name XYZ as an additional insured, if requested by XYZ. XYZ agrees to maintain, at its expense, comprehensive general liability insurance with similar limits of coverage as set forth above for and during the Event in connection with its participation in the Event, including for the conduct of any promotion. The parties shall furnish each other, at the other's request, with a certificate (or certificates) prior to commencement of the Event evidencing such insurance coverage, which certificate shall state in substantial part:

"Thirty (30) days advance notice shall be given in writing of cancellation, termination, or any modification of the policy or policies evidenced by this Certificate."

9. Assignment. Unless otherwise stated herein, neither TTI nor XYZ shall have the right to grant sublicenses hereunder or to otherwise assign, transfer, encumber, or hypothecate any of its rights or obligations hereunder, except that TTI shall have the right to assign the financial benefits hereof and XYZ hereby consents to such assignment. Notwithstanding the above, the parties agree that if the majority of the assets of either party are sold and/or transferred to a third party, then the assignment of this Agreement (rights and obligations) to said third party shall be deemed approved.

10. Waiver. The failure of either party at any time to demand strict performance by the other of any of the terms, covenants, or conditions set forth herein shall not be construed as a continuing waiver or relinquishment thereof, and either party may, at any time, demand strict and complete performance by the other of said terms, covenants, and conditions.

11. Employer/Employee Relationship. TTI's relationship with XYZ shall be that of an independent contractor, and nothing contained in this Agreement shall be construed as establishing an employer/employee relationship, partnership, or joint venture between XYZ and TTI. Accordingly, there shall be no withholding for tax purposes from any payment by XYZ to TTI hereunder.

12. Notices. All notices and/or submissions hereunder shall be sent via Certified Mail, Return Receipt Requested, to the parties at the following addresses, or such other addresses as may be designated in writing from time to time:

   XYZ: address

   TTI: address

   Copy to: your respective attorneys

   Notices shall be deemed given upon deposit of same with the postal authority.

13. Terms of Agreement Confidential. It is hereby agreed that the specific terms and conditions of this Agreement, including, but not limited to, the financial terms and the duration, are strictly confidential and shall not be divulged to any third parties without the prior written consent of both XYZ and TTI, unless otherwise required by law or for purposes of carrying out the terms of this Agreement.

14. Significance of Paragraph Headings. Paragraph headings contained hereunder are solely for the purpose of aiding in the speedy location of subject matter and are not in any sense to be given weight in the construction of this Agreement. Accordingly, in the case of any question with respect to the construction of this Agreement, it is to be construed as though paragraph headings had been omitted.

15. Governing Law. This Agreement shall be governed by and construed in accordance with the laws of (your state), regardless of the fact that any of the parties hereto may be or may become a resident of a different state or jurisdiction. Any suit or action arising shall be filed in a court of competent jurisdiction within (your state). The parties hereby consent to the personal jurisdiction of said court within (your state).

16. Severability. If any provision of this Agreement of the application thereof shall be invalid or unenforceable to any extent, the remainder of this Agreement or the application thereof shall not be affected, and each remaining provision of the Agreement shall be valid and enforceable to the fullest extent permitted by law.

17. Force Majeure. The parties herein shall not be liable for their failure to conduct the Event by reason of fire, strike, war, insurrection, government restrictions, force majeure, or other causes beyond their control, provided that the parties shall provide prompt written notice of the force majeure condition to the other party as soon as it is practicable to do so, and further, the parties shall use their best efforts to cure such force majeure condition and conduct the Event as quickly as possible. In the event of cancellation, said canceled Event shall be rescheduled at the earliest possible convenient date at the same location as set forth herein.

18. Entire Agreement. This Agreement constitutes the entire understanding between XYZ and TTI and cannot be altered or modified except by an agreement in writing signed by both XYZ and TTI. Upon its execution, this Agreement shall supersede all prior negotiations, understandings, and agreements, whether oral or written, and such prior agreements shall thereupon be null and void and without further legal effect.

ACCEPTED AND AGREED:

XYZ

By:_____   Date: _____

Title: _____

TTI

By: _____   Date: _____

Title: _____

Chapter FIVE

Getting in Touch With Your Customer

By this time you probably consider the people who manage your site, the sponsor contacts, charity organizers, licensees, television executives, and athletes as your customers. In a sense, that is correct. However, in most cases, I prefer to look at these people as event *partners*. They are customers in that they buy rights and other goods and services from you, but they generally don't define themselves as customers. They look at themselves in terms of the benefits that they provide to you. You must see them through the same set of eyes and treat them accordingly.

However, the person buying your tickets or merchandise, making a donation to your charity, buying a spot in your clinic for their kid . . . those are your customers by any definition of the term. They think of themselves that way and react as a customer if things go wrong. If someone is in their seat when they get to it, they want service. If the T-shirt they buy shrinks in the wash, they want a remedy. If the clinic gets rained out, they want a refund or a rescheduling. "They" are the public, and "they" can be tough. You should know. When

you are not putting on an event, you are one of them!

The public, at the end of the day, makes or breaks your event because they have the ultimate votes on whether there is a market for your project. If you have great sponsorship and site deals but no one shows up to attend the event, it will not be long lived. If your television ratings barely register because no one watches your telecast, you won't be on television in the future. So, while you have to treat your sponsors, television distributor, site, vendors, and so forth with great respect, you need a whole different mentality with the public, the people who pay $25 (or more) per ticket for a family of four, $4 to park, $25 for programs and T-shirts, $15 for food—in other words, $144 for a couple of hours of entertainment. They are the ones that can and do make a huge difference.

So, you need to communicate with the audience; let them know you are coming to town; tell them what to expect, how they can buy tickets, where they can participate, and how they can buy merchandise. You also need to price your event so that it is affordable and a good value. Finally, you need to make them feel wanted, that you are glad they attended or participated, and that you hope they come back again. In short, you need to attract, cater to, and deliver value to the fans.

As an event organizer or promoter, you are a link in a long chain that is made up of some pretty formidable historic figures. Each member of this fraternity understood that he was putting on an event for the public. The list includes the likes of P.T. Barnum; John Ringling; Charlie Chaplin; Walt Disney; Pete Rozelle; and more recently, Kenneth Feld and David Stern. These were and are some of the great promoters of all time. They each had great vision and marketing savvy, understood the desires of the public, and knew how to deliver value by putting on a great show. Theirs are tough footsteps in which to follow, but I think it is worth your while trying to live up to the standards they have set. In that regard, it can't hurt to study each of these innovators and perhaps borrow some ideas from them.

One thing you are sure to learn from each of them is that being in touch with your customer is critically important. To understand your customer, you have to learn about what they want, analyze what you sell to them, know what they consider to be of value, and carefully analyze the various means by which you communicate with them.

To begin with, we will look at some of the ways in which you might find out who your customer is. Then we will look at what you sell to them (tickets, merchandise, and so on). Later, we will examine how you actually talk to your target audience.

KNOWING YOUR CUSTOMER

There are certainly bigger users of research than I have been over the course of my career. This has been a mistake, however. A little more research probably would have helped me to avoid a few mistakes. I was able to see the value of research while operating the Association of Volleyball Professionals (AVP).

In 1996 we undertook a fairly extensive (although not necessarily the most scientific) on-site survey program that told us in pretty clear terms who our audience was. Frankly, what we learned in that case was pretty much in contradiction to what the press and our sponsors had thought about the AVP audience and their primary attraction to the sport in the first place. Everyone thought that the beach volleyball audience was young, hip, and without a great deal of disposable income. We found that in reality the AVP audience was older, more settled (i.e., had families), and had more money than expected. While we didn't go around flaunting that information for fear that it would turn certain sponsors away, it

Your customers may be as diverse as this audience at a football game. Do your research and find out who your customers are so you can anticipate how to attract them to your event.

did help us to communicate better with the current market and to direct our efforts to attracting a younger audience.

The message here is that research—uncovering facts about the audience for your event—whether it confirms or contradicts your beliefs about the sport, venue, or audience itself, can be important in helping you shape your strategy for communicating with your target market. While the term *research* may conjure up unpleasant thoughts of term papers and science experiments, gathering this information really is not that difficult and can be quite painless.

Conducting Surveys

Your research may require little more than a survey, which can be a one- or two-page questionnaire with questions pointed specifically at your needs. These surveys can be implemented in several places, including on site at your event, by mail, by phone, and if you have a Web site, over the Internet. Certain questions can be asked before the event, others during or following the event. Even though some of these methods (i.e., on-site or postevent surveys) only give you the information after the fact, there is always next year. Plus, your sponsors will love getting the information after the event, particularly if it helps them justify the expense of sponsorship! In fact, you might suggest that your sponsors get involved with the survey as a means of asking specific questions that are relevant to their product or service. As discussed earlier, it is only a benefit to get the sponsors more invested in the event, and in this case you can be the direct beneficiary of their seemingly selfish effort.

To put your survey together, you can either enlist the help of a research company or simply use your common sense to figure out what kind of information you need. Some of the basic things are obvious: age, marital status, number and age of kids, income range, a few likes and dislikes (so you get a bit of a character sketch), what products they like (with emphasis on your sponsors or potential sponsors), and their feelings about your sport.

Figure 5.1 is a list of questions from a survey we did to understand the volleyball audience better. Keep in mind that this survey had as its goal to find out the general age, income, and family status of the volleyball fan. The secondary purpose was to get a feel for various lifestyle issues that could be helpful to promoters (for advertising and promotional purposes) and sponsors.

You can glean a lot of information from surprisingly few questions, and you can do this relatively inexpensively. First of all, if you conduct your survey on site, it can be photocopied. It doesn't have to be anything fancy. Further, you can get interns or volunteers to ask the questions and compile the answers. Finally, you can do the survey at your site, or you can even do this on a street corner where you probably don't have to pay any fees for authorization to ask the questions (research the local ordinances just to be sure).

Obviously, if you conduct your survey by mail or phone, it will be more costly (postage, printing, phone lines, and the like). But the point is that a survey does not have to be intimidating—to you or to the person being questioned! It does not have to be scientifically correct (as long as you explain how it was done) or conducted by an independent party. And it does not have to be expensive.

The key is doing it. Some of the most successful promoters live by their research. I have been impressed by the amount of research the Feld Organization (Disney on Ice, Ringling Brothers Circus) does, and they organize all of their properties around what they learn from it. The information that we learned at the AVP was critically important and really foretold some of the problems that the sport of beach volleyball was facing. The research

■ ■ ■ ■ ■ ■ ■ ■ ■ ■ ■

Some of the most successful promoters live by their research.

■ ■ ■ ■ ■ ■ ■ ■ ■ ■ ■

NAME: (optional) _____

ADDRESS: (optional) _____

AGE: ❑ 12–18; ❑ 19–21; ❑ 22–25; ❑ 26–35; ❑ 36–45; ❑ over 45

MARITAL STATUS: ❑ single; ❑ married; ❑ divorced

CHILDREN: (number) _____

INCOME: ❑ under $20,000; ❑ $20,000–$35,000; ❑ $36,000–$50,000; ❑ $51,000–$75,000;
    ❑ $75,000 and above

OWN A COMPUTER: ❑ yes; ❑ no

OWN A CAR: ❑ yes; ❑ no

OWN A DOMESTICALLY MADE CAR: ❑ yes; ❑ no

OWN A FOREIGN MADE CAR: ❑ yes; ❑ no

TYPE OF MUSIC YOU LISTEN TO: ❑ top 40; ❑ oldies; ❑ country & western; ❑ jazz; ❑ classical;
    ❑ hip-hop; ❑ other

ATTENDED BEACH VOLLEYBALL EVENTS IN THE PAST YEAR: ❑ yes; ❑ no

IF YES, HOW MANY: _____

ATTENDED OTHER PROFESSIONAL SPORTS EVENTS IN THE PAST YEAR: ❑ yes; ❑ no

IF YES, WHAT SPORTS: (list) _____

Figure 5.1 Sample survey.

you conduct will help in many ways, including helping you fine-tune your advertising and other communication while also supporting your sponsorship sales.

Creating Mailing Lists

One of the secondary benefits of questionnaires, whether done via the phone, mail, Internet, or in person, is building a database of names and addresses. These are becoming increasingly important in today's business environment. In fact, the Internet is, in some respects, nothing more than a database collector. People and companies are prepared to pay handsomely for access to lists targeted specifically to potential customers. Mailing lists can be mightily beneficial to you in your ticket sales campaign because they allow you to get direct mail pieces about your event into the hands of people who are predisposed to attending events like yours. You can also make the use of lists a benefit to your sponsors and venue. So don't overlook this side effect of your research.

TO SELL OR NOT TO SELL

To sell or not to sell—*that* is the question. If you have determined who your customer is, the next question is, Will they buy tickets to the event? If so, what should your pricing be? Through what outlets will tickets be sold? How will you get the word out about available tickets? Should there be any discount or other promotional offers? How many seats do you need to hold back for "comps" and "kills"? How many should you allocate to each sponsor? These are just some of the many questions that will come up at this point. Before you deal with all of these issues, though, the first ticketing decision is whether you should be charging for your tickets at all.

Deciding to Sell Tickets

In some cases whether or not to sell tickets will be an easy decision. If you are organizing a professional sporting event, such as a ten-

Proper Technique

As with the research into the local market that we discussed in chapter 3, some of you may be uncomfortable with a survey that is not more scientifically based and that does not employ "proper technique." If that is the case, there are many research organizations that will be happy to help you develop, implement, and compile information that will be statistically sound. Ad agencies, public relations agencies, and promotions companies often have divisions dedicated to this activity. There are also many companies whose sole business is to do research. They can be pretty expensive, though.

To save money, you might go to a university that will be interested in helping you as part of a class activity. You may also find a professor who is looking for a research project to support a study that he or she is involved with. In most cases this will save you a lot of money and give you the added benefit of the university imprimatur on your data.

For me, all of this is an added benefit, and if you have the time and possibly the budget, there is only an upside to getting a more scientific survey compiled for you. On the other hand, as a person who has not employed a great deal of research over the years, even a survey that is not 100 percent statistically accurate can prove to be very beneficial (my mother, a professor of biostatistics, will probably cringe at the thought of this!). As far as I'm concerned, the more information, the better.

nis or golf tournament, NASCAR race, or major championship such as the U.S. Gymnastics Olympic Trials, people usually want to buy tickets to ensure themselves of good seating (or in the case of a golf tournament, to make sure that they can get on the grounds of the course). With events such as these, there is a history of high ticket pricing (and even ticket scalping) and an understanding by the public that these are expensive events to put on. As a result, people accept the fact that they have to pay to attend.

But what about a marathon, 10K, or junior tennis event? If you are putting on an "extreme sports" event in which there is no history of ticket sales, should you charge for seats? Just the other day I was shown a tape for a new event involving acrobatic airplanes. It had never been done before but was being taped for a cable television broadcast. Should the promoter have charged spectators to see these daredevils?

As we discussed earlier, we were faced with just this question when we first put on the King of the Beach Invitational. At the time,

back in 1990, the AVP had never charged for general admission tickets and had just recently begun selling the seats closest to the action. The players and the promoters of the sport were afraid that by charging for tickets, they would both keep people away and change the nature of the crowd.

At the same time, however, the players (who also owned the tour) wanted to play for more prize money because they were having a hard time making a living at events that had total purses of $40,000 to $50,000 for 32 teams (or 64 players). We were proposing that the King of the Beach pay $200,000 in prize money for 14 players! That money had to come from somewhere.

I felt very strongly that for the King of the Beach Invitational to be recognized as an important event, we had to make being at that event valuable to the audience. We had to create an atmosphere that made people *want* to be there. As such, they should be willing to pay to watch the best players in the world compete. Further, and perhaps more important, if we were to put on an event that paid out record prize money and still had a chance to make a profit, the revenue had to come from sources other than sponsorship. Ticket sales was a logical place to start. I insisted that if we were going to hold this event, we had to sell tickets.

There were a number of skeptics among the players and AVP executives, but we decided to sell tickets anyway, although not for a lot of money. I think that general admission seats were $5 at the first event, with the most expensive "sandbox" seat being $15. As it turned out, we sold out the event in Daytona Beach, surprising all of the critics and putting the King of the Beach Invitational on the map.

Before deciding whether to sell tickets to your event, consider the following questions:

• **Is there a history of selling tickets to similar events?** If, for example, you are going to be the first to sell tickets to an "extreme sports" event, you need to understand that there may be some negative backlash.

• **Does the event depend on ticket revenue?** If your profit and loss projection shows that you can't make ends meet without revenue from ticket sales, that pretty much determines that you have to either sell tickets or not run the event.

• **Will there be pricing sensitivity?** Is yours one of those events that people will pay virtually anything to attend, or is there a very specific breaking point at which people will choose to do something else?

• **Does the event lose prestige if the spectators get in for free . . . and does this matter?** This was an issue at the King of the Beach Invitational. We wanted the press to take the sport seriously, and we didn't believe they would unless spectators had to pay to get into the event.

• **How will you sell tickets, and can your ad budget support the necessary communication to support ticket sales?** If you can't advertise the fact that your tickets are going on sale, you have to think through whether it is worth the effort since no one will know how, when, or where to purchase their tickets.

Deciding to Give Free Entry

If you choose not to sell tickets, you will still need to communicate to the public that the event is happening and that they are welcome to attend. In fact, you could make quite a bit of noise (through your PR campaign) about the fact that there is no charge to come to your event, thus creating a large crowd, an exciting atmosphere, and potentially a lot of word of mouth about the event (which could enable you to sell tickets in the future). You also might make up for any lack of ticket sales revenue with on-site merchandising and souvenir sales. There is a lot to be said for events that do *not* charge an entry fee, so you need to weigh this decision carefully.

As we have found, however, one of the real downsides to not charging is that you tend to get a different type of audience. In other words, you will get your hard-core fan, but you will also get what I call "casual observers." These are people who may have no interest in your event but just happen to be walking or driving by. Also, if there is no charge to get in, some of your spectators will come with no money in their pockets. This means that they can't buy souvenirs, concessions, or merchandise from your sponsors and other vendors. People without money at your event—particularly if you are trying to raise money for profit or charity or simply trying to provide an attractive audience for your sponsors—really don't do you, the promoter, nearly as much good as people who come ready to buy.

When running the AVP Tour, we instituted ticket sales at every event. A lot of people did not like this, but ticket sales added much-needed revenue to the coffers of the tour. However, in the first year of what was essentially a new ticket sales initiative, we did not always communicate well enough to the fans that they could no longer get in for free. That is how we found that many people came to the events without any money.

We learned this when we had to turn them away at the gate, as they were unable to buy even the most inexpensive general admission seats when they arrived. However, the people that did buy tickets came with money and bought concessions, sponsor products, and food. We know this because revenue generated from each of these sources increased over prior years. We also found that sponsors much preferred giving their message to people with money in their pockets—real fans who demonstrated a desire to be there—rather than to the casual observer who just happened upon the event and stopped by for a while out of curiosity, boredom, or spare time.

If you are in the developmental stages of your event (or sport for that matter), you might not care about this distinction. In many cases, though, your sponsors will. Thus, there are a lot of issues to consider if you have what I would characterize a borderline event with respect to selling tickets.

Regardless of whether you choose to sell tickets, you will need to address a number of items. One major point, and we will come back to this in detail later, is that you need to let people know that the event is coming to town and happening in their area. Going back to the earlier 10K hypothetical example, you don't want to have the local police plan for a crowd of 2,000 and have only 200 show up because no one knew the event was taking place. But more on that later. Let's first focus on some of the ticketing decisions that you have to address before you start your communications campaign. First and foremost is pricing.

PRICING TICKETS

There are many issues to consider when setting the price for the tickets to your event. First of all, who is your event catering to, and what can this target audience afford?

Different demographic groups can afford to pay different levels for tickets. You have to be very sensitive to this issue. If your tickets are priced incorrectly, you might get some backlash from the very people you are trying to appeal to. Worse, they may simply be unable to afford tickets and thus not attend an event that was, in a sense, planned for them. Don't price yourself out of the market!

Further, ticket pricing is where you will be competing against every other form of entertainment—from the movie theater to movie rentals to concerts to television to the Internet. Each person has a finite amount of time and money. If you price your event at a point greater than its perceived value, you risk losing all but the hard-core fans. That can spell disaster for you if you are counting on revenue from ticket sales to help you cover costs and make a profit.

If you price your event at a point greater than its perceived value, you risk losing all but the hard-core fans.

Finally, major events (or others for which the tickets will be at a premium) can charge more than events that are building and have to almost coax the audience to attend. I think this is all best illustrated by examples. So, using some of our properties, let's examine the ticket prices.

King of the Beach

When we first started this event, it fell into the category of possibly having to coax people into the stands. Nevertheless, we wanted to charge something for the tickets just to establish that there was some value to coming to see guys play beach volleyball. We thought that if people could get in free, there might be a sense that the event is a sideshow or not professionally organized. Free admission might also suggest an air of nonimportance. If people have to pay to get in, the whole nature of the event changes—the expectations are higher from everyone, players perform better, the staff is more on its toes, the sponsors treat the situation differently, and so forth. I think establishing this type of atmosphere is important particularly given today's "first impression" mind-set.

We still wanted tickets to be inexpensive enough so that the price would not be a deterrent to anyone thinking about coming. Someone suggested that we charge a dollar or perhaps two. I felt that was almost an insult to the sport and the players. No one would take an event seriously that charged a dollar. We ended up charging $5 for general admission in the first year. We had a sellout.

As the event grew, we still never felt comfortable with ticket prices getting too high, so general admission has never gotten higher than $12. I think that is a pretty good value considering that we deliver six hours of entertainment for that price. The "sandbox" seats are a different story, however.

From our experience in other sports, we knew that people were willing to pay a premium to sit at courtside. This makes them feel a part of the action and gives them a chance to interact with the players. We thought this same behavior would apply to beach volleyball. Over about a two-year period we watched the sales pattern, which showed that the "sandbox" seats sold out first, even as we increased the price. Even with this track record a sandbox seat, which can only be bought in a package for all three days of the event, today only costs $85 (or less than $30 per day for an entire day of entertainment, which compares well with the alternatives in Las Vegas—and elsewhere for that matter. What does it cost to go to an NBA game, which lasts only two and a half hours?).

The bottom line on the King of the Beach event is that we established ticket sales as viable. We chose to keep prices affordable; we generated reasonable revenue, and the customers always knew that they were getting a very good value.

Halloween on Ice

When we first began this show, figure skating was experiencing a boom to the point at which certain shows and events that were charging as much as $50 or more for rinkside seats were selling out.

To her credit, Nancy Kerrigan, who is our partner on this show, always felt that it was important to keep the prices low so that the average working family with a couple of kids could afford to attend. Since this was in part Nancy's event, we agreed to keep the ticket prices down.

When certain other skating events were coming into the same arenas and charging $45 for a top-price seat, our highest price of $32 looked like a bargain. We have kept this theory going throughout the life of the show, and I think it is one of the reasons the event has received such a positive reception in the community.

The issue of affordable ticket pricing leads to an important point. In most cases you work and live in the community in which your event is taking place. As a result, for a variety of reasons you will be best served if the public judges you as a fair and supportive person or organization. Part of this equation will be the price of the tickets to your event. Remember, you are in part putting on this event for the people in your community, so having them think you are reasonable can only be a plus. Shaving a bit off the ticket price to gain some goodwill in the community is not a bad thing.

Skating Goes Country

This show represented the highest ticket price we ever presented to the public. In retrospect, we might have misjudged the public's level of enthusiasm for this new concept. We felt that by combining some of the biggest names in figure skating with some of the most popular acts in country music, we would have a blockbuster event that could command the highest prices in a market that does not get a lot of skating and loves country music.

Ticket prices for Skating Goes Country started at $125 for a Gold Circle pass that got you into an after-show party attended by the talent and went down to $25 for the upper level. At the time of this writing, the jury is still out, but suffice it to say that ticket sales are slower than we expected.

The lesson to be learned here is that we probably did not research the market well enough. We spoke to several people about ticket prices, but we never really undertook an in-depth study that compared our prices to those of other concerts and sports events in Nashville. As I mentioned before, I believe in research, but I have never been a big user of it, going from my gut instinct and experience instead. This has gotten me into trouble from time to time. While there is no substitute for experience, it can always be aided by some hard facts! A little time and money spent researching Nashville ticket prices would have been resources well spent.

The bottom line on ticket pricing is that your decisions here will affect many things, from revenue to ambiance at the event. In making your decision, remember the following:

- Know your audience.
- Research prices at comparable events.
- Don't overprice.
- Create perceived value.

ON-SITE REVENUE SOURCES

The sale of souvenirs has always been a pretty big business in the world of sports. I remember going to baseball games as a kid and always wanting something at the game. However, in those days, not only were the options pretty much limited to a program, hat, miniature bat, "bobble head" doll, and a shirt but

also the presentation was pretty basic—a guy hawking at a stand. In today's marketplace, merchandising has become an art form. The merchandise is diverse and the displays are attractive. Teams and leagues even have their own stores. Licensing has become so influential that some of the styles that start out as souvenir merchandise set the tone for everyday dress. Entire industries, including New York Stock Exchange companies, have grown up around licensing and memorabilia items.

While we will get into licensing a bit later, for purposes of this section let's define merchandising as souvenir sales, recognizing that the term *souvenir* has taken on a much broader meaning over the last 10 years.

Merchandise sales at events of every level, both on site and in store, can be a great source of revenue for you if you have the right items, price them correctly, design them so that they are in fashion, don't get the wrong weather, and present them in a manner that is fan friendly. Easy, right?

Well, the fact is that selling merchandise requires making an investment in inventory, hiring salespeople, making displays, dealing with cash, outfitting the salespeople, and on and on. In effect, you are getting into the retail business. In addition to tending to the event and its never-ending stream of details, you are now a merchant. Be careful that you are not taken in by the allure of the big bucks here because they may not materialize and the whole exercise may not be worth the effort.

Working Model: Tournament Ticket Prices

Because of the nature of the event (i.e., this is its first year, participation is limited to top juniors from the region, and there is limited initial interest from the general public and the private club location), we are planning to build only 400 seats. Also, since we never envisioned ticket sales as a major part of the revenue stream, we plan to keep ticket prices low. With that in mind, it is important to charge an entry fee because we want to set a precedent as we build toward the future. Moreover, we are raising money for junior tennis programs, which are perceived as a worthy cause. As a result, we do not think people will be offended by having to pay a nominal fee to get on the grounds.

Before making the final decision on the $10 ticket price, we researched similarly situated events in the region and found that this price was at the top end of the spectrum, but tolerable.

As you may know, T-shirt sales at rock concerts are the biggest money makers. At the 1999 Ryder Cup in Boston they literally sold out of every T-shirt. By the time my son and I got to the event on Saturday afternoon, there were no T-shirts left . . . none. I had never before seen an absolutely bare cupboard.

On the other hand, we still have shirts in storage from the 1996 Miller Lite Championships of New England, one day of which was wiped out by Hurricane Bob. We sold all of our sweatshirts that year but had only produced a small quantity because we did not anticipate cold and rain in the middle of the summer. We use those T-shirts as samples from time to time, but other than that, they have no value to us because the event no longer exists.

I only bring this to your attention because I don't want you to think that merchandising sales represents easy money. It might. But it also takes some expertise, up-front cash, and a little luck. Plan your merchandising strategy carefully and make sure you can afford the cash flow and the risk of loss.

Then you have to figure out what items to sell.

Programs

Most events have a program. They make a nice statement about your event, they provide information to the fans, sponsors like them for running traditional advertising, they make a great tool for autograph seekers, and they are popular remembrances for attendees.

We have cut back on producing programs lately unless having one is important to the sponsors. This is a financial decision. Programs can be expensive to produce if you try to make them look special (and if you are going to go to the trouble of producing a program, you should make it a nice one. I hate those that really look and feel cheap!) and

Consider the need very carefully before you spend the time and money to produce a program.

they typically don't sell that well. You might sell one to every five to eight people that come through the gate. Programs often lose money unless they contain a lot of ads or the event is truly memorable. At major events such as the Super Bowl, the Ryder Cup, or the U.S. Open in tennis, people may want the program for its collector value. Clearly, most events are not of that magnitude. I urge you to consider the need very carefully before you spend the time and money to produce a program.

If you decide to proceed with the production of a program for your event, you should plan to include the following elements: bios on the participants, a story or two about the event, lots of pictures, perhaps something to promote your company, and *as many ads as you can sell*. It has also become fairly well accepted to include letters from VIPs, such as the local mayor, your charity affiliate, and lead sponsors.

Remember that a nice program takes time to produce, as you need to find a printer you can work with, locate photos, collect ad copy, write editorial, and proofread every line. Whatever you do, don't leave this until the last minute. One of my pet peeves is a program that has mistakes in it (typos or photos in backwards).

T-Shirts

Perhaps the most popular souvenir item is a commemorative T-shirt. T-shirts provide an ongoing walking billboard for your event and sponsors. They also make great gift items for you to send to people as a reminder of your event when it comes time to start selling it in future years.

However, again, you have to be careful with the details when producing shirts. For example, you may not want to put a date on them. If they have a date and you are left with inventory, you won't be able to sell them again the next year. On the other hand, spectators like having the date on what they purchase. This is another of those small but sometimes difficult choices. In my mind, there is some safety in leaving off the date.

Besides being a popular souvenir, T-shirts also advertise your event.

Then there is the artwork. What is more attractive: art on the front or on the back? How should you deal with the sleeves: blank or with your logo . . . or your sponsor's logo? Personally, I like the event logo on the front breast with the major artwork on the back. I think putting the logo on the sleeves is a cool idea, but some people won't like it. Anyway, this is all a matter of fashion, so if you question your own taste on this type of thing, don't hesitate to bring someone in to help you design this and any other items, such as sweatshirts, hats (very popular these days), or fleece (fleece vests are a great winter sports item) that might involve fashion design. Getting the right look for your merchandise is tricky and could very likely affect your sales totals.

Other Items

If you think it might be helpful to extend your product line, things like autographed photos of the stars of your event always seem to work well. Also, don't be afraid to get creative here. Now that virtually everyone has a computer in their home or office, mousepads are an effective item. You can also get mouses made with your logo on them. Screensavers might work well too. The new technology opens up a whole new line of souvenir products. I urge you to explore these items . . . but remember the cost involved.

Presentation

Last, like any good retailer, you have to present your merchandise in an attractive manner. Many events will simply set up a booth or table and sell from there. People expect that and will not be offended by it. However, if the booth is too small, you might not be able to handle a big crowd. If items are too easily accessible, you might leave yourself open for having items stolen (which is going to happen, so be prepared, try to keep it to a minimum, and don't let it bother you too much). If items aren't accessible enough, it may turn people off. What if people need to try things on? Do you want to provide your customers with a dressing room? (We tried this at AVP events and it really complicated matters. I say, pass on the dressing rooms.) Should you have one booth or several (this depends somewhat on the size of your site), and how do you staff the booth(s)? Do they need one person or two (one to sell and one to work the cash register) or more? And don't forget the petty cash, cash register(s), and credit card hookup.

Each of these decisions is going to be specific to your event, so I can't give you any all-encompassing direction. What I can reiterate is that merchandising is a pretty big undertaking, and while I am not meaning to discourage you from it, I do mean to heighten your awareness to the potential pitfalls. One way to deal with the entire subject is to license out the whole thing to a third party.

Licensing

In most cases we define licensing as the selling of your logo or event name to others so that they can sell merchandise based on the marketing power of those marks. For the purposes of this discussion licensing will also include granting a third party the right to be financially responsible for the merchandise sales in conjunction with your event, be it on site, in stores or catalogs, on the Internet, and so on. While the vast majority of events won't command the attention necessary to warrant this kind of attention, there are some real benefits to having someone else take over this role. First and foremost, you don't have to worry about a lot of what we just reviewed! If you can find someone to come in and do all of this for you (with your approval of course at each step of the way), I think you will be a lot better off.

In addition to not having to worry about all the details associated with merchandising and retail sales, you might be able to make a deal with a third party vendor that guarantees you some money up front and then a royalty on all sales. When I say "all sales," this could include items that have your logo or name on them plus revenue from any other items they might sell. At the King of the Beach event we "licensed" all our merchandising to Speedo. In so doing we let them determine the look of the event merchandise, manufacture it, stock it, and pay us a guarantee against a royalty on event items and any regular Speedo merchandise they sold. Merchandise sales is their business, they do a good job at it, they put us at ease, and they send their checks on time. What more could you ask for?

If you decide that you want to control all of your merchandising, no problem. Just follow

> ■ ■ ■ ■ ■ ■ ■ ■ ■ ■ ■
>
> *Just because you have licensed out the responsibility for production or sales does not mean that you are not in the wholesale and retail business!*
>
> ■ ■ ■ ■ ■ ■ ■ ■ ■ ■ ■

the basic steps described earlier, but think twice before you take on this task.

Another form of licensing is simply the sale of your event name and logo. I am not going to dwell on this too much here because it usually requires a pretty big or well-established event to be able to command attention from the licensing marketplace. If you are able to attract interest in a licensing relationship, you should again be looking for an up-front guarantee plus a royalty on all sales. Often the guarantee will first be applied against the royalty, meaning that you won't receive any additional distribution over and above the guarantee until the licensee has recouped the guarantee. As a practical matter, let's say you have a $10,000 guarantee against an 8 percent royalty on a $10 item. You earn 80 cents per item sold. Therefore, the licensee would have to sell 12,500 units before you reached the guarantee and began to earn additional royalty payments.

In either case remember that just like ticketing, the selling of merchandise is putting you in direct contact with the consumer, so you need to be sure that your licensee is set up to do business in a manner that is not going to reflect poorly on you. In this regard they have to have everything from good customer service to a return policy that you can live with to a reporting procedure that allows you to know what is going on with your product. These reports should include sales activity, returns, damaged goods, inventory on hand, and so on. Just because you have licensed out the responsibility for production or sales does not mean that you are not in the wholesale and retail business! No matter the outcome, whatever happens with your licensees, it all reflects on you and your event, which affects your relationship with your audience. So watch over your licensees closely.

Pricing Merchandise

With all of the souvenir items come pricing issues. Similar to tickets, you need to evaluate your audience, know the competitive situation, and recognize the potential value of souvenir merchandise. If you have a good group of vendors, they can help you determine your pricing because they will be familiar with the market. The bottom line is that you must remember that you are a retailer. As such you will have cash flow and inventory issues, pricing decisions, accounting concerns, and collection problems to worry about.

If you have the right merchandise and price it correctly, you just might make some important revenue. If you are wrong on these issues, you might have a warehouse full of shirts, posters, autographed photos, and coffee mugs!

GETTING YOUR MESSAGE OUT

Once you have decided what you are going to sell and for how much, you had better tell as many people as possible about your product. A fully comprehensive, complimentary, and coordinated communications program includes public relations, advertising, and promotion. To me, no one element is more important than the other, and they should each reinforce the other. This is not easy, but it should be the goal.

Public Relations

Working with the press can be challenging, interesting, or just plain distasteful, depending on your orientation. It can also be rewarding, as from time to time you will achieve exposure that could not have been accomplished without the aid of the press. But some of those writers . . . well, you can't live with them and you can't live without them.

Publicity can and should be an integral part of your event plan. A good public relations campaign can properly position you, your event, your sponsors, and your participants in the mind of the public, and it all appears as arms-length editorial from a writer that is supposed to be an objective reporter.

The press can kill you too. While it is not an example from an event, I was involved in one of the great media circuses of all time when Nancy Kerrigan was attacked by Tonya Harding's group of thugs. First the press built Nancy into the perfect human being. Then they criticized her every move. All of this happened in a matter of weeks. The media can do that to you and your event too, so you have to be careful about how you handle the press.

The press can make you if managed properly or break you if not handled well.

I suggest that you hire experts to handle the press properly. While certain aspects of putting on an event do not require great expertise (a little experience and some common sense can go a long way in some areas), dealing with the press is another matter altogether. The members of the press have their agendas, and unless you live with them on a daily basis, you won't know them, you won't get any special treatment, and you may not get any coverage at all. In short, the press can make you if managed properly or break you if not handled well.

In all likelihood you will not have the experience or contacts to know how to manage the press effectively. If you can make room for it in your budget, hire a PR agency and send everything through them. Let them make the calls to the newspapers and magazines. Let them get you on the 6 o'clock news. Let them get a photo in the paper of the chief executive of your title sponsor.

Remember, the press—be it radio, television, print, or the Internet—is a powerful tool that can aid you by supplying coverage that you could never buy even if you wanted to. The press can be your best communication tool because of the credibility they have with the public. Think of the power of a bad review for a movie or a musical. The critics can kill you. But think of the flip side. If the evening news says something is coming to town and recommends that you go see it, the repercussions are fantastic. This is what every producer and promoter strives for.

So make your public relations campaign an essential part of your program, and either hire an outside agency or bring someone in "on staff" who can do the job.

When hiring an agency, don't always accept their fee structure. I have long been an advocate of putting a PR agency on a retainer with bonuses based on their actual results. For example, an article in *Sports Illustrated*—not out of the question even for a grassroots event—might be worth a $5,000 bonus, while an article in the local weekly might only be worth $150. This is all over and above the agency retainer, and it does two things: it helps keep the retainer at a lower level and it keeps the agency hungry because they know they can earn more for better results. Some PR agencies don't like the retainer/bonus method of payment, and you may lose a good agency as a result from time to time. But I have seen it work time and again, as the bonuses can be a real motivator. I know that Ira Silverman, whom I have worked with for years in New York, hates the concept but knows that it works. He has picked up quite a few bonuses over the years, and we are both happy whenever he does.

Anyway, make the press your friend if you can. They will come back to help you many times over.

PR on a Shoestring

If you can't work an agency's fee into your budget and you can't hire someone on your staff to work with the press, this does not mean that you should just throw in the towel. There are ways to make the press aware of your event even on a limited budget. Some basic PR strategies include the following:

• **Get a list of all of the local press.** This includes television anchors and sports reporters on network affiliates and cable stations; sports writers at all of the local newspapers—major and minor; gossip columnists at the major papers; and contacts at city magazines, both those with paid circulation and giveaways (there are usually many of the latter).

• **Hold a press conference announcing your event.** You might hold this at a place that is centrally located so that as many of the press can attend as possible. Don't make it hard to get to. Send out an invitation to all of the people on the press list that you compiled. Try to hold your press conference midmorning so that deadlines can be met. If you serve food, you are likely to get a better response.

• **Send out periodic press releases announcing various issues that show progress in your event.** This can include signing new sponsors, attracting new participants, finding a venue, securing television distribution, and so on. Anything that you perceive as enhancing your event can be considered newsworthy. Trumpet your successes.

• **Send out photos if possible.** These might be of participants, of you with the venue manager, or anything else that could be of interest.

- **Put your Web site address on everything.** If you have an Internet site for your event, make sure the press knows that they can get archived information on your site at all times.

- **Try to advise the press of your news on slow news days.** This is hard to judge because you never know when a significant figure will die, a major fire will start, or some other big news story will break. If it happens to coincide with the timing of your press release or press conference, bad luck. However, if you can time your announcements for slow news days, you will be more likely to get coverage. Don't put your information out on weekends or holidays, though. You will either not get picked up, or if you do, it will be on the day that the fewest people read the paper (Saturdays and holidays).

- **Make sure you invite the press to your event.** Send them reminders and invitations and make follow-up phone calls. They will come if you make it easy for them, and they will cover the event if they show up.

PR does not have to cost a lot of money. Event promoters with small budgets who have chosen to court the press themselves have been successful. If you go this route, just remember to provide an area at the event for the press and remember to feed them. Also, they need servicing, so pay attention to the press during the event.

Advertising

Advertising, along with your PR campaign, will probably be your primary vehicle for communicating with the public. As such, it is also the most important means by which you will sell tickets. As we discussed in chapter 4, advertising will also be important to your sponsors, as it will allow them to reach their audience through your efforts. In short, with respect to your relationship with your target market, advertising is key.

Your advertising has to be carefully planned so that it works within your budget and gets your message out to as many people as possible. And remember, your message might be about tickets, free entry, an invitation to participate in the event, the time of the event, entry deadlines for participants, or all of the above!

Trade-Outs

There are many ways to approach your advertising campaign. If you have a small event with little or no advertising budget, you will rely primarily on trade-outs or barter. This is where you provide certain benefits to a newspaper or radio/television station (e.g., tickets, banner space, and booth space) in exchange for ad space in their paper or on their station. Projects with a big budget won't be as concerned with trades, although they are *always* helpful. I suggest that the ideal situation is a combination of paid and trade advertising.

In other words, plan to spend a certain amount of money on advertising that you can control (i.e., pick the day, program, section of the paper), while at the same time trading for additional ad space over which you may not have any control (i.e., your ad runs when and where the paper or station has time or space).

As you get into the "trade business," I think that you will find that local papers, cable networks, and radio are more likely to make trade deals than are the major papers and network affiliates. Many of these trade deals will include promotions in the form of ticket giveaways and other contests instead of more traditional advertising. Don't let this dissuade you, as the line between the two is a fine one anyway.

We have made many a trade deal over the years, and I can assure you that they were in

Trades With Sponsors

Trades with sponsors is another area for you to consider. Sponsors love them because they are cheaper than cash, and you can benefit from them in several ways.

On the advertising and promotion side, sponsors can provide all-important exposure. Examples of this include supermarkets, local retailers, and outdoor advertising outlets. Think "trade" when you approach any of these potential partners.

If you can trade tickets, display space, etc. with the local bus or metro authority and, in exchange, get ads on or in their buses or subway cars, you will reach a lot of people. Similarly, if a trade with a supermarket will cause them to stuff all their bags with a flyer about your event, you may gain a significant number of customers. Trades work everywhere!

Trade-out situations don't only exist with respect to advertising and promotion. You can employ trade deals with sponsors as well. In some cases a barter of your event benefits for the company's product or services will be of equal or greater value to you than cash would be. For example, if you can trade an official sponsorship package with an airline so that instead of paying you hard dollars they give you airline tickets, they may be able to justify giving you more in trade than they would have in cash. In fact, oftentimes, just like in the advertising and promotions area, a company will have a policy in which they will give you a multiple of the agreed value if they can pay you in kind rather than cash (e.g., three for one in an airline deal, so if you were asking for $5,000 in cash and are willing to take trade instead, they would give you $15,000 in trade value). There really is no difference between the two if you are going to have to fly talent, staff, television crew, and the like to your event anyway. The same thing is true with printers (i.e., they print your program for no cash and in exchange you give them tickets, on-site exposure). This goes back to the hard versus soft costs of sponsorship that we discussed in chapter 4.

most cases equally as valuable as those in which we got cash. At Skating Goes Country we traded tickets and a credit on the television show with a local limousine company that then handled all of the local transportation for the skaters, musicians, staff, and so on. At the Janet Evans Invitational, which had a very small budget for everything including food for the athletes, we traded on-site exposure with In n' Out Burger, who provided food for the swimmers, staff, and press. Even Northwest Airlines' title sponsorship for Halloween on Ice included a portion of cash and trade.

The point is that trade deals don't only apply to advertising. The products and services that sponsors can deliver have a lot of value that can be just as important as cash.

Where to Advertise

I think it was Sam Wannamaker, the founder of Wannamaker's department stores, who said something along the lines of "50 percent of your advertising will be effective; the trick is being able to determine which 50 percent." In other words, some of your advertising will actually reach your market *and* deliver the message that leads to action by the recipient of the message. The rest will be wasted on an audience that doesn't care or doesn't get your message.

I totally agree with Sam Wannamaker, except that he may have understated the issue a bit. Determining where to advertise, when to run the ads, and for how long is a very difficult job. If you have a big event, you probably should hire an advertising agency loaded with people trained to read research, create advertising strategies, and design the ads themselves. Even if you have a medium-sized event, you might be able to employ a smaller, localized agency that specializes in sports or the region in which your event is being held. Regardless of whether you can hire an agency to design and implement your ad campaign, at a minimum your advertising should include some of the following elements.

Print

Given the fact that for most events the audience will be local or at most regional, your primary means of advertising should include the following:

- The major local newspaper
- Regional papers
- City and other local and regional magazines

The goal of your print advertising is to reach as many people as possible as often as possible so that there is no chance that anyone can say after the fact, "I didn't know that your event was in town." These are nine of the worst words an event organizer can hear. If people know that your event is coming but don't want to attend, fine. But make sure they know you are coming!

You may want to plan your ad campaign around the biggest newspaper in town. When opening a discussion with them about your ad buy, keep in mind that the major local newspaper might be a good sponsor of your event (particularly on a trade deal). So don't be afraid to approach them on that basis. If you do, keep in mind that most big cities today have only one major paper. Thus, they have a monopoly and might think they don't have to make a deal. They also might think you have no choice but to advertise with them

> ■ ■ ■ ■ ■ ■ ■ ■ ■ ■ ■
>
> *The goal of your print advertising is to reach as many people as possible as often as possible.*
>
> ■ ■ ■ ■ ■ ■ ■ ■ ■ ■ ■

. . . and they are probably right. But don't let that stop you from asking.

After you factor the bigger paper(s) into your plan, you need to focus on the smaller papers. In many cases, they may be more important than the major paper. In the average city with a strong suburban population, each town might have its own weekly paper. These papers are read diligently and may have more influence than any other vehicle that you find. Table 5.1 illustrates a sample event advertising schedule that was created for Halloween on Ice. Making a chart like this one can be helpful in tracking which ad will appear where and when.

The same issues apply to local magazines. Many cities and towns have their own sports newsmagazine that reports on local events and other happenings. Be sure to make them part of your plan along with any other magazine that might reach your target market. For example, in Nashville we advertised in *Parent's Monthly* because it had a strong circulation that was made up of mothers, a perfect fit with our customer profile.

Radio

Most of the same principles that apply to print also apply to radio, television, and the Internet, or the electronic media, as they have come to be known. Radio probably gives you the most options in terms of flexibility because it is not expensive and most stations are pretty open to trying new things.

However, before you make a deal, you have to go through all of the same evaluations that you made for print and then some. Ask yourself the following questions:

- Which stations are geared to your audience?
- Should the commercial spots be 30 or 60 seconds long?

Table 5.1   Sample Event Advertising Schedule

Paper	Ad size	Date
Boston Globe	1/4 page	9/3; 9/10; 9/17; 9/30; 10/5; 10/6; 10/7; 10/8; 10/9
Boston Herald	1/4 page	9/3; 9/17; 9/30; 10/6; 10/7; 10/8; 10/9
Phoenix	1/4 page	9/3; 9/30; 10/7; 10/9
Lynnfield	1/2 page	9/3; 9/17; 9/30; 10/6
Stoneham	1/2 page	9/3; 9/17; 9/30; 10/6
Danvers	1/4 page	9/17; 9/30
Cape Cod	1/2 page	9/3; 9/17; 9/30

- How much can the listener digest in a short period of time?
- Do you need a catchy jingle?
- Should you use a male or female voice?
- When should the campaign start? (For Skating Goes Country we started advertising about 10 days before tickets went on sale, which is the first time I had ever done that. It was a good idea in concept, although I am not sure it worked.)
- When should the campaign end?
- How many tickets can you give to the various stations for promotional trade? (As I discuss later, radio loves to trade out and run promotions, such as call-ins.)
- How far outside the local area should you advertise?

Each of these questions applies equally to radio, print, and television. You might ask, Why even use radio? Well, it is very effective during certain periods of the day, and some formats deliver pretty big audiences. Finally, radio reaches a very segmented audience; if you are trying to reach a male sports fan, for instance, you know that you have a pretty good chance on sports-talk radio. The same can be said for young adults, who listen to rock stations. Because the demographic profile of radio listeners is pretty accurate, radio should be a part of your plan.

Television

Without rehashing all of the issues, television requires the same analysis as print and radio. The obvious benefit to television is that it delivers the largest audience of any medium. A commercial spot on the Super Bowl (which I know you won't be buying) is going to get your product seen by millions of people at one time. On a local level, advertising during a pro or college football or basketball game is bound to deliver a significant male audience. A spot on *Friends* or another prime-time show is going to reach a large cross section of people. You simply reach more people on television than on radio or in print. However, you have to know whom you are trying to reach. Otherwise, you can waste a lot of money.

Here again, it's not the worst idea to hire an agency. We have done this on occasion, and it generally works pretty well. However, recognize one thing about television: It can be expensive and inefficient. Local cable time can be purchased pretty cheaply, but once you get into network time or even network affiliate time, the cost goes way up in comparison to radio and print. You also have to produce a commercial for television, which can get costly as compared to a radio spot, which doesn't have to cost much at all.

Since most of you will be producing local events, I want to stress the value of local cable advertising. Frankly, if you buy the right spots, it can be the most effective advertising of all.

Similar to radio, cable television is highly segmented. People looking for sports information tend to watch ESPN and Fox Sports Net. If kids are involved, they are likely to watch Nickelodeon, the Disney Channel, or Fox Family. When most people look for the news, CNN is often the network of choice. Each of these networks and their local cable affiliates can tell you who their audience is, what they watch, and when, based on the Nielsen ratings and other information.

This detailed information allows you to pinpoint with some degree of accuracy where to run your advertising. If you are looking to get the word out to participants about a junior tennis event, you might skew your ads to Nickelodeon or the Disney Channel. If you are trying to sell tickets to a three-on-three basketball event, you might be better served by going heavier on ESPN or TNT during their basketball broadcasts.

Irrespective of your event or audience, cable television has become so well accepted and pervasive that it is often the best delivery system for your message.

The bottom line here is that you want to communicate your message to the broadest yet most targeted audience for the least amount of dollars. Efficiency is the goal. It is easy in theory. It is damn difficult in practice.

The Internet

The importance and impact of the Internet change and grow daily. As a result, you have to factor it into your communications plan. You might want to create an Internet site for your event (and since they are not particularly expensive to get started, you should). I love the idea of linking your site to various others (sponsors' sites, for example) to have your message spread to Web surfers. But the banner ads don't do that much for me. In fact, at this point I think the Internet's impact is still hit and miss. However, every day more people, young and old, are using the Internet to get information and to make purchases, so you have to be there. If you use all of the other advertising tools to let people know that your site exists (in other words, tag all of your ads—print, television, and radio—with **www.yourevent.com**), you will drive traffic to your site, thus making it an even more important advertising tool. Once you get viewers to your site, you can offer promotions, contests, and so forth to generate additional interest. The Internet presents a great addition to your advertising arsenal, so use it aggressively.

Ad Copy

Simultaneous with deciding where to place it, you have to figure out what your ad should say. Deciding what to say may be a lot easier than determining *how* to say it.

In terms of content, you want to communicate the following:

- Date
- Time
- Location
- Stars (or in the case of a grassroots event that is open to anyone, how to sign up)
- Where tickets can be purchased and how much they cost

In keeping with your sponsorship and site agreements, you also need to make sure that, at a minimum, you have fulfilled any contractual obligations, such as logo placement. You should put your sponsors in a position that helps them with the public. If you can accomplish all this while also effectively

■ ■ ■ ■ ■ ■ ■ ■ ■ ■ ■

*Y*ou want to communicate your message to the broadest yet most targeted audience for the least amount of dollars.

■ ■ ■ ■ ■ ■ ■ ■ ■ ■ ■

The Internet

While the Internet has made its way into several areas within this book, it hasn't taken a dominant position in any one chapter. Were I writing this book five years from now, the Internet might take up as much room as television does.

To make the point even clearer, from the time that I began writing until the time that I completed the final draft of this manuscript, the Internet has become almost all-pervasive throughout our society. I find that you can access the Internet now at your health club while on the exercise bike and on your phone from just about anywhere. It is delivered by broadband, telephone wires, cable, and satellite. You can send e-mail from almost anyplace.

The message here is that the Internet, while still in its infancy, is daily becoming the most dominant means of distribution on the planet. As a result, the impact on sports events is going to be significant in every respect, although the nature and format of that impact is still not entirely clear.

For event promoters and managers this means that in addition to everything that has been discussed during the course of this book, you must keep a careful watch on where the Internet is going, how people view it (a recent ESPN poll showed that 56.7 percent of children aged 7 to 11 visit the Web sites of the pro sports leagues and 77.5 percent play Internet games), how advertising is bought and sold, what the revenue potential is for e-commerce, and how this medium can work to supplement your activities for promoting and selling your event.

We have just announced a new Web initiative called SportsInstruction.com, through which I am learning more about the technical end of the Internet than I ever imagined I would. I don't think you need to become a technical wizard to understand how to put this phenomenal resource to work for you. The Internet world changes rapidly because of a number of factors. So watch the development of the Web very closely, as it could enable you to approach the positioning of your event in a manner that we could not have imagined even 10 years ago.

The Internet makes for exciting times. Don't be caught napping on this one.

communicating the critical elements related to the event itself, then you have created one hell of an ad.

Think about your own day. You are bombarded with advertising messages for everything from food to clothes to necessities to luxuries. Every product that relies on advertising is trying to "break through the clutter." Now it is your turn to try to do the same thing. In so doing, consider the following:

- The size of the ad
- Whether to focus on the stars in the event
- What size type to use for which aspect of the message
- Where in the layout to put the location and the time
- How to explain the ticket purchasing process

None of this is easy; there are no right answers, and you won't know for sure whether your ads have been effective until after the event is over.

If the point of your ad is ticket sales, you can track the impact of your ads by watching the ticket sales results each time you run an ad. If you see sales increase after an ad, then you can assume that your ad is reaching your audience. If you see no activity, you might conclude that your ad is not working. This is a major generalization, but you get the picture. Your ad should be a call to action for the recipients of your message. If it isn't, it may not be properly conceived. If you conclude that your ad is not working, don't be afraid to change it. Change a losing game before it is too late.

Promotion

I don't think the value of promotion can be reinforced enough, which is why this topic appears throughout the book. Make sure that promotion is high on your list of priorities.

Defining promotion is pretty easy, and in fact, implementing promotion, as long as you keep it rather simple, should be pretty easy too.

I define promotion as any interactive activity that you undertake to try to entice people to come to your event. This is *not* advertising; it requires the customer to *do* something in return for special offers. Promotions can take the shape of free tickets, two tickets for the price of one, discount tickets (rebates, for example), early-payment discounts (purchase *now* and get 15 percent off), free tickets with the purchase of a product, coupon redemptions, and so forth. The list is pretty long, but the goal is the same in every case: lure people into attending your event.

The implementation of a promotion can go through a myriad of channels. Some of the more popular methods of promotion are through radio. As mentioned earlier, most stations love to give away tickets to callers. You can package promotions with your radio advertising buy to extend the frequency of your on-air advertising. For example, you might agree to spend a certain amount with a station if they provide a like amount in promotional time. This just requires a bit more deal making than does a straight ad buy.

Because you have been the target of ticket promotions many times, you can probably think of several ideas right off the bat. Following are several ticket giveaway radio promotions that we have used for various events:

- The first caller after a commercial for the King of the Beach Invitational won a pair of tickets.
- The third caller after a Billy Ray Cyrus song won tickets to Skating Goes Country and to the after-show party.
- For Halloween on Ice we had a costume contest in which the person with the best costume won tickets to the show or a chance to meet the cast backstage.
- I have referred earlier to ball-guessing contests. On the tennis tour we would fill a Volvo with tennis balls, and the person who guessed the number of balls in the car won tickets to the event.

The list of this type of promotion is endless, and you are limited only by your imagination—so go for it. The return is very worthwhile.

As with the surveys that we discussed earlier in this chapter, one of the benefits of certain promotions is that you obtain names, addresses, and phone numbers of prospective customers because they have to enter to win. If you plan on holding your event for a long period of time, the more names and addresses you can collect, the better off you will be. Mailing lists even have a value in the marketplace, as you can rent your lists to certain organizations if you so desire. (Given the amount of junk mail I get, I am not a big proponent of renting out lists because I know that it is just adding to the recipients' junk mail collection. From a business point of view, however, it might make sense at certain times.)

Don't forget the value of getting your sponsors to run promotions. In the perfect world, you would team up with one of your sponsors to put together a promotional program that is helpful to both of you. If you have a package goods sponsor, a free pair of tickets

> **M**ake sure that promotion is high on your list of priorities.

with the purchase of product (the sponsor buys the tickets from you for a deep discount) is a win–win situation for everyone. If you can achieve this level of interaction between your event and your sponsor, you will have hit a home run.

You should not shy away from the many opportunities to run promotions; just be sure you are familiar with the laws that govern them. In most states, for example, you cannot require a person to purchase something or pay to enter a promotion such as a sweepstakes. If you do, it is considered gambling. Check out the legal implications carefully *before* you institute a great offer; otherwise, you may find yourself in trouble.

■ ■ ■ ■ ■ ■ ■ ■ ■ ■ ■ ■

You should not shy away from the many opportunities to run promotions; just be sure you are familiar with the laws that govern them.

■ ■ ■ ■ ■ ■ ■ ■ ■ ■ ■ ■

Your customers, the ticket-buying public, like nothing better than a good contest with a great prize. If people perceive that they are getting a good deal, they will certainly be attracted to your event, and the word will get around. A well-thought-out promotion can easily start a "buzz" about your event that affects its perception in the marketplace.

A positive buzz will lead to a hot ticket, which is, after all, what this is all about in the first place!

Charity Affiliations

Similar to promotion, charity affiliations are pretty easy to define and also fairly easy to implement. Over the years we have involved several charitable groups with our events, and every one has created a positive spin for the event while also making all of us involved with the event feel a little better.

I define a charitable organization as any group that qualifies to receive money with a corresponding tax deduction for the donor. The Internal Revenue Service calls this a 501(C)(3) organization, and most charitable organizations fall into this category (if they don't, you need to start asking a lot of questions!). Every one of these organizations operates differently, and you should check them out before you get them involved with your event. Assuming the organization you are considering passes muster, you will usually find them more than willing to help support and promote your event.

Don't be surprised if some charitable organizations don't jump at the opportunity to affiliate with your project. These groups hold themselves and their partners to high standards, and so they need time to research you as thoroughly as you researched them. Once you and your chosen charity agree to work together, the benefits should be several.

Start by choosing a group that you feel some sense of commitment to personally. At times we have no choice but to make our charity the local volleyball, tennis, or figure skating club. That is fine, and in most cases we have a nice relationship with them. However, there often is no passion in these relationships. On the other hand, we have had affiliations with the Lion's Club, which does work for the blind; the American Heart Association; and Mothers Against Drunk Driving, each of which had a personal meaning for someone related to our company or the event. While almost any charitable organization will lend some benefit to your event, it is more rewarding, I think, to get involved with a cause that you are passionate about.

Don't be bashful about making your association with a charity a two-way street. You might be uncomfortable with this at first, but remember that charity organizations are businesses too and understand the need for the benefits to flow both ways. They will have mailing lists, newsletters, volunteer groups, and the like, all of which can be of major benefit to you in trying to build awareness for your event.

Certain organizations will give you a great deal of credibility in the marketplace and make your event more attractive to sponsors and the public. People are generally willing to pay more to attend an event that is raising money for a good and established cause than they would to attend one whose sole purpose is to line the pockets of the promoter.

Most charities will be well connected in the local marketplace, potentially helping you get better value with trades. They also can tap into their donor and membership lists to help you sell tickets, sponsorships, and so forth in an effort to raise money.

The charity will have an incentive to make sure that you do well. This depends on the deal you make with the charity (I suggest that they get a percentage of some portion of the revenues, such as a dollar for every ticket sold). Charities are used to fund-raising and in most cases are very good at it. Tap into their expertise. It can only help you.

Again, a charity affiliation serves a multitude of purposes, from making you feel good to making the participants, sponsors, and spectators feel that they are contributing to a good cause. In the final analysis, however, no matter how much good feeling comes from the association, you and your charity are both looking to generate money for and from the event. Don't be afraid to use this tool to your advantage.

Ancillary Events

Along with the rest of your communications plan you have the opportunity to create activities around your event that have tremendous PR value and draw a lot of attention to the event that you are promoting. I call these ancillary events. They are not really necessary. They don't really add direct value to the event itself. But they are quite helpful in getting the word out that your event is coming to town or about to take place.

Ancillary events, which can take many shapes and forms, include the following:

- Clinics
- Autograph sessions
- Celebrity golf outings
- Bar, restaurant, or mall promotions (before Skating Goes Country we sponsored a booth promotion in conjunction with the Country Music Association [CMA] Awards in one of Nashville's most well-known bars)
- Pre-event parties to announce anything from sponsors to participants
- Grassroots programs that get kids involved before the event. This could include visits to schools, fund-raisers through ticket sales, ballboy/ballgirl training, and celebrity visits to schools.
- Contests (the Volvo ball-guessing contests were always a big success in drawing attention to the event)

■ ■ ■ ■ ■ ■ ■ ■ ■ ■ ■

Don't be bashful about making your association with a charity a two-way street.

■ ■ ■ ■ ■ ■ ■ ■ ■ ■ ■

In short, anything that encourages participation by your prospective audience can fall under the umbrella of ancillary activities. These do not have to be expensive. In fact, oftentimes you might get one of your sponsors to put up some extra money to underwrite something like this. The key is to make sure that your ancillary activities are well covered by the press and get people involved emotionally in your event. These activities are designed primarily to draw attention to your event and "hook" people into buying tickets or otherwise attending the event when it takes place; so the more "noise," the better.

✔ Customer Checklist

From advertising to autograph sessions, there are numerous ways in which to get in touch with your customer—the ticket buyer—directly. Each method is an important element within the overall communication campaign. They should work together to create a good feeling about your event and generate ticket and other sales. Without those revenues, there is no event. Without spectators, in most instances, there won't be an event either. So keep your customers in mind at all times.

In so doing, don't forget the following steps and issues:

✔ Do your best to know your customer before you price your tickets and merchandise.

✔ Carefully consider whether your event justifies ticket sales or whether it should be open to spectators for free.

✔ Create a spectator program that delivers value and develops a relationship with the customer.

✔ Move toward being on the social calendar so that your target market has your event on its "radar screen" throughout the year.

✔ Check that your tickets are priced to sell.

✔ Try to determine what merchandise is important.

✔ Decide whether you want to be a retailer or would rather license merchandising to a third party.

✔ Decide whether you need or want a program.

✔ Determine what kind of ad campaign you can afford.

✔ Plan your ad campaign using the most efficient channels of communication.

✔ Ask yourself whether everyone knows that your event is coming to town.

✔ Ask yourself whether you have appealed to your customer.

Finding and keeping your customer is difficult under the best of circumstances. Tastes change. What is "cool" is always shifting. What works one year might be viewed as corny in another. If you can be consistent in talking to your customer, understanding the shifting sands and making the adjustments that your market demands, you can withstand the test of time. It can be very difficult, though. The King of the Beach event is in its ninth year. We feel that is quite an accomplishment considering the ebb and flow in the popularity of beach volleyball. If you can stay on top of the issues, though, you can be around for a long time.

Now that we have addressed your relationship with your customers, it is time to move on to the people your customers come to see—the participants.

Working Model: Tournament Communications Plan

Primary PR Goal
Your underlying goal for this year is to increase the general awareness of the tournament to both the tennis world and the regional business world to grow this event to a larger entity for future years. Essentially, this is an introductory year for the event.

Secondary Goals

• Use local and regional public/consumer media to attract general interest.

• Involve local business media to attract sponsors.

• Use local/regional tennis media to attract participant attention and to raise awareness of the event in the tennis world.

These goals will be achieved by the following:

Local and Regional Public/Consumer Media

• Develop a press release to announce the date and those eligible to participate in the event.

• Issue updates as new details are developed, such as the site, sponsors, and the like.

- Approach the lead sports-talk radio station to become a sponsor/partner in the event.
- Announce the manner in which funds raised from the event will be used (i.e., build courts, hire coaches, etc.).
- Pitch profiles on top players and the tournament director.
- Make the tournament director available for radio and print interviews.
- Hire a photographer to take photos at the event to be issued to all interested media.
- Issue a press release announcing the amount of money raised by the event for the establishment of further junior tennis initiatives.

Local Business Media

- Develop a press release to announce the date and sponsors that have already committed to the event.
- Issue secondary releases as additional sponsors are confirmed.
- Develop a business angle to pitch to local papers.
- Issue a release announcing the amount of money raised and how it will be used to further junior tennis in the region.
- Be prepared to discuss the intent of growing the event into one with national significance.

Regional Sports/Tennis Media

- Develop a press release to announce the date, location, draw sizes, potential participants, and other issues related to the event.
- Issue updates as top players commit to the event.
- Pitch interviews with top players.
- Issue photos of players and site.
- Issue tournament facts and figures to encourage coverage.

Sports Broadcast Media

- Announce television coverage with broadcast details to sports broadcast reporters throughout the region.

Chapter SIX

Working With Your Participants

Now that you have committed to your event and begun working on your sanction, selling sponsorships, working out the details of the site, and so on (you have started all of this, right?), you will have to begin immediately determining the list or caliber of athletes whom you would like to have participate in your event. Then you have to figure out how you are going to attract them. On the professional side, if you thought prize money was enough, think again. Even at the grassroots level it takes more than just announcing a time and place and providing a nice trophy.

If you are planning a local 10K, you will go about soliciting participants very differently than if you are operating a major LPGA event or ATP tennis tournament. Regardless of the level of your event, as I indicated in the opening chapter, the participants are what make the event viable no matter where on the spectrum your event falls.

You might think that the entry list is only important to major league sports events. But consider what would happen if you organized a 10K road race, signed on a sponsor that expected to expose its product to 2,000 runners, arranged for a city police force to in essence dedicate its force to shutting down the streets for the two hours you expected your race to last . . . and then only 150 runners showed up. Your sponsor would not be happy, the police force would not be happy, you would be embarrassed, and the prospects for ever mounting that race again would be minimal.

In that same vein, let's say you wanted to promote a major tennis exhibition with the intent of raising money for junior tennis. In order to solicit sponsors, sell tickets at premium prices, possibly obtain television coverage, and get the attention of the community, you would need to deliver an event that had some of the top players in the world *and* be prepared with worthy replacements in case one of the players got sick or hurt or decided not to play at the last minute. This is a daunting task in a world in which the top players are in great demand and have at least one important tournament on the ATP tour every month.

No matter what the example, *the athletes are critical,* so how do you go about securing a player field that will suit your event?

A PLAYER-FRIENDLY TOURNAMENT

To begin with, you should approach your event with a "player-friendly" mentality. Your mind-set should be to design an event with the athletes in mind and thereby make it easy

It is important to design your event with the participants in mind. For example, make sure you provide plenty of water to keep athletes hydrated and cool on a hot event day.

for them to decide to participate in your event. This attitude can manifest itself in many forms. Here are a few examples related to grassroots or local events:

• Don't schedule your event at a time when other major events are taking place in your city. Put the event in a place that is readily accessible. Schedule it at a time of year when the weather is conducive to your sport (our 5K Racquet Run may have been troubled from the start since it took place in Washington, D.C., in mid-July—traditionally the hottest week of the summer).

• Make sure to provide ample and convenient parking or other transportation, such as shuttle buses from the parking lot. The last thing you want to do is make the participants walk a long distance to the field of play.

• Arrange for prizes, gifts, and other benefits that will be interesting to the athletes you are looking to attract.

• Don't forget to communicate throughout your community the fact that your event is taking place. We lost the opportunity to raise quite a bit of additional money for charity through entry fees at our race because it wasn't publicized well enough.

• Many grassroots events will charge the participants for entering. In that case you need to be sure that your entry fee is in keeping with the cost of other similarly situated events so that you don't turn off potential participants. When running an event in which the participants have to pay, it helps to have a charity involved, as that makes the fee a bit more palatable.

For professional events, compensation, prestige, and convenience will be major considerations for the athletes when they are making their schedules (although some events are cause or charity related and entice people to participate almost irrespective of these major factors). However, in addition to money, prestige, and convenience, the athletes on the professional side are going to be looking for the extra touches that make their participation in your event a great experience. These are the things that make them want to come back year after year. Some of these will be seemingly small things, such as adequate and easy-to-use transportation to and from the event. Others will be much bigger, such as taking care of their families. Still others, such as having access to tickets for local sporting events, will be much more difficult to pinpoint. We have tried a lot of these "extras" and find that they are very much appreciated and thus worthwhile even though they can be very time consuming to put together. As events proliferate, thus intensifying the competition for the players, the "perks" become that much more of a necessity.

When we began the King of the Beach Invitational in 1990, we were determined to make it the most important event in beach volleyball. One way to accomplish this was to make it a major title in the minds of the players. Over time we thought we would be able to accomplish this by virtue of the fact that the event was going to establish a new measurement for the best individual player in a sport made up of two-man teams.

To achieve this status quickly, though, we felt we had to go that extra mile to make sure that the top players wanted to play in the first year or two of the event. To reinforce that this was an event designed specifically for the athletes, we included the following:

■ ■ ■ ■ ■ ■ ■ ■ ■ ■ ■ ■

In addition to money, prestige, and convenience, the athletes are going to look for the extra touches that make their participation in your event a great experience.

■ ■ ■ ■ ■ ■ ■ ■ ■ ■ ■

• **A golf tournament for the players.** So many people play golf today that this is bound to be popular. This ultimately turned into a fund-raiser for the local volleyball association, which provided volunteers for the tournament.

• **A player welcome party.** This is held the night before the tournament starts and is exclusively for the players and their families and friends.

• **Free hotel rooms.** None of the other events on the tour offered to pay for the players' hotel rooms. In a sport in which the earnings were not enormous, we knew that this would be well received.

• **Free air transportation.** Similar to the hotel rooms, paying for the players' airfare turned out to be very popular, as you might expect. Some sports leagues or tours may not allow this. Others may require it. So, make sure you know the rules.

• **Black jack tournament.** Obviously, not all events can have this type of gambling event, but we took advantage of the fact that we were in Las Vegas and could do this legally. The tournament also turned into a fund-raiser for local charities and expanded to include the public, but the players love it and they all participate . . . even though they don't get to keep their earnings!

• **The Bash.** This has become our annual Saturday night party complete with band, food, and dancing. Over time this has become open to the public as well. However, we still have a private room for the players and their guests as well as the sponsors. It has proved to be as popular as the tournament itself.

Not every sport and not every event is as conducive to some of these specific player activities. Beach volleyball connotes a party atmosphere to begin with. A golf tournament probably requires a different approach. However, regardless of the sport, some things are constants in the minds of the players. For instance, consider the following examples:

• When we ran the **LPGA** event in Stratton Mountain, Vermont, the free hotel rooms were a big player feature.

• At the **AT&T Challenge** the players had access to a championship golf course.

• Perhaps the best player feature I have ever seen was the softball game at the **Volvo International tennis tournament** in North Conway, New Hampshire. There the Americans played the non-Americans in an annual event that, for some of the players, was more of a draw than the tennis tournament.

• On the **Champions on Ice Tour** promoter Tom Collins treats the skaters to a variety of special events, including baseball games and Broadway shows. However, Sneaker Day, in which everyone gets to pick out a pair of athletic shoes of their choice, seems to be the most popular and most fun.

Don't think that these player extras always have to cost a lot of money either. Sponsors

The Participation Fee

As mentioned earlier, a grassroots event may require participants to pay an entry fee. This is not unusual and won't be frowned on by the athletes. However, if you want to make your event stand out among the amateur runners, tennis players, golfers, and the like, I strongly suggest that you make sure they get something for their money in addition to just a good run or round of golf. Following are some things that come to mind:

• **Beverages.** All athletes get thirsty. If you can supply plenty of liquid, you will be a step ahead of the game.

• **Souvenirs.** Give them something that they can proudly display or use. For a golf tournament, a bag tag is always a safe gift. Runners like to keep their jersey numbers. Tennis players love bags for their paraphernalia. Cups or mugs, jackets (as opposed to T-shirts), fleece vests, and so on are all good gifts and help to justify the expense of competing. Having said that, if the event is for charity, don't go overboard, as the money should really be passed through to the charitable cause.

• **Prime seating for friends and relatives.** If your event is conducive to seating, make sure that the participants have passes for the people that are close to them. Making their "entourage" feel important will surely be a big plus for you.

• **Tax deduction.** If your event is charity related, make sure that you make it easy for the participants to get a tax deduction. One thing that I like is when I get a letter from the organization confirming that the donation was made and thanking me. This serves as an easy reminder that a deduction can be taken.

are often willing and eager to donate products or foot the bill for the cost of a party, as they want to have a great field as well. Colgate-Palmolive used to make product shipments to all of the tennis players twice a year. Volvo offered players deep discounts on their cars. Miller Brewing threw parties throughout the year for players on the AVP tour, and Coppertone made plenty of sunblock available to the participants at their events. At Skating Goes Country, Lane provided gift bags for all of the skaters and musicians. Getting your sponsors invested like this can only be beneficial to you and the event. It also brings them in contact with the athletes, which makes them feel more a part of the action.

Goody Bags and Other Gifts

Being player friendly does not always require a major effort or expenditure. The ever-popular goody bag can be very attractive to the participants, particularly at the grassroots level. It is amazing how far a T-shirt, duffel bag, or hat can go! Athletes love to use something that they got from an event in which they participated, and you benefit from getting the free exposure when they use that gift in public.

Another nice remembrance is a picture sent to the participants after the event. This has the added benefit of enabling you to communicate with the athletes at another time during the year. Dick Button sends a group photo every year after the World Professional Skating Championships. We recently did this with our One Enchanted Evening show. We happened to have some great pictures of the skaters in settings in which they are not usually photographed. We had copies made for everyone and sent them out a couple of months after the show. Some events will send the competitors a tape of the television show; others will send a copy of the program as a memento; still others will simply write a thank-you note.

You will know that you have truly arrived as a player-friendly event when *you* get a thank-you note from one of the participants! At the professional level, this doesn't happen too often since the athletes are pretty busy, but every now and then we get one, which makes us all feel pretty good.

As you can see, there are a number of little things you can do in your effort to make your event one that the participants will want to come back to year after year. Having a beautiful setting helps; having a good date on the calendar helps; being a prestigious title helps. However, creating a good environment for the players and their families or friends, including added touches such as food, day care, towels, transportation, and the like (we will discuss some of these things in the operations section of the book in chapter 8 as well), goes a long way.

In addition, especially at the professional level, you may want to get out to see the athletes from time to time so that they remember you and your event. They are bombarded all of the time by people who want something from them, so it doesn't hurt if they know you and like you as well. On the ATP Tour, one of the best at that is Barry McKay, who runs the successful San Francisco stop on the tour. He somehow manages to remain friends with the players despite the fact that there is always a new crop coming along. This has paid off handsomely for him, as he has had great fields for his tournament year in and year out.

Athletes appreciate even the smallest gifts and souvenirs from an event.

For professional events, no matter how player friendly you are known to be, you will still probably have to go through the athlete's agent to get confirmation of his or her participation. If the athlete really likes you or your event, your interaction with the agent will be that much easier.

Agents

Don't be intimidated by agents. Their reputations are blown out of proportion, and their bark greatly exceeds their bite . . . but then, as a longtime athlete representative, I guess I have to say that!

For virtually any big spectator event (or any event at which you want to have a big-name athlete/celebrity appear), the process for attracting a participant field can be fairly involved. To begin with, most of the top-ranked athletes in the world have agents or business managers that help them sort through the many offers and opportunities presented to them.

If you want big-time athletes in your event, the first step is to find out who represents them.

When I represented Ivan Lendl (who was at the time the number one tennis player in the world), he and I used to meet at least every other week to go over his schedule and the offers that had been presented. Top performers in virtually every sport go through the same procedure with their managers or agents. If you want big-time athletes in your event, the first step is to find out who represents them.

Finding out who represents the athletes will not be that hard in most cases. As with sanctioning and scheduling issues, the sport's governing body can be very helpful. I suggest that you start by calling the sport's federation and asking them how to get in touch with the athlete's representative. In all likelihood, they will have that information. To help you out, I have also listed some of the major agencies in appendix F. I encourage you to get to know some of the agents, as not only will you have to work closely with them but also they have some level of influence over their clients' decisions on whether to play in your event.

Agents will look for some very specific information when trying to determine if your event makes sense for their client. We like to present the agents with this information in a memo form that we send out when we start the player solicitation process. This process can begin anywhere from 6 to 15 months prior to the event depending on the sport and its scheduling cycles (tennis players make their schedules much farther in advance than do figure skaters, for example).

The Offer

To illustrate the range of issues you will need to solidify with a prospective participant, let's take a look at a memorandum that was used to invite skaters to appear in One Enchanted Evening, which StarGames produced for the Romance Classics Network for Valentine's Day 1999. Figure 6.1 shows all of the fundamental elements that should be clarified among you, the athlete, and his or her agent.

This letter is short, but it is very much to the point in that it

- describes the show and the skaters' responsibilities, including any restrictions on their prior or future performances;
- itemizes the benefits we are specifically willing to pay for;
- specifies the full extent of the rights that the skaters must grant; and

---

To: Skater Agent

Re: Valentine's Day Skating Special

Date: (It is always important to date your documents.)

In follow-up to our various discussions regarding our Valentine's Day show to air on the Romance Classics Network, this memorandum shall serve to formally invite the pairs team of _____ and_____ to participate.

As you know, each team will be required to skate two numbers to music either approved by us or chosen by us. The numbers must not have been seen on television for one year prior to the airing of our show (February 1999) and can also not be seen on television in the United States for three months following the show. The skaters must provide their own costumes.

We are planning to shoot the show during the week of December 14 in Amherst, Massachusetts, subject to the schedules and availability of all of the skaters. I anticipate that the shoot will take two days, but given the fact that _____ and _____ are participating in your Holiday Skating Tour, we will try to get them in and out of Amherst in one day. We will pay for all transportation, accommodations, and meals for the skaters.

We are prepared to offer _____ and _____ $_____ to participate in the show. They will be required to grant us all rights to their performance and endorsement (i.e., name, likeness, etc.) in perpetuity for this show for all forms of media including television, video, sound track, and the like.

Please let me know at your earliest convenience if _____ and _____ are interested in participating. I look forward to hearing from you soon.

Best regards.

Figure 6.1 Memorandum from One Enchanted Evening.

Entry Procedures

I don't mean to completely contradict everything that we have just discussed, but your event might be part of an organized circuit of events that is governed by very specific entry procedures. ATP and WTA tennis events fall into this category, as do PGA and LPGA tournaments. If you are running an event that falls under the auspices of a league or tour, you may not have to worry about soliciting your entire field, as a certain number of players are going to enter on their own. Even in this situation, all of the same issues of player friendliness, agent communication, and so on should apply but on a less formal basis, as the tour will take care of the entry process for the bulk of your field.

- delineates the fees that we are proposing for their appearance.

Because this letter was intended to serve as the basis for any future negotiations that ultimately took place between us and the talent's representative, the more comprehensive we could be, the better. For example, in this situation, the restriction on the use of the performance numbers (paragraph two) was very important. Most skaters want to be able to use the same number on multiple occasions. However, if we were going to produce a unique show for the Romance Classics Network, we had to be sure that the skating numbers were either new or had not been seen on television for quite some time.

Every event will have its own set of characteristics, and they should be conveyed in this initial solicitation letter to the athletes. On the other hand, certain issues will apply to virtually any event. We will cover some of these in the following sections.

Media Rights

Of paramount importance is the need for the participants to grant you all rights from the event in perpetuity (paragraph four of figure 6.1). This is often a major point of contention and negotiation.

As an agent for athletes I can tell you that the very idea of granting such broad rights does not sit well. My instincts are always to minimize the rights we are granting so that we maintain control over the amount of exposure the client receives. When presented with this type of offer on behalf of Nancy Kerrigan, I have been very reluctant to agree unless it was for a competition. Whatever the final agreement on this topic, I always insist that the promoter of an event or show grant her the rights to each of her performances at no cost in case we want to produce a Nancy Kerrigan retrospective (television show, home video, or CD-ROM) at some point in the future.

■ ■ ■ ■ ■ ■ ■ ■ ■ ■ ■ ■

You should do everything possible to obtain the broadest media rights from the participants.

■ ■ ■ ■ ■ ■ ■ ■ ■ ■ ■ ■

For you, as the event organizer and producer, the need for these rights on a very broad basis is critical. With the constantly changing landscape in television, video, the Internet, and satellite distribution, the control over these rights in the long term is becoming increasingly important. The ownership of a library of recorded events and other programming can, in and of itself, create tremendous future value as networks (and Web sites) look to fill their airtime with high-quality content.

The big media companies, such as Disney and Time Warner, make significant revenue from their library of programs. StarGames, which was founded in 1995, has seen revenue streams develop from old programs that have been resold for regional cable telecasts or inclusion in home videos long after the original show aired. Therefore, as an event organizer you should do everything possible to obtain the broadest media rights from the participants.

In some cases media rights is not an issue because the athletes, by virtue of their agreeing to compete on a tour or in a league, grant these rights as a matter of their collective bargaining agreements or entry procedures (for example, the LPGA or ATP tour entry procedure covers all of this for you). This is yet another example of why you need to know the "industry standards" of the specific sport in which you are dealing.

The area of media rights has not really been of much interest at the local, regional, junior, or grassroots levels. Here too, however, I encourage you to get releases from the participants (or their parent or guardian in the case of minors) granting you the worldwide media rights in perpetuity as it relates to their participation in your event. If it is not too intimidating to the athletes, you might use one of my favorite clauses, which grants you the "rights to all media now known or that may later become known throughout the universe." Talk about covering all your bases!

It may seem silly to worry about procuring these rights for your local 10K, but you never know what direction the sports and entertainment worlds are going to take. Also, you may not think that having the rights to the guy who finished 407th are worth anything, but what if that person turns out to be Bill Gates, Hillary Clinton, or Michael Jordan! Any footage that you have just might be valuable someday, so don't overlook what might appear on the surface to be a worthless detail.

ATHLETE CONTRACT

Assuming that your initial invitation to participate in the event is accepted (or negotiated so that both parties are in agreement),

you should then move to either a memorandum of understanding (or a deal memo) or a full-blown contract. I recommend that you go straight to a contract if possible because this eliminates a step and reduces the chances for misunderstandings.

However, because contracts often require more extensive legal review and negotiation of all the important but more minor language, the memorandum route (which details the terms and conditions of the athlete's participation without most of the legalese) can be more expeditious. In fact, of late we have taken to turning the initial invitation letters (similar to the one in figure 6.1) into deal memos by having a signature line at the bottom. We then go to a more formal agreement after all of the participants are in place. By having the deal memo signed, we know there is something in writing in case a question crops up prior to the formal contract being written or signed.

Sometimes the formal contract never gets signed because of timing. This makes the memorandum or letter of intent that much more important. As an aside, during the deal making for one of my clients involving a potential made-for-television movie about his life, our Hollywood-based attorney advised me that it is standard practice in the television and movie industry for final contracts not to get signed so that there is some murkiness in case of a lawsuit!

I have included one of our standard participant contracts in appendix B. However, there are a few critical paragraphs from that agreement that I want to point out in detail at this juncture. These are discussed in the following sections.

Athlete Obligations

This is the paragraph in which everything that you will require from the participants in your event should be spelled out. In this clause you can stipulate everything, from time of arrival and departure to length of the activity, requirement to attend postevent parties and press conferences, and anything else that you might request of the athlete. A typical clause, taken from our One Enchanted Evening skating show but certainly applicable to any sporting event, might look like this:

Athlete Obligations. In connection with this Agreement, Athlete agrees to carry out the following obligations:

a) Athlete shall participate in the Event as described herein.

b) Athlete shall perform two (2) numbers specifically tailored to the romance theme in both costume and music. Said music is subject to approval by StarGames. Further, Athlete understands that the production of each number shall consist of multiple takes with different camera angles in order to achieve the desired look for the Event. In addition, Athlete shall participate in interviews and pose for photographs during taping if asked to do so for the Event and/or publicity purposes.

c) Athlete shall provide StarGames with still photographs that he/she may have that could be used in the broadcast as part of the theme of the Event.

d) Athlete agrees that at least one (1) of the numbers performed in the Event must not have been televised during the twelve (12) months immediately prior to the original broadcast of the Event and three (3) months after the original broadcast of the Event.

e) Athlete shall provide StarGames with the music for his/her performance by no later than fifteen (15) days prior to the taping of the Event. Athlete agrees that said music shall strictly conform to the romance theme of the Event. StarGames

agrees that it shall be responsible for obtaining the necessary music clearances, including the cost therefor.

f) Athlete shall arrive in Amherst, Massachusetts, in time for rehearsal by no later than 12:00 P.M. on December 14, 1998, and depart no earlier than the conclusion of taping, but in no event later than the evening of December 16, 1998.

g) Athlete shall be responsible for supplying his/her costumes with StarGames' approval, not to be unreasonably withheld. StarGames will supply all necessary makeup.

h) Athlete shall participate in one (1) "meet and greet" with network affiliates during the taping.

i) Athlete shall sign, subject to Athlete's (or Athlete's representative's) prior review and approval, a standard release form furnished by the broadcasting network.

As I said earlier, this paragraph is where you put in everything that you expect from the participants in your event, so be thorough.

Promoter Obligations

This paragraph will be the corollary to the previous clause in that it will stipulate your obligations as the event organizer. Again, from our One Enchanted Evening contract:

StarGames Obligations. In addition to the Fee set forth in Paragraph __ above, StarGames shall provide Athlete with one (1) coach-class round trip airfare to the Event, hotel accommodations, local transportation, and on-site meals. The expenses and accommodations provided for herein shall be no less favorable than those provided to any other Athlete in the Event.

In this case, our obligations were not too extensive, and the fees payable to the participant were dealt with in a separate clause. However, I can assure you that there will be instances in which an athlete may be a bit more demanding. If so, it is in this paragraph that you will formally commit to these details. Be prepared for anything. It is not beyond the pale for the stars to ask you to provide other items, such as specific insurance, certain food, private dressing rooms, transportation and accommodations for coaches and family members, and so on. To illustrate the point, for one of our shows, a participant submitted the following requests for her dressing room (we did *not* agree to this, although we tried to be accommodating where possible): 12 cans of Pepsi, 6 glasses, 12 fresh-cut roses daily, cinnamon and apple air freshener, precut fresh fruit, and 12 bottles of Evian water. Some superstars can be very picky!

Advertising and Promotion

Not to be overlooked in the negotiation of the rights that you will seek from the athlete is the fact that you will want to obtain the right to use the participant's name, likeness (meaning drawing or other reproduction), signature, and photo in the advertising and promotion of the event. This will, in all likelihood, be a key element of your marketing plan, so you must be very clear in outlining your needs. These rights should include use of the athlete's name and likeness in everything from television and radio advertising to print advertising and other graphic materials, such as posters, flyers, and ticket order forms. You will want the right to use photos without getting constant approval from the athlete or his representative, so you might require the ath-

You will want to obtain the right to use the participant's name, likeness, signature, and photo in the advertising and promotion of the event.

lete to provide preapproved photos. The paragraph that covers these rights might read as follows:

> *Use of Name and Likeness; Prohibition of Endorsement. Athlete agrees that throughout the Term his/her name and approved likeness may be used in connection with all advertising and promotion created, placed, or otherwise distributed by or on behalf of the Event. However, it is clearly understood that no such advertisement or promotion shall contain any direct or indirect endorsement or indication of use by Athlete of any product or service without Athlete's express written consent, which Athlete may withhold for any reason whatsoever.*

In thinking ahead to your sponsors and remembering that we want to encourage them to participate actively in the event wherever possible, you might want to be in a position to provide them with the use of an athlete's likeness for inclusion in any advertising and promotion that they might create for your event. The language in the preceding paragraph would require specific written consent from the athlete, which you might never get without paying additional fees. Therefore, you may want to use a different approach with regard to the "prohibition of endorsement" section of this clause.

If you look at it from the athletes' point of view, they are going to want to prohibit, or at least approve, any use of their likeness that might give the impression they are endorsing any particular company or product. The reason for this is that athletes can command high fees for this type of endorsement, and so they want to control the use of their image. This resulted in the advent of restrictive language, such as "... provided such use does not imply an endorsement of any product or service, which the athlete may withhold in his/her sole judgment for any reason."

In order to find a compromise on this topic, we have from time to time employed the concept of group rights. Instead of allowing any sponsor to use a single athlete in their advertising campaign, we specify that they must use at least three or four athletes from the event in a group shot. This stipulation makes it difficult to convey a message about a specific athlete, thus diluting the potential for the public to assume that a particular person is in any way linked with a specific product or service. In fact, most often the use of athletes in group rights situations ends up with the company using an action photo, which waters down the link between an athlete and product to what should be an acceptable level. In conveying these group rights, you will have to include a paragraph in both your athlete and sponsor agreement that protects the athlete. The athlete contract might read as follows:

Group Rights. Athlete agrees to grant to StarGames his/her exclusive marketing rights as part of a group of Players (four or more Players) for purposes of StarGames confirming sponsorship and licensing agreements for the Event, so long as the use of said rights does not constitute an individual endorsement of any product or service, nor conflict with a preexisting individual endorsement of which Athlete is a part. Athlete shall have the reasonable right of approval over the use of Athlete's photograph, likeness, and/or endorsement, but not the approval over the terms of

the sponsorship or licensing agreement itself. In this connection, Athlete acknowledges and agrees that StarGames shall have the right to solicit and confirm sponsors and licensees for the Event on a worldwide basis; however, nothing contained herein shall preclude Athlete from entering into individual endorsement agreements that may be in conflict with Event sponsors and licensees.

The company contract might read like this:

Group Rights. Company shall have the right to use the names, photographs, likenesses, or facsimiles thereof ("Endorsement") of the athletes in groups of four (4) or more in advertising, promotions, direct mail, television advertising, and/or in-store materials produced specifically to support Company's sponsorship of the Event itself. Notwithstanding the above, nothing contained herein shall grant the right to Company to use an Athlete Endorsement, individually and/or collectively, for purposes of endorsing any product, other event, service, and/or third party without the express written consent of the Athlete, which may be withheld for any reason.

When it comes to group rights, I should caution you that not every athlete will agree to even this less direct use of their name and likeness. However, there is a better chance of them granting these limited rights than there is of them granting the full right to their individual endorsement. Even though it may be a long shot, this is a right worth asking for from participants in your event; group rights will make sponsorship in your event more valuable. In turn, that will allow you to increase your sponsorship fees, which will make your event more financially viable.

Media Rights

Given the value of content rights in today's market, the language in this paragraph is of particular importance and can be tricky. It is also an area of the law that is constantly evolving, so there is a lot of potential for creating new language and new definitions. This can help you or hurt you depending on your level of knowledge, so try to cover all of the loopholes. But fight hard for these rights! The language that we like is as follows:

> *Exhibition of Show. Athlete expressly agrees that Event shall have the unlimited right and authority to utilize the coverage of the Event, and any and all pre- and post-Event interviews by Athlete, including the videotape and any and all forms of reproduction thereof in all media including, but not limited to, television, Internet, home video, and musical sound track, in perpetuity, in whatever manner and by whatever means now known or hereafter developed and wherever desired on a worldwide basis, provided that no such coverage shall constitute an endorsement for any product or service by Athlete. There shall be no obligation to pay any monies to Athlete for said coverage except as set forth in Paragraph ___ herein.*

The last sentence refers to the paragraph in the contract related to the athlete's fee to participate in the event.

I do not want to give you the mistaken impression that we get this language approved all the time. In fact, more often than not we have to dilute this paragraph a bit. In some cases we have had to negotiate additional fees for certain uses, such as a home video, in which we might agree to pay the talent a royalty based on some pro rata split of the royalties that we earn. However, even if you have to pay additional fees for these ancillary rights, try to negotiate them up front; only pay for them if you actually exploit them; and by all means, try to make sure that these elements are included in your agreement.

Indemnification

While this clause constitutes perhaps more "legalese" than you were bargaining for, the indemnity paragraph is one that I am always concerned about. This is where one party to the agreement is legally, financially, and otherwise protected by the other party or parties if they get sued because of something someone else does.

Does that sound confusing? A simple example should serve to clarify. Let's say one of the stars of your event, without your knowledge or permission, claims in a promotion on her Web site that a contest winner will win an all-expenses-paid trip to your event, front row seats, and dinner with the star. When it comes time to pay off, they can't deliver because you don't have the seats and the star decides not to go to dinner. As a result, the contest winner decides to sue the athlete and you. Since you did not authorize or approve the deal, the indemnity clause would dictate that if you lose the suit, the athlete pays. And, win or lose, they cover your legal fees.

You hope that this paragraph never gets used, but it is of great importance in my mind because you cannot control the actions of

> ■ ■ ■ ■ ■ ■ ■ ■ ■ ■ ■ ■
>
> *You cannot control the actions of others and don't want to be held liable for their negligence.*
>
> ■ ■ ■ ■ ■ ■ ■ ■ ■ ■ ■ ■

others and don't want to be held liable for their negligence.

Negligence, and degrees thereof, becomes the important issue here. Negligence is defined as the failure to exercise such care as would normally be expected of a reasonable person. Gross negligence results from a person acting with a certain amount of recklessness or willfulness. You will want the broadest definition possible, and the athlete (or any other party, for that matter, because there should be an indemnity clause in *all* of your contracts) will want the most narrow definition possible (negligence versus gross negligence). You will no doubt come to an agreement on the language, but I urge you to make sure that, at a minimum, the indemnification is equally onerous for everyone.

Warranty

Once you become familiar with these agreements, you may take this clause for granted. That is OK as long as you simply make sure it is included. This paragraph requires everyone who is signing the agreement to confirm that they actually have the right to enter into it and do not have any prior conflicts. Again, this paragraph only comes into play if there is a real problem down the road in which you need protection. For example, let's suppose you get sued by another promoter who claims that a particular athlete was supposed to participate in his event and thus couldn't be in yours as well. The warranty clause would be what you would point to in your defense.

This paragraph, in combination with others in the agreement, is important because it validates the enforceability of the contract. This clause can come into play in countless ways. However, because most people are pretty careful, it is rarely invoked. One simple example from One Enchanted Evening illustrates how easy it would be for this paragraph to become applicable. Let's say a skater agreed to be in our show with the perfor-

■ ■ ■ ■ ■ ■ ■ ■ ■ ■ ■

Have an attorney review all of your agreements.

■ ■ ■ ■ ■ ■ ■ ■ ■ ■ ■

mance restrictions that we required (music and choreography that had not been used before) only to realize later that they had already agreed to skate to the same music two days later for another television show. When we go to stop them from using the same music in the latter show, this clause would be quite helpful and important. Perhaps a more direct example would be one in which the athlete claimed that the person signing the agreement on his behalf (often athletes have their agents sign for them; this is called "power of attorney") did not have the authority to bind him to the deal. This would be the paragraph on which your case for damages would be built.

Release

It may seem that the clauses we have reviewed only relate to major stars at major events, but the fact is that promoters of events at every level need protection. For a grassroots event a simple release can cover many of these issues in much abbreviated language. A release of this nature might take a sentence or two out of each of the key paragraphs discussed previously. Even in an abbreviated state, this type of protection, both for you and the athletes, is of utmost importance (see working model, next page).

Even though you get used to the language after being involved with these contracts for 20 years, you still should have an attorney review all of your agreements.

✔ Checklist for Creating a Player-Friendly Event

In case I haven't gotten the message across, I can't stress enough the need for you to become known as a player-friendly event promoter. Treat your participants well and it will come back to help you out many times over. The athletes talk to each other as well as to sponsors and members of the press. The word of mouth from the athletes will be your best advertisement (or worst!). Therefore in order to attract the best athletes to your event, follow these guidelines:

✔ Design your event with the athletes in mind.

✔ Know the rules and the entry procedures for your sport.

✔ If you are running an event for professionals, find out if the athletes have agents.

✔ Communicate well the fact that your event is happening so that prospective participants are aware of its existence (particularly at the grassroots level at which the information flow is not as well organized).

✔ Send out a letter of invitation that spells out what you are asking from the athletes.

✔ Obtain the broadest possible media and promotional rights.

✔ Write a contract (or simple release) that covers all of the business and legal points between you and the athlete.

✔ Have your attorney review the player contracts.

✔ Create an atmosphere that is fun and relaxed yet caters to the competitive needs of the participants.

✔ Keep in touch with the athletes after the event.

Always remember that your event is competing for talent and that athletes can receive benefits similar to those you are offering at other events. Whether yours is a local grassroots event or a major professional event, the athletes will always have a chance to compete somewhere else.

If you focus on some of the elements discussed in this chapter, you will establish a fair and respectful working relationship with the athletes, both personally and through your contract, at the same time as you create an environment in which they like to participate. Remember, there is no event without the athletes.

Working Model: Tournament Release Form

In order to compete in the Regional Junior Tennis Tournament, players will have to enter by a certain date, confirm their birth date, agree to play on certain days, and agree to play a prescribed number of matches. In addition, we will want them, through their parent or guardian, to give us certain general releases as described throughout this chapter. The release portion of the entry form might read like this:

As a condition of entering the Regional Junior Tennis Tournament ("Event"), which shall take place August 10-14 at the Tennis Club of Anytown, USA, I, _____, hereby agree to release and hold harmless Tennis Tournament, Inc., the Tennis Club of Anytown, XYZ television network, the sponsors, vendors, and licensees of the Event, their officers, employees, agents, and assigns from any injury, death, or other claim sustained during the Event unless such injury, death, or other claim is as a result of their gross negligence.

I realize that by participating in the Event I may sustain injury due to the physical nature of the event. I warrant that I am in good physical shape and capable of performing at the level required by the Event.

I agree to abide by all the rules, regulations, and instructions set forth by the Event Management and that failure to do so may result in my being disqualified from the Event.

Further, I agree to grant to the Event the use of any television clips, interviews, highlight video, or other photos taken of me during the Event for use in any and all media now known or hereafter developed in perpetuity for which I will receive no compensation.

I have read the above and understand all of the elements contained herein and agree to abide by the contents of this entry form.

_____

Player (or legal guardian if under 18)

Working Model: Tournament Player Amenities

In an effort to make this event a good experience for everyone during its first year, it is important to go the extra mile in providing a nice environment for the players, parents, and coaches. Because we would like to see this event become a mainstay on the regional junior circuit, it will be important to get some word of mouth in the area about what a great event it was for the kids. With this in mind and keeping within the budget of $750 for entertainment (postevent parties), we might plan to have the following events:

• **Draw party on the night before the start of the tournament.** All of the players and their parents, plus the local newspapers and television stations, will be invited. Finger food will be served to the adults, along with beer, soft drinks, and coffee. Pizza will be served to the kids, along with milk and soft drinks. The draw for the event would be announced.

• **Quarterfinals party in the tent on site.** This will be a late-afternoon fun event for the kids. All of the participants and their coaches will be invited. Dessert-type food and maybe a cake celebrating the first year of the tournament will be served.

• **Postevent party.** Immediately after the event we will give a dinner at a local restaurant at which we make a trade deal. All of the participants will be invited, along with their parents, coaches, volunteers, officials, and sponsors. We will serve a limited menu of hamburgers, chicken, and salads. A lot of people will have already left town, but for those who hang around, this will be a great way of ending the event on a high note.

• **Tournament T-shirt and hat.** All participants will receive a T-shirt and hat commemorating the event.

Chapter SEVEN

Your Television Options

The history of sports was changed dramatically by the invention of the television. However, even the inventors of that little box could not have foreseen the growth in television and related delivery systems that has taken place over the last half century. In fact, television has created an explosion in sports that would have been laughed at as an impossibility when NBC delivered its first national baseball telecast in 1951.

I suspect that sports will continue to be altered significantly by the advent of the Internet, streaming video, and the new networks and distribution outlets that become available through still more new technology.

Amazingly, it was approximately 25 short years ago that we had three networks (plus PBS, which had Monday night tennis before Monday Night Football!) and a handful of independent local stations that could distribute programming. This limited amount of airtime made the creation of new events and leagues very difficult since so many of them only exist because of the television component that drives sponsorship and advertising dollars.

Today there are a myriad of options for transmitting television shows. This has resulted in a proliferation of sports events. The key questions then are, What does it all mean for you, the event manager and entrepreneur?

And, How do you take advantage of the opportunities that now exist?

At its most simplistic, the growth in television means that what once was not even thinkable is today at least a possibility. It seems that there is a television outlet somewhere for virtually every event, and as networks become even more niche oriented (for example, I have recently joined the board of TFN, The Football Network), the options will only grow. That does not necessarily mean that the economics of television will make sense for your event. Some events don't warrant or need television coverage, and some make for bad television. However, if you have an event you think will benefit from TV coverage, you should be able to find a distribution outlet that will, in theory, enhance your ability to sell sponsorships, create promotional partners, and so forth, all of which may allow you to bring your project to life.

If you are new to the world of television, it can be very intimidating and difficult to navigate. In order to help you out in this area, this chapter is designed to provide an overview of the television options. We will also briefly discuss some of the related media systems, such as home video, satellite distribution, pay-per-view, and the Internet. Following that discussion we will get into some specific deal points that will govern your relationships with the networks. With that said, I want to stress that this is an *overview*. If you want an in-depth study, I urge you to take a close look at the many books written about the complex world of television.

BROADCAST NETWORKS

Since broadcast television is the modern mother of all of today's mass distribution systems, it makes sense to start our discussion there. At the moment, there are seven broadcast or "over-the-air" networks: ABC, CBS, FOX, NBC, UPN, the WB, and PAX (some may include Univision in this group as well). Each network is made up of a group of affiliated stations throughout the country, some of which the parent corporation of the network owns (the "O & Os"—owned and operated). The more affiliates a network has, the more penetration throughout the country it can generate, thus giving a program on that network the best chance to reach the maximum number of homes with television sets. In fact, the more stations a network owns, the more coverage it can guarantee for a program (and the ownership laws and the ownership itself are changing very rapidly). All of that is important for providing a vehicle for a large audience. Audience size is tied to a program's "rating" and "share," which is tied to advertising, which is tied to network and affiliate profit. In short, this is a vicious circle.

Ratings and share are what interest the networks because these results drive the advertising rates. Sometimes you might even get the feeling that all anyone at the network cares about is ratings, even at the risk of bad programming. To some extent that might be true since the ratings and share are what determine advertising rates for the sale of commercial time, which is primarily where the networks make their money. I say *primarily* because, as we will discuss later, there is something called a "buy-on," in which event owners and other program suppliers pay the network to air their show. A buy-on can be an expensive way to get television coverage for your event, though. Unfortunately, for promoters of newer or marginal events, the

networks increasingly impose this option. But more on that later.

Ratings

Your event's attraction to television is going to depend primarily on its perceived ability to generate ratings and deliver a specific audience. An NFL game generally delivers a big rating with a large male audience. Figure skating reaches a large female audience. A local 10K does neither. The most common measuring standard for ratings and share are provided by the A.E. Nielson company, which has set up a system by which they follow the viewing habits of about 1,200 randomly chosen households (which change periodically to ensure consistently new input) around the country. Considering that there are about 95 million "television homes" (homes with television sets) in the United States, it is amazing what power this relatively small number of people has, as their viewing preferences influence which shows get on the air, how much advertisers pay for commercial time, what time of day certain programs will be seen, and so on.

The Nielson system measures a variety of demographic and other information as well, but the two measurements that you hear the most about are rating and share. The rating of a show is the percentage of households watching a particular program against the total number of television households in the country. The share is the percentage of households watching a show compared to the total number of households that are watching television at a given moment in time.

When Nancy Kerrigan and Friends aired on CBS in early February of 1994, it received a 10 rating and a 17 share. We thought, Not bad! Later that month the 1994 Winter Olympic figure skating competition, also on CBS, earned a 44 rating and a 62 share! In layman's terms, this means that 44 percent of all television households were watching the Olympics. It also means that an astounding 62 percent of those actually watching television were watching the Games.

The 1994 Winter Olympics were a historic moment for sports television and a boon for

CBS, as the telecast of ladies' figure skating became the third-highest-watched sporting event of all time and one that *Time* Magazine called one of the top 10 moments in the history of sports television. (As an aside, when Nancy says to me that she is sometimes surprised at how often people recognize her, I remind her that about half the people in the entire country watched her perform under intense pressure at the 1994 Olympics, many of whom will never forget that moment.)

A Saturday or Sunday afternoon sports telecast might normally earn about a 3 rating and a 7 share. The NBA Finals, in prime time, might earn a 14 rating and a 22 share. By way of contrast, in today's marketplace a top-rated prime-time show on a major network might regularly draw about a 15 rating and a 28 share. Thus, sports do not typically deliver the same size audience as do general interest programming such as *Friends, ER,* or *60 Minutes.*

With everything being driven by ratings, you can imagine that the decision-making process over what events are worth airing is quite an interesting one. Essentially, despite lots of research by the networks, it all boils down to individual taste and guesswork because no one can ever be absolutely sure that a particular event with certain athletes will deliver a rating.

As I write this book, there has been a movement toward breaking down the Nielson numbers in greater detail so that networks and advertisers know more about the audience. In today's marketplace most networks and advertisers care primarily about the 18- to 49-year-old audience. If you are 50 or older and watching a show, it just doesn't have the same impact because advertisers covet the younger audience that they think controls so much spending (as I get older, I tend to take issue with this thinking, by the way!). If a show wins the time period (meaning it had the highest rating and share) but loses that time period in the 18-to-49 demographic, it often is not valued as highly as is a show that finishes second in the aggregate but wins the time slot in the desired target range.

From a sports point of view, this has meant a strong interest in "extreme sports," which tend to draw from that younger audience. Events such as the X Games on ESPN and now the Gravity Games on NBC get far more attention from network programmers than do events, such as ballroom dancing, that have a much longer history and potentially greater following but draw from an older audience. Again, I am not sure that I agree with this approach (people over 50 control an awful lot of money!), but it is the one being taken by most of the networks at the moment and something you should figure into your thinking when trying to position your property to sell it to a network.

Cable

Turning from the broadcast networks, which are always reaching for the broadest audience possible, the cable networks, such as ESPN, USA, TNN, TNT, ESPN2, FOX Sports Net, and the rest, have moved to fill the gaping hole in the sports television marketplace by televising events that the broadcast networks have overlooked or find financially unattractive. The advent of all of these cable networks has allowed many events, both new and old, to receive television coverage. In fact, if you have noticed, the majority of our events have aired on cable networks, which is fine for us because most of our events attract a niche audience that has become loyal to networks such as ESPN (which is in about 72 million homes by comparison to the broadcast networks' 95 million) and FOX Sports Net (which, through its affiliates, is in about 65 million homes).

Unless you are operating a reasonably major event or are prepared to ante up a large sum of money to buy your way onto a broadcast network, the likelihood is that your event, if it is going to get TV coverage at all, will air on cable television. Lately it seems as though a new cable outlet for sports is announced at least monthly. Some of these provide regional coverage, and some are for niche sports, such as horse racing. There is even a movement to start TFN, The Football Network. The point is that because of ever-evolving technology and the fierce competition among the media giants, such as Disney, Time Warner, and FOX, networks are proliferating. All of this can work to your advantage.

Some promoters shy away from cable networks saying that they don't deliver a large enough audience, but such attitudes should not dissuade you from considering cable. People watch programs, not networks. When we chose to air Skating Goes Country on TNN (because it was geared to the country music audience), some may have argued that we were limiting our audience by not going with a larger network. However, it is generally accepted that once a cable outlet is available in 50 million or more homes (and TNN is available in about 70 million), it has broad enough distribution to be considered a national network. While many people don't watch TNN on a regular basis, if the network is airing a show that interests them, they will find it and watch it. To make the point, if TNN carried the Super Bowl, virtually the same 40 to 50 million homes that watch it on FOX or NBC would be tuned in to TNN on Super Bowl Sunday.

> ■ ■ ■ ■ ■ ■ ■ ■ ■ ■ ■ ■
>
> ***T**he audience will find your show if they know about it.*
>
> ■ ■ ■ ■ ■ ■ ■ ■ ■ ■ ■ ■

The audience will find your show if they know about it, so you have to make sure that your television partner promotes it heavily in places other than within its own programming; and you have to support this with additional advertising if you want to get a solid rating.

The ratings for Skating Goes Country supported my theory, as the average rating on TNN during the week or so that the show aired was about a 0.7. A Holiday Celebration on Ice (which is what the show was called for television) garnered a 1.6 rating in its initial airing, more than doubling TNN's typical rating. The network was very pleased with this result and ended up running the show another seven times during the 1999 holiday season!

This leads me to one other point about the value of sports programming and why there might be a television outlet for your event.

Network Audience

Sports coalesce an audience better than most programming. What I mean by this is that if a network wants to reach a broad audience (which is what they are set up to do), certain sports programming—the Super Bowl, World Series, and so on—virtually guarantees this for them. That is why you see such huge rights fees paid to the NFL, Major League Baseball, and the NBA. It is also why some of the other major sports events (Wimbledon, the U.S. Open in golf, etc.) command big fees. Sports event programming can deliver the large audiences the networks need to satisfy their affiliates and advertisers and to promote their own shows. If a network promotes one of its prime-time entertainment shows during the Super Bowl, they are bound to see a bump in the ratings for that show. If you can create the right event, and this does *not* necessarily mean a mega-event like the Super Bowl, you too can be an audience builder for the network, whether over the air or cable.

TNN did not buy Skating Goes Country from us because they like skating necessarily. They chose to put a skating show on their network because they were trying to expand their audience and reach people who don't otherwise watch TNN. They hoped that by airing the skating show during the Christmas holiday period (when a lot of people watch television), they might attract a bigger and more diverse audience than normal. That would enable them to expose new people to TNN, promote a couple of their upcoming shows, and entice people to return at a later date either casually while channel surfing or to watch a show promoted during our show. TNN hoped to build its audience, which would ultimately lead to higher ratings and more revenue for the network. I believe that sports programming can help virtually any network in this same manner.

This line of thinking may open up outlets for your event that you would not have thought would even be candidates for sports programming (who would have thought that the Romance Classics Network would air sports!). So, think of your event as a tool for the network as much as television is a tool for you.

Regional Sports Networks

One other type of network exists specifically for sports programming. This is the "regional sports network." FOX Sports Net (FSN) is made up of 24 regional networks set up originally to air local sports programming. Each of these regional networks was initially created to stand independently and focus their programming on the local sports scene, be it professional teams, college teams, or other local/regional sports programming of interest. FOX has since come along and tied these local programming distributors together with a combination of local, regional, and national programming. By doing so, FOX has created a new delivery system for their national sports programming, and more important, given the regional networks a platform from which they can sell more advertising for increased dollars.

In addition to FSN (where our Telly Award–winning show Spike aired), there are other local cable outlets that carry additional local sports programming (FOX Sports New England in Boston carries our Sports Instruction: Learn From the Pros, for example). These regional sports networks—which really act similarly to local over-the-air television stations—provide great outlets for smaller, grassroots, and local events. The junior tennis tournament being developed in the working model of this book would be geared toward a regional sports network, for example.

For the promoter with a smaller event, the regional networks provide a perfect outlet. Airing your show on a regional network may not generate huge advertising and sponsor-

■ ■ ■ ■ ■ ■ ■ ■ ■ ■ ■ ■

*T*hink of your event as a tool for the network as much as television is a tool for you.

■ ■ ■ ■ ■ ■ ■ ■ ■ ■ ■ ■

ship dollars for you, but it can give you credibility and visibility while not costing you much.

When you add the regional outlets to the cable outlets and the broadcast networks, there are a myriad of potential television distributors for sports events. And this does not include the options offered through syndication, satellite, and pay-per-view coverage, which I will review briefly next.

Syndication

This is where you, in effect, create your own network. Remember, each local station that is affiliated with a broadcast network also is its own independent business, and while that station may take the bulk of its programming from the network, they have the right to program themselves during certain time slots each day. This gives flexibility to virtually every television station throughout the country. As a result, you can, in theory, take your show and shop it to each station in each television market to create a scenario in which your show airs in every market without going through a network. You might be on the CBS affiliate in Boston, the ABC affiliate in Washington, D.C., the UPN station in Chicago, and the FOX carrier in Los Angeles.

This is a hard way to go in most cases because if you are representing only one event that will air for two hours, you don't have much leverage; and to go to each of the stations around the country will require a huge effort. There are "syndicators" who specialize in this type of sell, and they can help you a lot. However, even if they are successful in selling—or clearing—your show into enough stations, you will also have the issue of when the show airs in each market.

One of the nice things about the networks (broadcast or cable) is that in most cases they are going to provide you with clearance to at least half the country and air your show in a uniform time slot. If your event airs at 5 P.M. EST on Saturday afternoon, it will air at that same time (with adjustments for the various time zones) throughout the country. This enables you and the network to promote the telecast at a certain time on a particular date.

In syndication, you will have to give each station a window during which they can air the show. If you hold your live event on a Saturday in June and you have the television show edited and ready to air by July 1, in syndication you might have to give each station a window from July 1 to July 10 during which they can air your show. In other words, the show may air on July 1 in Chicago at noon, July 2 in Los Angeles at 3 P.M., July 3 in New York at 10 P.M., and so on. This makes it a lot more difficult and expensive to advertise the time slot for your telecast. It also affects those all-important ratings, as it is simply more difficult for the audience to know when to look for your event. I recommend that you stay away from syndication unless you have a strong event and a powerful syndicator working on your behalf.

Satellite

One of the most aggressive and growing areas of television distribution is satellite delivery systems. As far as I can recall, satellite television began to invade the home about 15 years ago when big satellite dishes were made available to consumers. They were expensive, complicated, and took up a lot of space, but they were able to receive television transmissions from all over the country. You could sit in Washington, D.C., and watch the evening news from San Diego! That made the whole

When you add the regional outlets to the cable outlets and the broadcast networks, there are a myriad of potential television distributors for sports events.

idea of satellite broadcasting pretty compelling. When the technology improved to allow 18-inch receivers that cost under $250, direct broadcast satellite television transmission began to take off. While it is not yet seriously threatening cable and broadcast networks, the impact of satellite distribution has been felt, as about 7 million homes are currently able to receive this type of transmission.

In a world where the "500 channel universe" has been the mantra for several years, satellite distribution makes this a real possibility, providing endless options for broadcasters and viewers.

At the moment, satellite distribution does not offer individual event promoters too many opportunities. DirecTV and its competitors are becoming more of a factor, and sometime in the next decade we should see a real impact from this system.

Pay-Per-View

Interestingly, pay-per-view, with its Muhammad Ali closed circuit telecasts, was the first of the major broadcast alternatives. For all practical purposes, it has not really become a viable option for most events. While there are some successful pay-per-view boxing matches, wrestling spectaculars, and an occasional concert, unless the event is potentially a huge attraction, pay-per-view in its current format will not be much of an option for you. Certainly no grassroots event need even consider going this route. Only if you have something that is truly out of the ordinary should you spend any time exploring this option.

While the discussion about pay-per-view broadcasts of the Super Bowl and World Series continues (and I don't foresee this anytime soon), I don't expect that you will see many events on pay-per-view unless they are potential blockbusters. The only serious offer or discussion that I have ever been involved with was for a pay-per-view skate-off between Nancy Kerrigan and Tonya Harding. While the money offered was huge, Nancy never seriously considered it as a viable option.

A few other attempts at pay-per-view events have cropped up from time to time (a one-on-one basketball game involving Hakeem Olajuwon and a home run hitting contest come to mind); however, the ones that come to fruition—other than boxing and wrestling—are really few and far between.

The earnings potential offered by pay-per-view can be very tempting, but unless you think you have a huge event, it just won't be an option for you.

Now that we have discussed the many options television has to offer, keep in mind that it is not the only available delivery system. Home video, CD-ROM, and the Internet are markets that, under the right conditions, can provide great alternative distribution for you. A brief look at these markets follows.

Home Video

This market has been proclaimed "dead" several times. First, cable television was going to be the cause of its demise, then satellite distribution, DVD, digital delivery, and now the Internet. Through it all, home video endures.

For event promoters, home video does not present much of an option unless you have a major event or have built up a history so that a historical retrospective of your event might make sense. This is yet another reason to make sure that you have secured all of the media rights in perpetuity from the athletes, sponsors, television networks, venues, and any other entity that might think it has a claim to these rights.

Home video should not be at the top of your thought process as you create your event. However, as things unfold and you have some creative options, you can always consider this an ancillary distribution system for your property.

CD-ROM

I don't see CD-ROM much differently from home video, except that it is possibly an even tougher medium to crack. Frankly, the only place where we are starting to see some application for CD-ROM is in the exploitation of the sound tracks to our events and television shows.

As music, sports, and entertainment converge, we have seen a significant rise in the marketability of sound tracks with sports-related music. Through StarGames Music we have tried to create music tracks that are specific to our events in anticipation of eventually either releasing a sound track or simply earning royalties from the playing of music that we own (this also helps in the music rights area, which we will discuss shortly). This ties into the CD-ROM option through the developing market for "enhanced CDs," which can be played on your computer. This format allows you to hear the music and watch the broadcast footage created in conjunction with that music at the same time. As I write this book, we are in the process of negotiating a deal for such an album based on figure skating and some of the music and footage from One Enchanted Evening and Halloween on Ice.

Again, while I see this as an exciting new opportunity, it is not something to spend a lot of time on since the odds of creating something in this genre are slim and the financial return at this stage of development is not worth the effort.

The Internet

Last but certainly not least is the Internet. I suspect that if I were writing this book 15 years from now, I might be devoting as much space to the Internet as I am now to television.

There is no telling where the Internet will go and in what manner it will develop as a factor for your event. What we do know is that currently, no matter how big or small your event is, there is an opportunity to promote your event in advance either on your own site or through the various sports-related sites, such as CBS SportsLine, SportsInstruction.com, and so forth. Some of this promotion can take the form of simply making information available to Internet surfers through advertising, press releases, and so forth. However, it can also include chat sessions, e-commerce, contests, and the like.

During your event itself you can provide live reporting with the results, scores, and live updates over the Internet. When America Online first became a factor, we worked with them at both the King of the Beach Invitational and Halloween on Ice.

At the King of the Beach we "broadcast" (now known as a webcast) in real time from the event as play was going on. During Halloween on Ice we had a chat session going on from the arena with all of the participants, each of whom went online to answer questions between their performances during the show. We did not make much money on either of these efforts, so I could say that it may not have been worth it. However, in an attempt to be on the cutting edge of our industry, we felt that it was worthwhile. If you have the time and the staff, you may want to explore involving the Internet in some way with your event. (This does not include the fact that many Internet companies are prospective sponsors. Your audience may match up well with their target market, and as we have seen, the marketing plans for these businesses are more and more becoming very traditional in their approach.)

I suspect that when broadband matures, we will see an all-sports Internet site emerge, which, much the same as ESPN was 20 years ago, will carry sports event Webcasts over the Internet 24 hours a day. We will also see niche sites that webcast specific sports. In this respect, I think that we are entering one of the most exciting times in the history of sports and entertainment. However, to take advantage of these new developments (and seemingly there is a new "major" development daily) requires keeping close tabs on the industry and a recognition that at this stage there is not much money to be made with some of these new systems.

With all of these different options, the lure of television or other media distribution outlets can be mesmerizing. Being able to tell your friends, competitors, potential sponsors, or business partners to watch your show at such and such a time can be good for business and equally good for your self-esteem.

However, knowing *about* television is one thing. Making a deal that makes sense for your event is quite another. Let's take a look at what goes into "cutting the deal."

GETTING ON THE AIR

It has been said that everyone has one book in them (I hope this isn't my only one). If they don't have a book, they think they have multiple television shows! You will be competing with everyone who ever dreamed of writing or producing a show, whether it is sports related or not.

With all of the options we have just discussed, it would seem that there should not be a problem finding an hour or two to air your event. Not so. Television scheduling is a nightmare. With the already scheduled regular programming, previous commitments to specials and other programs, plus the fact that sports generally are slotted into specific day parts (and as we briefly discussed earlier, don't usually deliver the same ratings as entertainment-oriented shows), the windows of opportunity become very well defined and quite narrow, particularly for a newly created or grassroots event with no track record. While this has all become a bit easier with the proliferation of cable sports networks, both regional and national, getting your show on television still is not an easy task.

The Proposal

To begin to find a television home for your event, you will first have to create a proposal from which to sell your show. This should include some very specific points, which are illustrated in the outline we used for Skating Goes Country (figure 7.1).

Similar to your sponsorship proposal, this letter will be the basis for your television discussions. Also similar to your sponsorship

Skating Goes Country Television Proposal

"Skating Goes Country" is a new entertainment spectacular timed for the Christmas season and designed to take advantage of the popularity of two of America's favorite genres of entertainment, country music and figure skating, both of which have seen tremendous growth in their crossover appeal in the past five years.

1. Theme: The theme of the show will center on the Christmas holiday. Each skater will be asked to perform at least one number to a Christmas song by a major country artist. They will also perform a second number to select country music. In addition, a minimum of four country music artists will be asked to perform two songs, one of which will be a Christmas or holiday song. The other can be one of their recognized hits. We will set up a stage adjacent to the ice surface to feature these live performances in a concert setting.

2. Talent: It is anticipated that the show will include some of the top names in professional figure skating and country music. While no invitations have yet been extended, some of the targeted skaters include Nancy Kerrigan, Rudy Galindo, Philippe Candeloro, and Brasseur and Eisler. Musical artists will be of the same or similar caliber.

3. Location: The show will be taped in front of a live audience at the Nashville Arena on November 23, 1999. Delivery of the show will allow for an air date of mid-December. StarGames reserves the right to hold the event in a different venue if we are unable to make a satisfactory rental arrangement at the Nashville Arena.

4. Live show: It is anticipated that the live show will be of approximately 2 1/2 hours in duration including a 15-minute intermission. The live show can be edited to a one- or two-hour television show, which will include skating and musical performances, as well as select interviews.

5. StarGames obligations: StarGames will be responsible for all aspects of the show, including securing talent, pre-event promotion, ticket sales, event operations, etc. StarGames will be the promoter/owner of the show and the ultimate risk taker. StarGames will also oversee the television production on behalf of ____ and give the show a ____ look in terms of graphics, credits, etc. ____ shall supply its production guidelines well in advance of the live show. Further, we would like ____ to make its editing facility and television equipment (i.e., trucks, cameras) available to us at favorable rates.

6. Financial: We would be looking for a rights fee of $_____ for a fully delivered show (this does not include music clearances, which will be an incremental cost to you). We would request that payment be made in three equal installments, with the first on signing of an agreement, the second 30 days prior to the show, and the balance upon delivery of the final, approved version of the show. Finally, we would ask that ____ agree to actively promote the show on air and through other customary means available to ____ at no cost to StarGames. For this fee, ____ would own the right to five airings of the show in the United States over a three-year period, after which all rights would revert to StarGames. ____ shall also have input into creative elements of the show and the producer/director. All other rights to the show, including, but not limited to, home video, music sound track, international sales, etc., would remain the property of StarGames. However, we are prepared to split these ancillary revenue streams with you on a basis to be determined.

7. Sponsorship: ____ shall agree to meet with StarGames to explore the options available for sponsorship sales with an objective to provide StarGames with a vehicle through which it can sell a title sponsor for the live event and telecast.

We are confident that, similar to some of our other figure skating productions, we can produce a first class and unique show that will drive viewership for the network.

Figure 7.1 Television proposal for Skating Goes Country.

proposal, there are a few things that you need to take note of. These are discussed in the following sections.

Talent

Talent is a tricky area and one that really smacks of "which came first, the chicken or the egg?" In other words, when sending this proposal, you have to be careful with the names that you use because unless you have actually contracted with some of your talent, you really don't have the right to use their names without all kinds of caveats, like "such as," "invited," and so forth. In the previous example, we noted that no one had been contracted yet because the discussions with the network took place *before* any conversations with the talent. With that in mind, the reality is that it is hard to get a television commitment if the network does not have some idea of who is going to participate in your event. At the same time, it might be difficult to contract with any of the talent until you know that you have either television or a sponsor. In some instances, this is a "Catch-22" situation. So, just be careful and keep everyone informed as to what you are doing. In all likelihood, you will have conversations ongoing simultaneously with television and talent so that if a particular athlete says she is absolutely not going to be available for your event, you will know not to use her name. Remember too that if you sell your event based on a certain expectation level with regard to the talent, you had better be able to deliver.

As we discussed earlier, one way to deal with the talent issue is to make a marketable athlete your partner in the event. The bottom line is that if you have a deal with one of the "name" athletes to build an event around him or her, then you can confidently tell the network executives that the event will certainly include that person. This will give them some level of comfort right from the start.

■ ■ ■ ■ ■ ■ ■ ■ ■ ■ ■

One way to deal with the talent issue is to make a marketable athlete your partner in the event.

■ ■ ■ ■ ■ ■ ■ ■ ■ ■ ■

Theme

Along with the talent, the theme is what is going to drive the network's interest in your project. Some networks will not even consider exhibition events, such as Skating Goes Country or Halloween on Ice. They will only air serious competition. Others will have certain formats that have to be conformed with. For example, despite many discussions with VH-1, we have never been able to come up with a show concept that suited their requirement for projects that are based on music (you would think that all skating would fit this criterion, but there are other issues as well). They have very specific ideas as to what fits their formula. I urge you to define the theme of your event or show with care (your one-sentence mission statement might suffice), as this will form a picture in the mind of the network programmers that will determine whether they will be interested in your property.

Sponsorship

Because the Skating Goes Country deal was being proposed as one in which we were paid a rights fee (the network essentially buys the show from us for a negotiated fee), the network was going to retain control of all of the commercial time. As a result, we would not have any commercial time to sell, which would make the procurement of a title sponsor (which we needed to make the economics work) that much more difficult. We wanted to be in a position in which the title sponsor could buy the rights to the event as well as their commercial time through us in a "one-stop shopping" scenario. In order to do so, we were going to need the network's cooperation, so we built this into the proposal up front.

Limitation on Airings

In some respects, this is one of the most important elements of the deal. On the surface, you might think, "Let them air the show as often as they want to." However, in keeping with the seating capacity issue discussed earlier, here too sometimes less is more. In other words, if you have a big event that you have sold based on its exclusive nature, overexposure can dilute its value. By restricting the number of airings (or "plays"), the event potentially takes on a more special quality, which will increase its opportunity to get future (and better) television contracts. On the other hand, if you are running a smaller event (a local charity golf tournament, for example), you might be better served to have as many replays as possible to generate awareness for the future. (We will take exactly this approach in a new golf tournament that we are creating—the Nancy Kerrigan Pro-Celebrity Classic—which will air multiple times on FOX Sports New England.) As with virtually everything else we have covered, there are no hard and fast rules when it comes to the number of airings.

As we have discussed previously, one of the overriding goals throughout your event should be to retain the ownership of all of your media and other rights for future use. Therefore, if possible, you should try to make sure that at some point the right for the network to air your show comes to an end and that all of the rights to the event revert to your control. In this manner you control the exposure of the show, get back the rights in case there is ever a market to re-air the event, and control the use of footage from the event in other programming (e.g., anthology shows) unless you also control those other shows. (For example, we were able to use King of the Beach and Best of the Beach footage in Spike, our beach volleyball magazine show. If someone else wanted to use a clip from the King of the Beach, they would have to pay us a rights fee.) Retaining ownership is not always possible. It depends on the structure of your network deal. However, again, it is something to strive for.

Location

Note that in the Skating Goes Country television proposal I reserved the right to change the location of the event if we were unable to make a satisfactory deal with the venue. This is something that you always want to provide for because as we saw in chapter 3, the deals you make with your venue can vary greatly.

■ ■ ■ ■ ■ ■ ■ ■ ■ ■ ■ ■

You will want to get as much money up front and as far in advance as possible to help your cash flow and pay for preproduction costs.

■ ■ ■ ■ ■ ■ ■ ■ ■ ■ ■ ■

You don't want to have your leverage in that negotiation taken away by your network deal (or any other deal for that matter). In most cases this will not be a big issue unless you have a venue that is of particular significance and thus critical to the network. If that is the case you will be equally committed to making a deal with the specific venue that provides the benefits in question.

Payment Schedule

This is one of those issues that you and the network will approach from diametrically opposed positions. They will want to pay you after the show is finished and delivered. You will want to get as much money up front and as far in advance as possible to help your cash flow and pay for preproduction costs such as equipment rental. I don't expect that this will become a major issue between you, but it is something worth covering right up front so that the network understands your expectations.

Promotion

As discussed in more detail later, the network can deliver quite a bit of promotional support for your show, so I suggest that you get this discussion on the table right from the start.

The Pitch

Having written a television proposal for your event (figure 7.1), you need to send it out to various programming people for their consideration for broadcast. If you are new to the business, you probably won't know anyone to whom you can send the proposal. As a result, you will have to resort to the "cold calls" that we discussed for sponsors in chapter 4. Remember, television executives are bombarded by proposals and so have little reason to take your call. Therefore, you have to be prepared to be persistent (again, this is an area in which many people fail in our business because they are uncomfortable with the cold call process).

To pave your way a bit, I suggest that you first try to get through to people at the networks by phone or e-mail to make them aware of the fact that your written proposal is on its way. They receive so many pitches that unless you somehow flag yours, your letter will likely just go in another pile on their desk.

If you know someone who can make an introduction for you, so much the better. If not, I suggest that you think of a creative way to get the attention of network executives without going overboard. (A short video about your event may be worth the investment. You can probably produce a three-minute video without spending a lot of money, and it can have multiple applications.) In any case, you will need to be persistent.

Opening Discussions

Assuming that your proposal has made its way to the top of someone's desk and there is interest in your show at a particular network or networks, there are a number of things that you are going to have to consider in your initial discussions and negotiations. In no particular order, some of these are included in the following sections.

Air Date

Before there is any hope of making a deal for your event to air on television, you have to have an air date that is somewhat compatible with the date of your live event (which may be locked in because of venue, athlete schedules, and weather considerations). I say *somewhat* because sometimes the network and the event organizer are content to have the television show run on a tape-delayed

basis in which the air date is considerably after the running of the live event. For a grassroots event that will not otherwise get television coverage, there is probably only an upside to any television exposure, provided it is affordable financially, so tape delay should not be an issue.

For bigger events, tape delay is not ideal for a few reasons. First and foremost, live television, particularly for competitions, makes for better theater. When events are televised

> ■ ■ ■ ■ ■ ■ ■ ■ ■ ■ ■
>
> *Live television, particularly for competitions, makes for better theater.*
>
> ■ ■ ■ ■ ■ ■ ■ ■ ■ ■ ■

live, the athletes generally perform better and differently than they do when they are being taped. Second, by the time the show airs on tape, most people already know the outcome, which lessens the impact and the value of the event. Finally, for a competition, it is tough for the press to know how to deal with reporting the results.

For an exhibition, the timing is less significant. For example, I didn't really have a problem when Halloween on Ice or Skating Goes Country aired a couple of weeks after they were taped. There were no results to report, and the delay gave the network a chance to promote the show using actual footage. However, with the AVP Championships of New England, I felt very strongly that live or same-day coverage was critical to boosting the credibility of the event and beach volleyball in the minds of the press and public. After all, the NFL isn't shown on a delayed basis.

The decision of whether to televise live or to tape is largely subjective and based on personal opinion and taste. Sometimes, though, you won't have any choice in the matter. If you are seeking an air date for a newly created event, the network schedule will not likely have an opening that is exactly compatible with the timing of your live event. You may just have to take whatever is available.

Time Slot

Similar to air dates, time slots are precious commodities. To have your show run in prime time (8–11 P.M.) is of greatest value because it is when the largest number of people are watching television. Keeping in mind the all-important ratings, if your show runs in prime time, you have the best chance of achieving the highest rating. This will affect your sponsorship and other sales as well as give you a strong history for future airings of your event. In most cases you are not going to have a lot of leverage, particularly if you are in the first year of your event or if your sport does not typically command strong ratings. Beach volleyball, for example, has a tougher time getting a good time slot than does figure skating, which in turn doesn't command the same time slots as the NFL. Similarly, a grassroots event will have more difficulty than a professional event. As with the air date, you will have some decisions to make as to whether you think your time slot is a plus or a minus for your event. If your only option is to air on a cable network that reaches fewer than 50 million homes at 2 A.M., you may want to think twice. A poor time slot may reflect more negatively on your event than no television at all.

■ ■ ■ ■ ■ ■ ■ ■ ■ ■ ■

***W**hen the show is taped, in addition to the promotional benefits it allows, in most cases you will have the luxury of time.*

■ ■ ■ ■ ■ ■ ■ ■ ■ ■ ■

Length of Show

In descending order of importance (after air date and time slot) is the length of your show. If you are given one hour to tell a two-hour story, you again may have some hard choices to make. In 1996 we aired the King of the Beach Invitational on NBC on a tape-delayed basis in a late Saturday afternoon time slot. While we were excited about the exposure, the King of the Beach event is hard to depict on television because of its round-robin format and point system. As a result, it is almost impossible to tell the story of this three-day tournament in one hour, which, after commercials and station breaks, is only about 44 minutes of actual coverage. However, in an effort to

build the prestige of the event, we felt that an NBC broadcast was pretty important. What resulted was a show that was difficult to follow for the viewer and was a less than representative summary of the event for the audience and players. The following year we were able to air the show with same-day coverage on FOX Sports Net. While available to a smaller audience, FOX was able to give us same-day coverage including a Friday night half-hour wrap-up show, a Saturday afternoon telecast of 90 minutes, and a Sunday afternoon telecast of 90 minutes. Our sponsors were just as happy to have the longer coverage rather than one hour on a network, and the audience was able to understand fully the outcome of the competition.

Conversely, you may have a two-hour time slot for an event that takes only one hour to complete. This happens from time to time with live tennis telecasts or beach volleyball events. The "fill time" is brutal and perhaps more problematic than not having enough time.

Taped Versus Live

As mentioned earlier, one of the major decisions you may have to make will involve that of having your show air live or tape delayed. In many instances you will not have a choice. While I am a strong proponent of live television, there are some benefits to a taped show. When the show airs live, there is an enormous amount of pressure on everyone associated with the show to start on time (for a tennis event, the network might tell you "balls in the air at precisely four minutes after the hour," and you literally can't be a minute early or late or it could affect the whole show), end on time (if the network news follows your show and you run long, there is a real risk that they will have to leave while you are still in progress), come back from commercials in a timely manner (play can't begin too soon or the audience at home will miss some of the action), get all of the commercial spots into the show, and generally not make any mistakes.

When the show is taped, in addition to the promotional benefits it allows, in most cases you will have the luxury of time. While this is not always the case, it is more often the norm. In the King of the Beach example discussed earlier, we had "same-day coverage," meaning the tape delay was only a few hours. For the 1998 version of Halloween on Ice we had a two-day "turn around"; that is, the show was taped on Friday night and aired on Monday. These tight schedules don't afford you much in the way of edit time!

When you do have a few days or even weeks to deliver the show, the edit time will allow you to analyze the show, make changes in the edit room, delete things that you are not happy with, and so forth. In fact, in a skating exhibition you can go so far as to allow the performers to retake their routines so that you can edit out the mistakes before the show airs. Again, I think this takes away some of the pressure of a live telecast and some of the spontaneity as well, but in some cases the ability to edit is far more important. Also, taped coverage might be your only option.

Financial Options

Once you have come to an agreement with the network programming people regarding the air date, time slot, and length of the telecast, you will begin negotiating the financial elements of your deal. Some events will earn rights fees. Others must purchase the time from the network, pay for the production, and deliver the show. There are other options as well. I have listed some of them here with an explanation of each so that when you get into this discussion, you won't be left scratching your head!

Rights Fee

A rights fee is what the network pays for the right to air your program. Just as not every event will warrant television coverage, not every event will warrant a rights fee. There may be an underlying sense that only the major events will earn rights fees. That is not necessarily true. You might have a smaller event that meets the needs and desires of a network (broadcast, cable, satellite, or regional). The NFL, NBA, NHL, and Major League Baseball are not the only entities to receive rights fees. In the case of new events and local/grassroots events, rights fees will be the exception not the rule, but it is what you should strive for.

In some rights fee situations the network will pay you a lump sum for which you will be required to deliver the show with all the bells and whistles, including graphics, billboards, commercial breaks, and so on. In other situations the network pays you a fee and *they* produce the show at their cost. In either scenario the rights that you grant in exchange for the fee are negotiable and can range from a straight buyout, in which the network then owns the rights to your show in perpetuity on a worldwide basis, to a one-time-only airing in the United States, after which any additional replays of your show belong to you and can be sold elsewhere. There are no real guidelines as to what your rights fee will or should be, as this is truly a matter of what the market will bear. Also, in most rights fee deals, the network will own all of the commercial time. This is discussed further later.

Barter

In this scenario, the network does not pay you any rights fee in cash but instead grants you the right to air your show on their network. They contribute the air time plus all or a portion of the commercial time, all of which is negotiable. While this may sound like it is not as good a deal as the straight rights fee, it all depends on your sponsorship situation and cost structure. In the typical rights fee deal, the network will own all of the commercial time in the show and have the right to sell it to whomever they wish. In that structure, if you have a sponsor that wants to buy advertising time, you will have to make a deal with the network to pass some of the sponsorship fee through to the network; they will, in effect, sell you commercial spots for your sponsor. The alternative is to have your sponsor engage in two negotiations—one with you for the sponsorship position and the other with the network for the commercial time.

You may remember that in chapter 3 I talked about the need to clarify any sponsorship restrictions when negotiating with your venue. Similarly, if the network has paid you a rights fee and is selling the commercial time, there are likely to be issues related to exclusivity that you must clarify. In a barter arrangement in which you control the commercial inventory, this type of potential conflict will not likely come into play unless you are selling sponsorships in categories that the network will not allow (such as alcohol and tobacco) or unless the network itself has exclusivities.

Anyway, in the barter situation, in exchange for the air time and commercial time, you will be expected to deliver the full show to the network, complete with all of the graphic elements, commercial breaks, and so on. The entire cost of the broadcast will be yours. If you have a major sponsor that is underwriting your event, this can actually turn out to be better for you financially. For example, if the network is willing to pay you $100,000 as a rights fee and the cost of production is $80,000 for a one-hour show, your net profit on the telecast will be limited to $20,000 because you have no commercial time to sell. On the other hand, let's assume that you barter the show and the cost of production remains at $80,000. In a one-hour show you will probably have 16 minutes of commercial time, thus 32 thirty-second spots to sell. Let's assume your barter deal allows you to keep all of the commercial time. If you can sell all 32 of your commercial spots for an average of $4,000 each (pricing will depend on the network, air date, and time slot), you will make more money under the barter arrangement—$48,000—than you would under the rights fee deal (although with more risk and nervous moments). Thus, *if,* and this is a big *if,* you have a major sponsor that is committed to purchasing a large number of spots at a premium price in order to be the title sponsor of your event, you must seriously consider whether the barter approach is the better financial arrangement for you.

In a barter situation the rights to the show should revert to you immediately after it airs, although you may have some time restrictions on when you can air it again on another network (perhaps a 6- to 12-month blackout period).

Buy-On

The most expensive and risky proposition for getting your event on television is buying your way onto a network. Under the theory that everything has a price, networks (both cable and over-the-air) have come to realize that their air time has a big value for promoters and other producers who think they absolutely have to have their shows broadcast to a national audience. All I can do here is warn you: Don't let your ego get in the way and try not to have delusions of grandeur.

Remember, in a buy-on situation you not only are paying the network for the airtime but you have to produce the television show as well. Granted, you then have all of the commercial time to sell, can work your sponsors into the show more readily, and own all of the media rights to your program in perpetuity. However, the up-front cost for all of these benefits may mean that you take a bath financially if you take this risk "on spec" and find out later that you could not sell adequate sponsorship to cover your costs.

The risks related to a buy-on are something that you must take great pains to analyze in the early going. Try not to get caught up in the thinking that being on television will build the image and credibility of your event.

■ ■ ■ ■ ■ ■ ■ ■ ■ ■ ■

Don't let your ego get in the way and try not to have delusions of grandeur.

■ ■ ■ ■ ■ ■ ■ ■ ■ ■ ■

Remember, there is nothing wrong with having a low-profile event that makes a good profit and return on investment. The buy-on should, in most cases, be your last resort.

Joint Venture

In the last several years networks have been moving toward wanting to own all or a piece of the programming that appears on their air. This can be quite a benefit to you if you have a property that piques a network's interest. Basically, in this scenario, you partner with the network so that they contribute the air time and production costs while you contribute the event and management (the exact percentages and splits are negotiable). All the revenues go into a shared "pot," with the profits and/or losses being shared by the partnership. While you clearly give up control in this structure, you also minimize your risk and take on a partner who can bring much more to the table than simply money. Whenever possible (and it won't happen often), I suggest that you take a hard look at this scenario, particularly at a time when the networks are primarily owned by major conglomerates that can bring many elements into play, including on-air promotion, access to production facilities, Internet support, and so forth.

TELEVISION CONTRACT

Once you have agreed on the structural points required to get your event on television, you might think you have covered all of the major elements of your television deal. Wrong.

Similar to the agreements with your venue, athletes, or sponsors, the terminology of television can be difficult and tricky, and you can't leave any stone unturned. Read the fine print and make sure your attorney reviews every word. As the operator of the event, you should look for some of the following issues in the contract itself.

Term

While fairly straightforward in and of itself, the term, or length, of your television agreement can be quite important. Have you made the type of deal that warrants locking up your event for the long term (normally no longer than three years), or are you better off keeping your agreement short, say one year, because you are not sure what direction the event will take after the coming year? If you are in the first year of the event, this can be an especially difficult decision to make, assuming that you have a choice.

Announcing a long-term agreement for your event before it even gets off the ground can bode well for you in sponsorship and venue negotiations.

Keep in mind that, from a variety of viewpoints, announcing a long-term agreement for your event before it even gets off the ground can bode well for you in sponsorship and venue negotiations. Everything is a balancing act. Whereas you may give up more than you want on the television side by entering into a long-term deal, you may make all that up in your sponsorship and site deals if you walk into those discussions knowing that you can deliver television coverage of the event for the next several years.

The flip side, and this is a risk in virtually any deal, is that you may give away the store by making a longer-term deal that sounds good at the beginning but doesn't look so great when your event becomes a huge success. I would tend not to worry too much about that, though. If it happens, you will likely be able to make up the differential in the next round of television negotiations. Being conservative, if you can get a long-term television deal that makes sense for you in year one and protects you during the developmental stages of your event, on balance you will be better off. If you are creative (and I urge creativity in all of your negotiations), you might be able to build bonuses and extensions into a long-term agreement that make up for what you might have "lost" in the original deal. These might pay you additional fees for a high rating or add additional years at higher dollars if you achieve certain ratings or the network reaches certain revenues from the sale of commercial time during your show.

Territory

With the growth of television around the world and the accompanying desire for sports programming, the territory (i.e., the area that your contract covers) that you negotiate with a domestic broadcaster (for an event in the United States, FOX, CBS, TNT, ESPN, etc. are domestic broadcasters) can become very important because international rights can be worth quite a bit of money to you in some cases. The value of international rights for sports has increased dramatically in the last several years. Given that there really are not that many universally understood and appealing genres of programming (American comedy or drama may not work in Japan and vice versa), it stands to reason that sports is one of the few genres that can transcend cultures, languages, and borders. Tennis is tennis no matter what language you speak. The same is true of golf, basketball, figure skating, and track and field. While Australian rules football is more popular in Australia, cricket is more understood in the United Kingdom, and badminton is most popular in Asia, the drama of sports and competition translates well.

As the value of international television rights continues to escalate, you either want to make sure that you control your international rights or that the domestic rights holder is prepared to pay you for them. International rights can and should mean incremental dollars to you. To maximize these fees, I suggest you find a specialist in international rights sales. (Similar to syndication, there are agents who will sell your event internationally. I doubt you want to call, fax, or e-mail every network in every country around the world!)

Trademark

This is certainly one of the most important elements of your entire contract and goes back to an issue that we have seen in the athlete and venue contracts. You have an event that, in many respects, might qualify as what is called "intellectual property." As such, what you own is an idea, perhaps a scoring system or format, a name and logo, the right to hold your event in a specific geographic area, and so forth. If I have not been clear on this up until now, let me restate that you want to keep control of as many of these intellectual property rights as possible. For example, we own the name and logo for Halloween on Ice. No one else can put on a show called "Halloween on Ice" without our permission. One year, a third-party promoter was looking for an ice show during the October time frame. He came to us and had to pay us a license fee for the right to put on a show with the Halloween on Ice title. This provided us with some pretty easy fees and good exposure for the show in markets that we otherwise would not have played. (Conversely, we had to pay someone else to use the name "King of the Beach.")

With regard to television, this means very clearly delineating what rights your broadcast partner has negotiated for. In today's marketplace the media conglomerates are attempting to control as much as possible through

> *The value of international rights for sports has increased dramatically in the last several years.*

their own mergers and acquisitions. Take ESPN as an example. They are owned by Disney, which owns ABC, several Internet sites, Buena Vista Home Entertainment (video), ESPN2, ESPN radio, and Hyperion books. They also have magazine publishing, movies, theme parks, and international distribution capability. As a result, they could in theory attempt to control all of your rights from venue to television distribution to production if they so chose *and* were willing to pay for it. FOX is in virtually the same situation, with the exception of the theme parks. AOL's merger with Time Warner is another example. For the moment, the different divisions of these conglomerates work pretty independently, so they don't usually negotiate for all of these rights. As a result, you may be in a position to sell television to one entity, distribute your international rights through someone else, handle your Internet rights through another party and your home video through yet another. I suspect that this will soon change as these companies figure out how to amalgamate all of their entities.

I am not necessarily suggesting that this lack of cohesion is a plus for you. If, for example, instead of just airing the event on ESPN2, we could have convinced Disney to really get behind the Best of the Beach Invitational by hosting the event at Walt Disney World, airing it on ESPN, promoting it on espn.com, giving results on ESPN radio, and so on, I think it would have been in our best interests *and theirs*. However, it is unusual for the smaller properties to command this type of attention and equally difficult to coalesce these big companies. As a result, for the time being, some of these "synergistic" opportunities go unnoticed or are not acted on.

With that in mind, remember to write the language in your television agreement carefully so that you don't find yourself in a position in which your network partner, which in almost every case will be a big media conglomerate, has stopped you from exploiting your property as broadly as you would like by not agreeing to participate in your event across the board. In other words, if ESPN airs the event but Disney does not want to host it, fine. But try not to let Disney then restrict you from holding the event at a Six Flags property.

> ■ ■ ■ ■ ■ ■ ■ ■ ■ ■ ■
>
> *You want to keep control of as many of these intellectual property rights as possible.*
>
> ■ ■ ■ ■ ■ ■ ■ ■ ■ ■ ■

While there are a lot of networks, increasingly they are all owned by only a few companies, so the competition at the top level is intense. This can be a plus for you but also can create big problems, so write the language related to rights very carefully and make sure you understand the ramifications.

Whether you refer to this issue as ownership of your trademark, protection of your intellectual property, exclusivity, or granting of rights, the key here is to be painfully aware of the issues that are in any way related to the exploitation of your event either by you or by third parties. Whether this means trademark registration, copyright protection, limitation on replay rights, or the number of runs a network might have of your show, it is absolutely critical that this all be spelled out very clearly so that you are protected and others know where the lines are drawn.

Creative Control

This doesn't seem like something that should be that big of an issue (and it usually isn't) since after all, the event is yours. However, networks are very picky about what goes on their air, as they should be. As a result, they may ask for approval over the content of the show, the producer/director, talent, number of cameras, budget, and so on. While some of this is reasonable (your event is in some respects going to be a reflection on them), you should be careful not to let them have so much input that it steps over the line and becomes controlling. In many respects, this is a judgment call on your part and one that you will have to feel out. I simply warn you that just as the network will be protective, so too will you when it comes down to how your event is presented on television. Make sure that you don't give away too much in this area.

Commercial Inventory

The ability to sell commercial inventory on your show will be directly related to the financial deal that you make with the network. If they pay you a rights fee, they are probably going to own all of the commercial time. If you barter, then the control over advertising sales will be based on the split that you negotiate; if you buy the time, you will most likely have the right to sell all of it.

As an aside, when I use the word *control* here, bear in mind that the network will have the ultimate control over what companies can advertise on their network and what commercials they can run. This will be governed by their standards and practices department, and they will have the final say on what commercials run on the air. For example, one year at the King of the Beach event we had a potential deal with a condom manufacturer, which was contingent on our ability to get the network to agree to run their commercials. The network gave us an emphatic no, which nixed the deal. This is an issue that you should review in detail before you go out into the market to sell sponsorships.

Regardless of who has the right to sell the commercial time on your show, commercial sales are going to be of utmost importance to your sponsors because they will want to air commercials on the telecast of your event. As a result, similar to what we did with TNN on Skating Goes Country, you must have an understanding on how to deal with commercial spots that *you* sell to *your* sponsors if the net-

work controls the commercial time. One way to deal with this is to work together on the sales of sponsorships. In this manner you might have the network out selling sponsorships for you. Some of their advertisers might want signage and other benefits at the live event just as your sponsors will want commercial time. If you can develop a joint sales strategy with the network, it should work to your benefit and theirs, as neither of you will question the income generated by the other.

Right of First Negotiation

This is another one of those critical paragraphs that always reads terribly one sided in the initial draft of the agreement and, unless you have a lot of leverage, tends to stay that way. Essentially, this paragraph will read something like this:

> *In the event of a Termination for any reason, the parties agree to negotiate in good faith the terms of a new agreement for a period beginning with the date of the termination and concluding ninety (90) days after the expiration date of the Term (the "Negotiating Period"). During the Negotiating Period, Rights Owner [that's you] agrees to negotiate exclusively with Network with respect to all television rights to future Events. In the event Rights Owner and Network fail to enter into an agreement during the Negotiating Period for the television rights to future Events (the "Future Rights"), Rights Owner shall be free to negotiate with third parties for the Future Rights, provided Rights Owner does not enter into an*

■ ■ ■ ■ ■ ■ ■ ■ ■ ■ ■

W*rite the language related to rights very carefully and make sure you understand the ramifications.*

■ ■ ■ ■ ■ ■ ■ ■ ■ ■ ■

agreement with any such third party without first offering to Network the opportunity to enter into an agreement with Rights Owner on terms at least as favorable to Network as those offered to Rights Owner by any such third party, which Rights Owner is willing to accept (the "Third Party Offer"). Network shall have thirty (30) business days from the date of written advice from Rights Owner of any such third party offer, containing full details, in which to accept or reject same. Network shall be deemed to have accepted said third party offer by acceptance of only the terms thereof that are reducible to a determinable amount of money. If Network rejects said third party offer or fails to accept same within the time above specified, then and only then shall Rights Owner be free to enter into an agreement with such third party. If Rights Owner does not accept such third party offer, the terms hereof shall apply to any subsequent offer received or made by Rights Owner.

Rights Owner shall not accept and Network shall not be required to meet the provisions of any such third party offer unless it has been reduced to writing, signed by the offeror, and delivered to Network with Rights

Owner's written advice to Network as provided above, together with Rights Owner's written acknowledgment of its willingness to accept same. Network's failure to accept shall not constitute a waiver of the first refusal rights described herein with respect to subsequent offers. This Paragraph shall survive the termination or expiration of the Agreement, and compliance with this Paragraph is deemed a material term of this Agreement.

In short, this language ties you up in every way imaginable with respect to future negotiations for the television rights to your event. What the above basically says is that the network has the first right to negotiate a new agreement if the current one expires or is terminated for any reason. Following termination, if you are unable to come to an agreement within a certain time frame (90 days in this case), then you will be able to go out and shop your event to other broadcasters. However, if you get an offer that is at least as good as the last offer made by the network with whom you were under contract, then they will have the right to match the offer from the new network and you have to stay with the old network if they, in their sole discretion, choose to match the new offer. Further, if you don't make a deal with the first new network to make an offer, the right to match goes on until you get another offer that you are willing to accept.

I hate this type of language because I can't stand letting someone else have that much

■ ■ ■ ■ ■ ■ ■ ■ ■ ■ ■

It is a fact of life
for most event organizers
that their network partner
is going to have some level
of right of first negotiation
and right to match
after the term
of their agreement expires.

■ ■ ■ ■ ■ ■ ■ ■ ■ ■ ■

leverage and control over what I want to do. However, it is a fact of life for most event organizers that their network partner is going to have some level of right of first negotiation and right to match after the term of their agreement expires. In some cases this can be a good thing and nothing to worry about. If you and the network have a good experience together, this is probably not a problem. However, if things get testy and you want to move to a new network when your agreement ends, you could have a sticky situation on your hands.

My advice here is to give as little as possible in this area, with the understanding that it is probably not the place to make your toughest stand. Ultimately, this could become a deal breaker for the network, which may not be to your advantage in the bigger picture. Keep in mind that it is going to be difficult negotiating with third parties for future rights when you are saddled with this "right to match" language. You will have to disclose this fact in your third party discussions (this will not come as a big surprise to anyone), which will make everyone reticent to make an offer because they won't want to be viewed as a "stalking horse" (i.e., you are using them to get a better deal with the incumbent broadcaster). Thus, the exact wording of this language provides another opportunity to be creative in your negotiations.

Promotional Benefits

In my experience, this is an area that is easily overlooked. A television network (or a local station or cable outlet) provides a very powerful communications tool that can be used in several ways other than just to televise your event. During the course of their other programming, the network will typically promote many of their shows. You should strive to have them push your show hard. Some of the highest-rated shows that we have been involved with were actively promoted by the networks during other highly rated programming. Your sponsors will also love the additional exposure that you can get for them at no extra cost.

Of equal benefit is the local commercial time that a network can provide through its local affiliates. You can use this time to promote ticket sales or simply create an image for the event. A certain percentage of the networks' or their affiliates' commercial spots either go unsold (and commercial time is a commodity that, once the time passes, can never be gotten back!) or are held back to be used in a variety of ways, including public service announcements for charity or other educational purposes. These spots can and should be available to you if you ask for them early in the negotiations. Believe me, these spots can be *very* valuable. They can save you money out of your ad budget and don't really cost the network or its local affiliate much.

We have negotiated for commercial spots many times, with the most effective being with TBS for Halloween on Ice. TBS arranged for the local cable company to provide us with 200 commercial spots in exchange for tickets to the event. They entertained their guests; we used the time to sell tickets. As mentioned earlier, these promotional elements can simply get overlooked because people are focused on the broadcast details. Make sure that promotion is on your list of negotiation points. Offering commercial spots should be attractive to networks because it lets them look extremely generous and it doesn't cost them much, if anything.

Music, Footage, and Other Clearances

During the last 15 years those who own the rights to names, likenesses, footage, photos, music, and anything else that might have value have become much more protective of their intellectual properties and more savvy about pricing them for third-party usage. As a result, in order to avoid messy situations after your event and television broadcast, you must research and contract for the use of these items in advance. In the world of sports, virtually every television show uses music, and many use photos and film clips of old action. You need to determine in advance what music and clips you are going to use so that you can get these "cleared" (i.e., obtain the rights to use them). In the alternative, you might determine that you are going to produce your own music and use your own photos and clips so as to stay clear of any rights entanglements. (Even if your event is not on television, you may need to clear music, costumes, and other items for the live event.)

This is a complex area because it is seemingly always in the process of being clarified from a legal perspective. In order to make your life easier, there are clearinghouses and experts in the field of music and footage clearances. If you are planning to use these items often, I suggest that you hire an expert (they are not particularly expensive), as otherwise you are going to spend a lot of time trying to uncover this information, and it will be slow going at best. You don't want to learn the hard way.

When we first produced Halloween on Ice, Nancy did a number to the music from the Broadway hit *Annie* in which she dressed like Little Orphan Annie. We cleared the music but did not know that the Annie outfit was copyrighted. Thus, in order for Nancy to wear an outfit similar to Annie's (which was specially designed for Nancy), we had to get permission from the owners of the show and pay them a rights fee. We found that out a few days after the show aired when we received a letter from the attorney for the show and the character. We were able to settle this issue for a modest fee, but we could have avoided some headaches and probably paid less money for the rights if we had negotiated this up front.

With regard specifically to music (which is probably the area to be most concerned with), there are vast libraries of precleared music that you can rent for reasonable fees. You can also produce your own music, as we have done on several occasions (our partner in StarGames Music, Michael Visconti, is very talented and can create a vast array of music). In either case, this avoids discussions

■ ■ ■ ■ ■ ■ ■ ■ ■ ■ ■ ■

***D**on't let clearance issues slip through the cracks.*

■ ■ ■ ■ ■ ■ ■ ■ ■ ■ ■ ■

with the major labels and publishing companies who may have the rights to songs from various artists. Also, your network partner is bound to have a library of music that they have already cleared. There are many ways to deal with this issue, and it need not be too problematic if you focus on it in advance and deal with it up front. Just remember, don't let clearance issues slip through the cracks.

If you can make the music clearance and other rights issues the responsibility of the network (or the venue for the live event), you will also save yourself the burden of this task, so keep this at the top of your negotiation list as well.

While it may seem that there are an interminable number of points to be negotiated with your television partner, most of this will be dealt with rather easily. I have gone into great detail here only because television is so high profile and potentially important to your event.

Deal Memo

When you have finished your television negotiations, you should try to end up with a deal memo, which might look something like the one in figure 7.2. This is based on our barter agreement (and not a particularly favorable one for us, I might add!) with one of the cable networks for the 1999 Best of the Beach Invitational (which, as you might recall, never took place because of site-related issues).

As you can see, this deal memo tracks pretty closely the points discussed earlier and delineates the major elements of the agreement. (I hope you do better than this in your negotiations!)

While a deal memo is probably a good idea for all of your agreements, I particularly recommend that you sign one with your television partner. This is not because they are less trustworthy but because, to begin with, it is a format that they understand and are used to dealing with. Second, if your experience

To: Network Executive

From: Event Organizer

Date: *as far in advance of your event as possible*

Re: Television Deal Points

The following points outline my understanding of our deal with _____ for the telecast of the Best of the Beach Invitational ("BOBI"), which will take place at the Trump Marina Hotel in Atlantic City on August 20-22, 1999. These include:

- The show will air on _____. This includes the original airing in prime time and one guaranteed replay in non–prime time.

- The show will be 60 minutes in length, inclusive of 16 minutes of national commercial time, plus 3 minutes for network promotions and local commercial spots.

- _____ will sell the show internationally and split the revenue with us on a 60/40 basis in our favor.

- We shall have two (2) commercial minutes (4 spots) to sell and retain the revenue in each original broadcast and 2 1/2 minutes (5 spots) to sell in each re-air.

- Each show can have three (3) opening and three (3) closing billboards.

- The on-site title sponsor of the event will be in a presenting sponsor role on the telecast (Best of the Beach Invitational presented by XYZ).

- We can include one sixty-second (:60) vignette in each show for the sponsor or site.

- _____ will have a one-year exclusivity on the show from the first air date, after which all rights shall revert to us. The copyright shall be owned by StarGames.

- With the exception of on-air talent and direct expenses incurred by the network, all production costs shall be the responsibility of StarGames.

- We can have a BOBI Web site and Web site sponsor, but we cannot advertise a competitor to your corporate site. We can link our site to yours if we so choose.

- If we sell more than our allotment of commercial spots, we can purchase spots out of your inventory. We will pay you for these spots at your rate card, which is $1,500 per :30 spot for weekday airings and $2,500 per :30 for weekend airings.

- _____ will have first right of negotiation to air the event for 2000 for 45 days following the event.

- The air date for the original broadcast shall be Friday, September 10, 1999.

If you are in agreement that the above accurately summarizes our discussions, please so indicate by signing in the space provided below. This deal memo shall then serve as the basis for a more formal agreement between us.

Best regards,

Jerry Solomon on behalf of StarGames

_____

ACCEPTED AND AGREED ON BEHALF OF NETWORK

Figure 7.2 Sample deal memo.

with the network's legal department is anything like mine, it takes forever to get an agreement out of them. I would say that with at least half of our projects we operated the event and aired the television show without ever seeing a draft contract and certainly without signing one. On the one hand, this means that most of the network executives are good for their word. On the other hand, it means that you had better have something in writing that everyone can refer to in case there are questions that the undrafted or unsigned contract would have answered. A deal memo can cover all of this.

THE SHOW

Assuming that you have worked your way through all the deal points and signed a television agreement in some form (deal memo or otherwise), you can now get on with the creative part of planning what parts of your live event will end up being televised (whether live or on tape) and what "look" your show will take. To put it mildly, this takes a ton of planning and creativity, not to mention attention to detail. Some of the things that you should plan for, guard against, and be prepared to deal with are included next.

Producer/Director

You may think I say this about a lot of issues, but your choice for producer and director (and they may be the same person, depending on the difficulty of your telecast) is one of the most important decisions that you will make in the planning process for your event and certainly for your television show. For those of you who have never been in a television truck, the director is the person responsible for positioning the cameras, telling the camera people what they should be shooting, deciding which camera is "on" at a particular moment, and so on. The producer is responsible for hiring all of the equipment, setting it up, monitoring the budget, overseeing the edit, and the like.

The producer and director will be the people ultimately responsible for the look, feel, and success of your telecast. While it is not rocket science, the telecast of an event is intricate and an art in and of itself. Some people will be more creative in their approach; others will be more conservative. You really need to match yourself with a director who shares your vision for the show; otherwise, you are destined for problems and disappointment. At the same time, you need to be able to articulate clearly what it is that you have in mind for that particular show. Without your explicit direction your television personnel will not be able to deliver the show you are looking for.

The producer and director are key and have to be able to not only take your vision and

Match yourself with a director who shares your vision for the show.

translate it to television but also work together closely, as they will, in a sense, be joined at the hip for the purposes of your show.

Running Order

Perhaps the best way to communicate to the producer and director what you have in mind for your event telecast is to give them a "running order" for the show. This serves as a road map for everyone to follow. The running order should be as detailed as possible, while recognizing that it must remain somewhat fluid as things change during the course of an event. The sample running order in table 7.1 from Halloween on Ice is instructive in this regard because the television show for the event was shorter (by about 30 minutes) than was the live show. We knew that we were going to have to cut certain parts of the live show in order to keep within the time allotted by the telecast. Having an idea of what we wanted to air on television in advance of the show was a big help to everyone, from the television production people to the lights and sound people to the participants themselves.

If you are airing a competition, the running order will be somewhat different from the outline for Halloween on Ice. First of all, it is difficult to judge the time of a live event because the players often dictate the flow of the competition. In skating you have the luxury of knowing the length of the music and therefore the length of each performance, which doesn't happen in other sports. Therefore, when putting together a running order for a telecast of a competition, you really need to determine in advance things such as interviews, when to go to the announcers, what type of sideline reports you are likely to run, and so on. Then you must fit those things in around the live action. (See the working model on page 164 for an example.)

Table 7.1 Sample Running Order From Halloween on Ice

Running time	Segment	Segment length
0:00	Opening animation with logo and quick scene set	0:45
0:45	Group opening	2:30
3:15	Nancy Kerrigan/Solo #1	3:00
6:15	Commercial break #1	1:30
7:45	Bumper with sponsor billboards	0:30
8:15	Hosts welcome audience; set scene	1:45
10:00	Kurt Browning/Solo #1	3:00
13:00	Bumper to commercial	0:10
13:10	Commercial break #2	2:00
15:10	Josee Chouinard/Solo #1	3:10
18:20	Urbanski and Marval/Pairs #1	4:14
22:34	Halloween Memory #1 (Rocky Marval); Note that these segments are sponsored by Ocean Spray with opening and closing animation.	1:26
24:00	Commercial break #3	1:30
25:30	Philippe Candeloro/Solo #1	3:00
28:30	Bumper	0:15
28:45	Commercial break #4	1:30
30:15	Brasseur and Eisler/Pairs #1	3:00
33:15	Ocean Spray Halloween Memory #2 (Isabelle Brasseur)	1:30
34:45	Commercial break #5	1:30
36:15	Baker and Dostatni/Dance #1	4:30
40:45	Josef Sabovcik/Solo #1	3:00
43:45	Commercial break #6	1:30
45:15	Liz Manley/Solo #1	3:00
48:15	Liz Manley interview	2:15
50:30	Commercial break #7	1:30
52:00	Backstage skater interaction	1:00
53:00	Gia Guddat/Solo #1	3:30

(continued)

Table 7.1 *(continued)*

Running time	Segment	Segment length
56:30	Bumper	0:10
56:40	Commercial break #8	1:30
58:10	Bumper with sponsor billboards	0:20
58:30	Josee Chouinard/Solo #2	3:00
61:30	Ocean Spray Halloween Memory # 3 (Kurt Browning)	1:15
62:15	Commercial break #9	1:30
63:45	Nancy Kerrigan and the Haydenettes	7:30
71:15	Commercial break #10	1:30
72:45	Philippe Candeloro/Solo #2	4:00
76:45	Candeloro interview	2:15
79:00	Commercial break #11	1:30
80:30	Salem Visit	3:00
83:30	Josef Sabovcik/Solo #2	5:45
89:15	Bumper to commercial	0:15
89:30	Commercial break #12	1:30
91:00	Ocean Spray characters	2:14
93:14	Liz Manley/Solo #2	2:50
96:04	Bumper	0:11
96:15	Commercial break #13	1:30
97:45	Kurt Browning/Solo #2	3:00
100:45	Kurt Browning interview	2:15
103:00	Commercial break #14	1:30
104:30	Brasseur and Eisler/Pairs #2	3:00
107:30	Ocean Spray Halloween Memory #4 (Liz Manley)	0:45
108:15	Commercial break #15	1:30
109:45	Nancy Kerrigan interview (includes footage from Grease on Ice)	3:15
113:00	Nancy Kerrigan/Solo #2	3:00
116:00	Commercial break #16	1:30
117:30	Bumper with sponsor billboards	0:20

Running time	Segment	Segment length
117:50	Hosts' closing comments	1:10
119:00	Closing from musical montage with credits	1:00
120:00	Show ends	

Note the various references to Ocean Spray, which was one of the show sponsors. Their role was pretty involved in this show. Also, be aware that the number of commercial breaks and their placement will be determined by the network. This is usually outlined in the production handbook they will give you before the event.

Personally, I enjoy creating the running order for the show, as it allows me a creative outlet. However, more important, it really serves to let everyone know what to expect. I suggest that you try to develop the running order at least 90 days prior to the event so that you have plenty of time to revise it as the event nears.

Production Needs

Certain elements of your television show will be affected by your venue. To begin with, you have to make sure that the facility can accommodate your production requirements, which will involve bringing in quite a bit of equipment. Most major arenas and stadiums will be set up for television, and newer buildings will even be cabled for the cameras. However, when you are building your own site or going to a public area, you must take some very basic television needs into consideration. For example, you will need room for at least one television truck, and if your show is live, you will no doubt have a second truck with the satellite transmission equipment necessary to provide the television signal. Also, these trucks and the cameras require a great deal of power, so if the site does not have a readily accessible power source, you are going to need generators. There has to be space made available for all of this, and it has to be relatively close to the playing area. (If you are televising a marathon, golf tournament, triathlon, or other event that takes place over a large area, then your issues are compounded.) All of this should be dealt with during a series of planning meetings and a walk-through of the site. However, when making your site deal, these television equipment issues should be at the forefront of your mind.

Develop the running order at least 90 days prior to the event so that you have plenty of time to revise it as the event nears.

Camera Placement

Camera placement is both a creative issue and a ticketing/seating issue. It is creative in the sense that you want to pick camera positions that will allow you to best and most creatively cover the action (figure 7.3). While I have often sought new and different camera locations, frankly this is sometimes a waste of energy. The more traditional camera positions are popular for the very reason that they have proved to be the most reliable in presenting the action in a way that best suits the viewer. For live events camera placement is also a seating issue: before tickets go on sale, you must be sure to block out (or "kill") the seats the cameras will be obstructing.

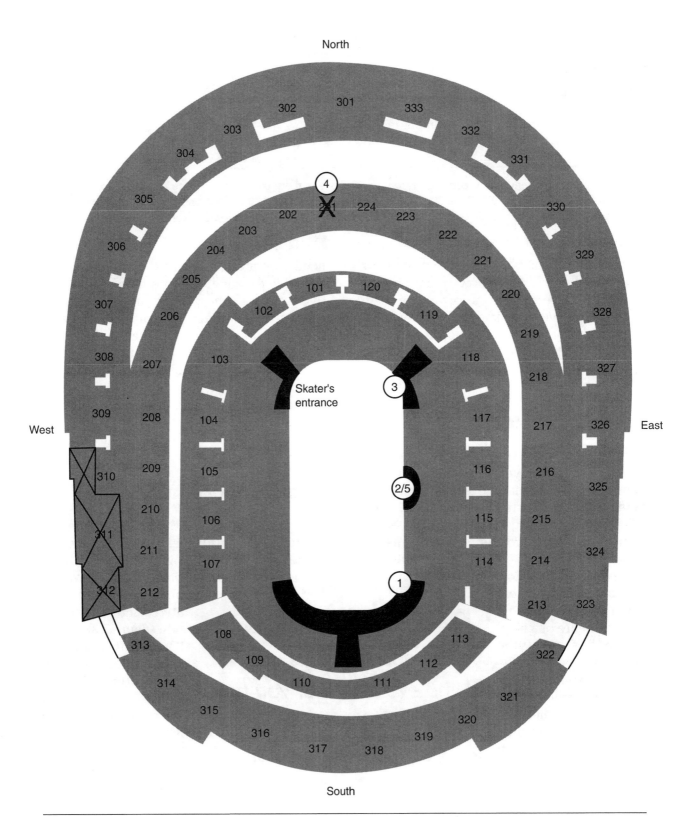

Figure 7.3 Diagram of an ice rink showing the seating chart and positions of cameras for televising the event. Make sure you have "killed" any seats that your camera placements will affect.

Perhaps my funniest experience with an impaired view (although this has nothing to do with camera positions) was at the Masters tennis tournament when a player's girlfriend asked me if the umpire's stand could be moved because it was blocking her view. We were able to move her seat (we obviously couldn't move the umpire's stand!). What would happen if a camera and cameraman were blocking the view of the people in the third row who had paid a premium for their seats? If you are lucky enough to also have a sellout, you won't have anywhere to move your customers, so you had better take care of this up front. Again, this is not an issue that requires a PhD, but it is one of those details that you *must* take into consideration.

Hiring a Production Company

One way to take yourself out of dealing with many of these issues is to hire an outside production company. There are many of them all over the country, and some are quite knowledgeable about sports production and do a very good job. They will be well versed in all of the production issues that have been raised in this chapter and can lift this pressure off you if you make the right kind of deal (your network partner can suggest production companies if you don't know of any).

The alternative as I have laid it out here is to hire independent contractors (i.e., the producer and director) and let them handle all of the details. In effect, there is not much difference in the two scenarios except that a company can handle all of the payments to the subcontractors, which also saves you a couple of steps.

If you do decide to go in this direction, I urge you to enter into a very explicit contract with your production company that covers a variety of issues, including finances, specific definitions of the show, timetables for delivery, equipment requirements, ownership rights of the footage and the program, approval over the show content, and postproduction expectations including the fact that the production will conform to the network guidelines (these can be very technical and cover details you don't really need to know). Finally, you will need to include the warranty, indemnification, governing law, and other boilerplate paragraphs, which should by now feel like standards.

Budget

Producing a television show from your event can be expensive, and the costs can get out of control in a hurry. You must have a tight budget from the outset. I have listed in appendix C the budget line items we use for an event's television production. Do not let the creative types set your budget. You have to determine in advance what you can afford and let the producer/director create the show from that rather than the reverse. The use of multiple cameras, state-of-the-art graphics, and so forth can get very expensive. Don't let the tail wag the dog here.

Credits

Before I got involved with television production, the credits never seemed like a big deal to me. Now that I am involved, I realize that to some people, the credits are *all* that count. It is only fair that you give credit at the end of the show to those who played an important role in the event. Be sure to give the producer a comprehensive list of the people you want to receive credits. This should include the tournament manager (or your closest assistant) and special thanks to the sponsors, volunteers, and people who donated food and transportation. Depending on your role in the event, you may want to give yourself an executive producer credit.

Do not let the creative types set your budget.

✔ Television Checklist

While the whole television area is difficult to summarize because of its scope, a brief synopsis is probably worthwhile and will serve to focus you on the most important issues. Be sure to do the following:

✔ Determine whether your event warrants or needs television coverage.

✔ Decide whether your event is likely to be a cable or broadcast network show.

✔ Create a proposal that illustrates that the telecast of your event can help the network build audience.

✔ Determine in advance if your show will benefit from any additional outlets such as the Internet.

✔ During the solicitation and negotiation stages, keep all parties abreast of what is going on so you don't misrepresent talent issues.

✔ Make sure your sponsors are properly protected in your television deal.

✔ Maintain control of as many of the rights and copyrights as possible and be sure to clear the use of anyone else's work product or intellectual property.

✔ Try to find air dates, time slots, and show lengths that are compatible with your live event.

✔ Know your financial situation before you commit to any deal structure other than a rights fee. *Television is expensive.*

✔ Make sure the term of your deal is comfortable. Length is not always a benefit here.

✔ Keep as much creative control as possible.

✔ Don't forget to include promotional benefits in your negotiation strategy.

✔ Put a deal memo in place and get it signed by all parties.

✔ Hire a strong, compatible television crew.

✔ Make sure your site can accommodate the television broadcast needs.

✔ Give everyone associated with the event a detailed running order of the show.

✔ Make the television part of your event fun and creative, *but not at the expense of your budget.*

The television portion of your event can take on a life of its own and in some senses is an event in and of itself. Therefore, I suggest that you surround yourself with experts in this area because while it may be fun and intoxicating, you should not have to become a producer/director at the same time as you are trying to organize an event.

Working Model: Tournament Television Deal

For illustration purposes let's assume that we were able to make a deal for a regional cable telecast of the semifinals and finals of the Regional Junior Tennis Tournament. The deal memo would look like this:

To: Regional Sports Network Executive

From: Regional Junior Tennis Tournament Director

Re: Television Deal Memo

Date: _____

It is my understanding that we have agreed to the following points between Tennis Tournament, Inc. (Promoter) and XYZ Network (XYZ) for purposes of televising the XYZ Cup (Event):

1. The Event will take place on August 10-14 at the Tennis Club.

2. The Event will feature the top junior boys and girls in the region between the ages of 16 and 18.

3. Promoter will be responsible for all aspects of the Event and agrees to provide all of the access required by XYZ for the telecast of the Event.

4. XYZ will provide to Promoter two (2) one-hour telecasts ("Show" or "Shows"), which will each air a minimum of five (5) times on XYZ's network, which reaches a minimum of __ million homes in the _____ region. XYZ shall fully produce the show at its own cost subject to reasonable approval by Promoter. The first Show will be a recap/highlights show of the semifinal and final singles matches for girls. The second Show will be a recap/highlights show of the semi-final and final singles matches for boys.

5. The Shows will each have no more than nine (9) minutes of commercial breaks and two (2) minutes for network promotional spots so that the actual content of the Shows shall be 49 minutes. Promoter shall be allowed to provide a 60-second vignette to the title sponsor of the Event subject to approval by XYZ.

6. All commercial time shall be controlled by XYZ subject to reasonable approval by Promoter. Should Promoter sell any commercial time, it shall be at XYZ's rate card. Promoter shall receive a twenty percent (20%) commission for such sales.

7. XYZ agrees that each telecast shall include an interview with a designee of the title sponsor of the Event, as well as with a designee of Promoter. XYZ further agrees to use the official name of the Event in all graphic and audio mentions of the Event both during the Shows and in any promotion of the Shows.

8. Promoter agrees to include XYZ's name and logo in all materials produced for the Event in a prominent position. Promoter shall also use best efforts to obligate all sponsors of the Event to provide XYZ with exposure on any materials that they produce for the Event including any promotional items.

9. XYZ shall have a 90-day right of first negotiation and a 10-day right to match for any future telecast of the Event. Such right of first negotiation shall commence on the day immediately following the airing of the first Show, which shall be no later than 30 days following the conclusion of the Event.

10. Both parties agree to fully indemnify the other from any and all actions taken by third parties that stem from a breach by the other party, provided such is not the result of the other party's gross negligence. Further, both parties agree to obtain a minimum of $1 million of insurance in which each shall name the other as additional insured.

If the above is consistent with your understanding of our agreement, please so indicate by signing in the space provided below. This memorandum shall serve as a binding agreement until such time as it is replaced by a more formal contract between the parties.

We are looking forward to a great event, which should be of benefit to junior tennis throughout the region.

Best regards,

Tournament Director

ACCEPTED AND AGREED:

_____

Tennis Tournament, Inc.

_____

XYZ Network

The beauty of this deal is that, because the network is going to produce the show at its own cost, it allows you to circumvent a number of issues discussed throughout this chapter, such as the need to hire a producer/director, equipment, and so forth. Considering this is the first time this event would have been attempted, it would be in everyone's interest to take as many of these obligations out of the hands of the tournament manager as possible.

Working Model: Site Survey

Ninety days prior to the event a site survey should be held with the tournament director, club manager, television producer, and director. Several issues should be discussed, including the number of cameras to be used to televise the shows, camera positions, the need for an electronic news gathering (ENG) crew for a handheld/portable camera, on-site power availability for the television truck, location of the truck, the need for a generator, talent positions for the commentators, and any other issues relevant to the telecast. For purposes of the regional tennis event, I would suggest three "hard" or stationary cameras (one at court level behind the court, one behind the court but up on a platform to give it some height, and one at courtside across from the chair umpire). In addition, I would want one ENG crew (portable cameramen) to be available to shoot parties, interviews, and general "color" footage for inclusion in the show.

Working Model: Show Running Order

Since both shows will essentially be edited versions of the semifinals and finals, there is little need for a running order for the show in the same sense as we used for Halloween on Ice. Nevertheless, there is a need to give some direction for each show. We would need to outline two similar shows that will keep the audience interested, each of which should include the following:

- Key portions of each semifinal
- Interview with the club manager
- Interview with former top-ranked junior player
- Interview with the kids playing in the two matches prior to the match (why this event is fun to play in)
- Key portions of the final
- Interviews with kids who won the doubles title
- Scenes from the player party
- Interview with the sponsor representative
- Interview with the finalists (why it is fun to play tennis)
- Interview with tournament director

Chapter EIGHT

Time to Play

So, event week is finally here. You have come miles since the idea of creating or acquiring your event popped into your head. There have been hundreds of meetings, thousands of phone calls, more negotiating than you ever anticipated, and nothing was easy. Every time you thought things were under control, something else came up that made you wonder if your project was ever going to come together. Well, lo and behold, you have made it to the eve of the event with everything intact, and you are (theoretically!) ready to go. But you haven't done it alone to this point, and you can't get through the event itself without the help of a great staff that is motivated to go the extra mile.

CREATING A TEAM ATMOSPHERE

Recently I was at an event at which I marveled at how polite everyone on the staff was to each other. There were more pleases and thank-yous passed around at that event than at an etiquette seminar. It was pretty impressive if only because it showed a high level of respect among the staff. I liked that a lot.

The best guy that I have ever seen at motivating an event team is Josh Ripple. He has a knack for getting everyone to want to walk through a wall to operate the event in the most efficient and effective manner. I wish I could just pass on his secrets and techniques, but I'm not sure his knack for management is explainable. As I said before, some people are "people people," and even though Josh isn't comfortable in every situation, if he is put in charge of an event staff he is really in his element. From my observation he is able to do the following:

• **He creates a sense of camaraderie among the staff** through staff meetings, staff social events, and a very intense focus on one-to-one managing. Josh spends a lot of time with his key people, both individually and in groups, so that they feel comfortable asking him questions and involving him in the process related to their specific area of responsibility.

• **He knows how to pick people for specific roles,** which results in people being comfortable in their job functions. Hiring is very difficult. There is nothing worse than when a person simply does not feel suited to his or her assigned task. By spending time with his staff, Josh is able to discern who is going to be most effective at what.

• **He delegates well.** Perhaps because of his closeness with the staff, Josh is not afraid to delegate, and he has confidence that his people will get the job done. He also is not a control freak like some others in the business. Giving up the reins is not easy, but managers who can do so really help the people around them develop to their full potential. This is where *managing* comes in, and while it is not the most visible part of operating an event, effective staff management is of equal importance as all of the other issues we have discussed thus far.

• **He spends a lot of time organizing staff meetings, social functions, and project assignments** so that there is never any confusion as to what is expected. Clarity of responsibility and clear delineation of authority, while not always easy to create, should be a goal of every manager. If the people on your staff know precisely what is expected of them, they will be a lot more likely to succeed.

• **He doesn't second-guess and micromanage.** Josh lets everyone do their thing, which gives the members of his staff a very secure feeling and enables them to do their jobs without looking over their shoulders.

I have been known to micro-manage from time to time, so the fact that Josh is able to give people their marching orders and then keep his distance always amazes me. Where I may want to know every detail, Josh is content with the big picture. I have to admit that his technique with the staff sometimes works more effectively than mine. You will have to find your own comfort zone, but I suspect that you will be better off giving your staff some room and letting them operate. Give them a defined level of authority and the right to make some mistakes. They will learn more, grow faster, and work better as a team.

If you can achieve 75 percent of the camaraderie and teamwork that Josh has been able to achieve, you will be in great shape.

> ■ ■ ■ ■ ■ ■ ■ ■ ■ ■ ■ ■
>
> *Giving up the reins is not easy, but managers who can do so really help the people around them develop to their full potential.*
>
> ■ ■ ■ ■ ■ ■ ■ ■ ■ ■ ■ ■

STAFFING

When putting your staff together, you will want to fill certain roles during the creation and planning of the event. Others are jobs specifically for event week.

Full-Time Jobs

I have always found hiring to be the most difficult part of my job. Nevertheless, you have to do it; so I look for people who are trustworthy, have had experience dealing with people, and most importantly, are willing to run through a wall to get the job done. Try to find people that will fill the job description but also be able to mesh with your personality.

Tournament Manager

The tournament manager is essentially the number two person on your staff. This person is akin to the chief operating officer of a company, while your job is akin to that of the chief executive officer. The tournament manager should be with you from as early in the event's creation as possible. This person will be the one to make sure all of the duties are being carried out by the staff, freeing you up to sell sponsorships and handle political issues and other big-picture items such as television. The tournament manager needs to know everything about the event. In a lot of grassroots or smaller-budget events the tournament director and tournament manager will be the same person. If so, this is a *big* job.

Sales Manager

If you can afford it, after the tournament manager I would hire someone to be responsible for generating revenue. As we have discussed throughout, sales is perhaps the toughest part of the entire event process. If you can have at least one person dedicated solely to beating the bushes to raise dollars, you will be well served. The earlier you can hire this person, the better. And don't be afraid to offer them incentives through commissions.

The payment of commissions is a very common practice in all areas of sales, be it sports or otherwise. By paying your salespeople commissions (a percentage of whatever revenue they can generate), you will reduce the amount of guaranteed salary on your payroll. We have typically worked on a 10 percent commission of the *gross* dollar amount brought in by a salesperson (for example, a $10,000 deal would pay a $1,000 commission).

In some cases, you might pay the commission based on the *net* amount that the event receives from the deal. This method is a bit more complicated, but it takes into consideration the fact that there is a cost to implementing each deal. Thus, using the same $10,000 deal, there might be $1,000 involved in implementing the deal, from the cost of banners to the printing of a sign to the cost of printing the ad in the program. You might pay your salesperson a commission on $9,000 in this case, making the commission $900. We have tried it this way, and while some people might argue that it accurately reflects the cost of doing business and saves you from "double paying," it is complicated and often leads to morale problems. I suggest you stay away from this method.

Because trade deals are also important, we pay a commission based on the dollar value of a trade. However, we have often paid a slightly lower commission rate (say, 7.5 percent) on trades because we want the motivation to be a bit stronger on the cash side of things. We have found that the full value of a trade is never quite equal to the value of cash.

Finally, if your event and staff are big enough, it is not a bad idea to pay commissions on the sale of box seats (again, 10 percent is a fair commission). These commissions should be paid only to those whose job is to make calls specifically to sell your box seats. If you can sell out your most expensive tickets for the duration of your event, you will

The tournament manager and tournament director can be one and the same in smaller, lower-budget events; she basically runs the show.

be ahead of the game and the commission will be money well spent.

Ticket Manager

Assuming that you are selling tickets, someone is going to have to be in charge of managing those sales. You should have your ticket manager in place at least a couple of weeks before tickets go on sale. The role of the ticket manager is to keep track of the money *and* the tickets. This person oversees the box seat chart, daily ticket sales totals, seat kills, and the money. The ticket manager must have a system in place for credit cards, deposits, bank accounts, checks, *and* cash, both prior to and during the event. This is going to be one of your key associates. You must have the highest level of trust in him or her.

Financial Officer

If you are working with a small staff, the financial manager might also be the ticket manager. If you have the luxury of a much bigger staff, you can split ticketing and overall financing into two positions. Regardless, your financial officer needs to be familiar with accounting procedures, cash flow, and cash management.

Advertising and Marketing Manager

This person is responsible for your communications plan and image building. This is a complex position that involves the coordination of all of the elements discussed in chapter 5. Don't underestimate the importance of this role. Remember, you never want to hear "We didn't hear about the event" when it is over. Publicity, advertising, promotion—these are all jobs for your marketing manager.

Event-Week Jobs

Whereas certain staff jobs are necessary from creation to completion, others are only needed during the event itself. These roles are generally filled by specialists.

Stage Manager

You will need someone to be responsible for getting the participants on and off the court (or stage or field) on a timely basis. The person in this role has to be able to interface with you, the athletes, the press, the television crew, and so on. This is a key position that could be performed by the lead referee if necessary. The stage manager needs to be able to handle a lot of pressure but always with an air of calm.

Talent Liaison

Someone has to be available at all times to deal with the needs of the participants. This doesn't sound like a difficult job, but handling all of the egos, particularly at a high-level professional event, requires a special demeanor and someone who is *not* star struck. You may want to bring someone in from another event where they have already proved themselves.

Cash Manager

You should have someone in place who can watch over the money and report to your financial officer. There will be a lot going on

Handling all of the egos requires a special demeanor and someone who is not star struck.

during the event. As the promoter you might lose track of cash inflows and outflows. People will buy tickets, merchandise, and food with cash. Also, there will surely be some last-minute things to pay for. I think it is best if someone that you completely trust is charged with keeping track of the cash and making sure that it flows properly. In a small event this will be your financial officer.

Press Officer

You will need to monitor which press people get on site and when, who has access to what athletes, and whether you are going to have press conferences or just let the press and the athletes fend for themselves. Regardless of the answers, you will need a press officer to make these decisions and control this flow. Managing the press during the event can be critical. They are on deadlines and need access and information on a timely basis.

Television Liaison

If you are on TV, someone is going to have to liaise with the television people throughout the event. The production crew requires a lot of attention because there is so much involved and so much at stake. During event week the intensity related to your telecast increases geometrically, so you will want someone who is familiar with the needs of the production crew.

Transportation Manager

This is another seemingly simple job that invariably becomes complicated when traffic is bad, cars are late (or don't show up), people are running late, and so forth. Someone has to be charged with managing your transportation. Make sure this person has access to cell phones, telephones, and walkie-talkies. This is often a volunteer job.

Obviously, if you have a mega-event, your staff will be much larger and include sponsor liaisons, housing managers, government relations experts, volunteer coordinators, and a host of others. In a smaller event these functions must still be performed—they just get delegated among the same people who then do double or triple duty. So, hire well!

GETTING IT ALL DONE

Once you have put your staff together, you need a very specific time line for event day or week, and then you need to implement your plan. At this point you may want to refer back to the introduction of this book to review the very detailed time line that was used by everyone involved in Skating Goes Country.

Operations Time Line

Every event should start out with a time line like the one we created for Skating Goes Country. In addition to this all-encompassing time line you will also want to create a time line that deals specifically with tournament week. To help create these time lines, I suggest you let the following be your guide.

• **18 to 24 months out:** This is the ideal lead time for planning your event. If you create your event this far out in front of the proposed date, you are likely to have ample time to complete everything that we have discussed in this book. Although an event can be organized and implemented in far less time than this, 18 to 24 months of lead time will enable you to do everything without being rushed, which is especially helpful if you are a first-time event manager. Additionally, this gives you the time needed to get in sync with the cycles of potential sponsors, sites, television distributors, and so on, all of whom plan pretty far in advance. During this time period you should create your mission statement and budget; contact federations and player's associations; and begin talking to potential sponsors, sites, and television outlets.

• **15 months out:** Confirm date; continue sponsor solicitations; revise budget; open bank accounts.

• **12 months out:** Confirm site and television deals; tie up all details with federation or players' association; confirm marquee participants.

• **10 months out:** Begin hiring staff; continue sponsor solicitations; create logo; design graphic materials; set ticket prices.

• **9 months out:** Send initial mailing to ticket buyer list; contact vendors; develop communications plan; begin international TV solicitation.

• **8 months out:** Begin press activity; sign contracts for venue, TV; hire TV producer/director.

• **7 months out:** Fine-tune TV production budget; conduct site survey; begin confirming additional participants; receive vendor bids.

• **6 months out:** Determine TV show format; contact referees, officials, volunteers; finalize hotel deal; determine ad/promotion plan; negotiate ad spot buys.

• **5 months out:** Review budget; continue press activity; sign sponsor deals.

• **4 months out:** Print ticket order forms; continue sales activity; write event day/week schedule.

• **3 months out:** Put general tickets on sale; hold press conference; begin ad/promotion schedule; get full staff on board; hold staff meetings regularly.

• **2 months out:** Develop TV show running order; revise budgets; sign vendor contracts; order awards.

• **6 weeks out:** Fine-tune all outstanding issues; send letter to sponsors and participants with update; distribute posters and other graphic materials; monitor ticket strategy.

• **30 days out:** Conduct site survey; hold vendor and operations meeting; finalize gift items; finalize food and beverages; place signage order; revisit TV issues; develop press/VIP list; finalize travel arrangements.

• **10 days out:** Confirm room list with hotel; review ad campaign, PR plan; review budget; confirm all music rights; receive awards; review all event logistics.

• **5 days out:** Move into tournament office; begin site construction; coordinate staff as they arrive on site; conduct staff meeting/TV production review.

• **2 days out:** Coordinate talent arrivals; conduct rehearsals/run-throughs if applicable; make final hotel room count; hold press conference with star(s); hold production meeting; load in.

• **Event day:** Follow event-day time line/to-do lists.

• **Postevent:** Load out; conduct settlement; hold postevent party; send thank-yous; review finances; edit television tapes.

When you get to event week, you may want a very specific time line that could be in 15-minute increments if necessary. Skating Goes Country did not require something quite that detailed. Remember that Skating Goes Country was only a one-evening event. It was an involved production that required more than just one day to load in, rehearse, run the show, and load out, but it was still only a one-day project. Thus, our four-day time line looked something like this.

Sunday, November 21 (shuttle transportation available throughout from hotel to arena)

by 8 A.M.	Ice painted, stage installed
8:00 A.M.	Lighting and sound load-in
1:00 P.M.	Crew lunch
2:00–6:00 P.M.	House curtain to be hung/props installed
6:00 P.M.	Crew dinner Group rehearsal
7:00 P.M.	Focus lights

Monday, November 22

9:30 A.M.	Ice make
10:00 A.M.	Open ice
12 noon	Ice make Skaters arrive Television load-in Furniture load-in from Lane's (furniture needs to arrive Monday morning)
12:30 P.M.	Skater runs through holiday/country program for television blocking
2:30 P.M.	Ice make
2:45 P.M.	Group number rehearsal
5:00–7:00 P.M.	Dinner at arena for all cast and crew
6:00 P.M.	Focus television cameras (arena dark)
7:00 P.M.	Dress rehearsal for lighting, television, and PA announcer
10:00 P.M.	Dress rehearsal concludes

Tuesday, November 23

9:30 A.M.	Skater interviews and sound bites at arena or hotel
11:00 A.M.	Group rehearsal and open ice
1:00 P.M.	Band sound checks
	Interaction between skaters and band members for television
4:00 P.M.	Run finale with entire cast
5:00 P.M.	Dinner for cast and crew
	Open ice for skaters
6:30 P.M.	Doors open
7:30 P.M.	Show begins

Note: Skater retakes (if necessary) from the first half of the show will take place at intermission; retakes from the second half of the show will take place at the conclusion of the show.

| 10:15 P.M. | Load-out begins |
| | After-show party |

Wednesday, November 24

| morning | Skaters, cast, etc., to airport |

As I mentioned, you might even want to get more detailed than this, particularly if you are dealing with an inexperienced staff. In Nashville we had compiled a pretty veteran group that did not need quite as much direction as other staffs that we have had in the past. If this is your first event or if you have a lot of first-timers, I suggest that you create a more precise time line.

To-Do List

In conjunction with the time line, I always carry a detailed list of what needs to get done each day during the event. I start this the week before the event and carry it through the week of the event. Even though modern management techniques and technology suggest that paper lists are no longer efficient, there is no substitute for a good, old-fashioned "to-do" list on three-by-five cards that you can carry around in your pocket. I might make a new one every day or every other day as the event approaches.

You need to update your to-do lists constantly and *live by them.* They should completely itemize what you need to accomplish on a particular day or during a week. As the tournament director, you might even have two lists: a list of specific things *you* need to accomplish during the event and a second list of what others on the staff have to accomplish. I strongly urge you to take a few minutes at the beginning or end of each day to put this list together, carry it with you at all times, and check off what has been done so that you don't repeat yourself.

Load-In and Site Preparation

Notwithstanding the importance of everything that has been done thus far, the site preparation and load-in might be the most important part of your event planning. Yes, you need sponsors, and yes, you need participants. Your contracts need to be correct, and the food has to be ordered. But, if your site is not prepared correctly and the load-in not thorough, all of your planning could go down the tubes in no time. This is particularly important if you are outdoors, although indoor events pose their own unique challenges. Some of the key elements to load-in and site preparation are discussed in the following sections.

Bleachers

Assuming that you have determined how many seats to build and where to rent the equipment (there are several companies around the country that specialize in bleacher rental), building your bleachers could take several days. As we discussed earlier, if you are building an outdoor facility, you probably need to move in a good 7 to 10 days in advance. Somehow, Association of Volleyball Professionals (AVP) events, such as the AVP Championship of New England, were able to get the bleachers and courts built and functioning in three days. Because the King of the Beach event required a more elaborate setup, we needed a week. We also had to bring in several tons of sand. Your move-in time line is directly related to the type of event you have and the extent to which you need to build out the site. If you are putting on a tennis event in which the courts are in place and the number of seats is few, you might only need a day or two to prepare. If you are putting on a 10K for which bleachers won't be needed, then you might show up the day before. For a charity golf outing you might arrive the morning of the event. There is no single answer to the amount of time you will need to load in, but just remember that it will no doubt take longer than you anticipate. Of course, the advantage to being indoors is that the seats are permanent!

Tents

The same issues that apply to bleachers apply to tents. These can generally be put up in

one day, but I suggest that you give yourself some extra time, particularly if you might decide that the layout you drew on paper doesn't flow well in reality.

Insurance

Don't forget to have all of your insurance in place before you begin setting up for your event. I emphasize this here (again!) because site setup is an area that points to all the issues for which you need coverage. Suppose you are putting in bleachers and a couple of screws come loose. Someone may then sit in that spot and fall through the stands. Need I say more? I hate to be repetitive, but insurance is one of those items that can easily slip through the cracks, and I just don't want you to forget it.

There are several types of insurance. We have discussed each of them already—liability, television production, errors and omissions, and even rain insurance. The best advice I can give you in this area is to sit down with an insurance expert, someone you trust or who comes highly recommended. Then go over all of your needs and tie that person into everything you do. This will seem like an unnecessary expense and an annoying detail until someone gets hurt on your site or something happens that leads to a major problem. Get the insurance and then you won't have to think about any of these issues!

Catering

Food becomes of paramount importance during the week of the event. Find a caterer who can provide an assortment of food groups to handle the various needs of your participants, sponsors, and crew members. They all eat differently (and at different times and places), and all are important in their own ways. If the food is good, someone *may* remember. If the food is bad, many people will *definitely* remember!

> **Y**ou need to update your to-do lists constantly and live by them.

Offices

You are going to need a place to work during the event. In fact, you are going to need a couple of places from which to deal with different situations. You may not care if anyone overhears some of your meetings and conversations, but you will want a separate space for more private conversations, including phone calls. Make sure that you have enough office space including a private area where you can deal with sensitive issues. This does not have to be traditional office space. It may be under a tent, in a trailer, or just a table away from all the action. If you go this route, don't forget a power source for telephones, computers, copying machines, and the like.

Dressing Rooms

We touched on this issue briefly in chapter 6. Participants need a place to prepare, to change, to get out of the heat or cold. Athletes need to be able to go through their routines in order to perform at their highest level. Make sure that you provide adequately for them. A cramped locker room with less than adequate facilities can be a real problem for the athletes and subsequently for you.

Access

Everyone who comes to your event, from participants to parents to sponsors, the press, television personnel, officials, and VIPs, is going to want full ac-

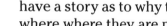

If the food is good, someone may remember. If the food is bad, many people will definitely remember!

cess to your site. If your event is at an indoor arena, they are going to want to get backstage. If your event is outdoors, they are going to want to be able to go into the player area, VIP lounge, or any place that is perceived to be a spot where only important people get to go. You need to control this flow of people, and while it will be a hassle in certain instances, you need to hold your ground. The best way to achieve this control is through a series of specifically notated credentials that flag where a person can go (see figure 8.1). Your security people will then be charged with saying no to a lot of people, each of whom will have a story as to why they need to go somewhere where they are not allowed.

Event-Day Management

Whether or not you are ready, when it is time for the event to start, you will be descended

Figure 8.1 Credentials.

Insurance

Throughout this book I have referred to various insurance needs. The different policies for different aspects of the event are listed here:

• **Liability.** This is similar to the insurance you might have on your house. Liability insurance covers you in the case of personal injury to a spectator, vendor, volunteer, or anyone else while on your site.

• **Errors and omissions.** E & O, as this is often referred to, is what protects you in case of a negligent act on your part that you or the officers of your company get sued for. This insurance covers you and your company for mistakes that are made related to an item or issue that you should have known about. I once heard of someone who wrote up a contract for a $10,000 deal and accidentally made it for $100,000. If the other party decides to sue over such a mistake, this is where E & O would kick in.

• **Auto.** This is pretty straightforward. Auto insurance covers anyone on your staff or otherwise related to the event who drives a car registered to the event. It protects the event in case the driver of one of your cars gets into an accident.

• **Rain.** I have alluded to this a couple of times throughout the book. Rain insurance protects you in case you are completely wiped out because of rain. It will cover situations as broad as cancellation fees that you might have to pay, as well as expenses that you had previously incurred and now cannot recoup.

• **Umbrella.** Your umbrella policy sits on top of all of these individual policies and provides you with extra protection over and above the levels that a specific auto or liability policy might pay out.

• **Television.** If you are putting your event on television and you are the responsible party for the production, you should look into broadcasters liability insurance. This covers you in case there are issues related to artist performances, music clearances, or other misuse. Suits related to television can get expensive, so this is pretty important coverage.

You should seriously consider all of these coverages to make sure you are fully protected.

---

on by athletes, vendors, spectators, VIP guests, and so forth. Everything you have worked toward will now become a reality. If you can, get a good night's sleep and wake up ready to meet the challenges that you have dreamed about.

Up until this point you have been a deal maker, promoter, salesperson, spokesperson, and mastermind of what you conceived months earlier. While you have also managed during the lead-up to the event, during the week of your event, "manager" will be your

primary role. You will potentially be at the eye of every storm, and you will need to be prepared to navigate through each one. This will require patience, vision, a grasp of the details, and the ability to delegate whenever possible.

As a manager you cannot be all things to all people during the course of your event. Believe me, I have tried managing the talent, being in the television truck, talking to the press, deciding on the schedule of play, taking care of VIPs, and so on, all at the same time. It doesn't work. Now is when all of the prior involvement with your staff, sponsors, site personnel, caterers, television production people, and so forth will pay off. You will have laid the groundwork for your colleagues to do their jobs. Now is the time to let them do just that, knowing that you are in the background as the final arbiter if things go wrong. But be prepared to manage.

There is no real trick to managing people. It takes hard work, compassion, and a sense of leadership. It takes the knowledge of when to interfere, when to stay out of things, when to set rules, and when to draw the line. In short, the best managers have a knack for motivating people and keeping them focused on their priorities. Some of the methods that might be helpful in managing during the event are discussed next.

Meetings

Although you don't want to have too many meetings, a daily get-together at which you go over the most important issues cannot hurt. It gets everyone on the same page, acts to disseminate information, creates a sense of camaraderie, and gives you a chance to motivate the troops.

Information Flow

This may be one of your most important tasks. Make sure that everyone who needs to know something knows it. You do not want a situation to arise in which someone acts out of lack of information, particularly if it is something that should have been communicated to him or her. I prefer to err on the side of over-communicating. You can use the daily meeting, a bulletin board, individual boxes where memos and other messages can be stored/ posted, or simple word of mouth. The bottom line is that information is key, so make sure that it gets to those who need to know.

Walking Around

One of the most effective management tools is walking around. If you have a big site, this can become even more important because staff members who are on the outer edge of your site might feel out of the flow. A regular walk of the site is a good tool, as it keeps you visible and in contact with your staff. Get out of your office and see what is going on.

Downtime

People may be asked to put in long hours during event days. Make sure that your staff gets some downtime if they are really being pushed. Remember, exhausted people make mistakes. Develop a system whereby people rotate in and out of being on duty so that they are fresh.

Meet and Greet

This is another form of walking around. If you are the tournament director, it is important that you be visible and that you say hello to all of the vendors, sponsors, television personnel, athletes, and so on. Go out and meet them all, shake some hands, and ask if everything is all right.

The Press

These guys are tricky. Are they for you or against you? Will they use your whole quote or just the part that fits their story? If they only use a portion, will it accurately mirror what you intended to say? Will their coverage be helpful or will you wish they never heard of your event?

When I first got into the sports business, I thought it was pretty cool to be in the newspaper. But then I was quoted out of context. And then I was criticized. Suddenly I didn't think it was so cool anymore. The moral of the story is that you

■ ■ ■ ■ ■ ■ ■ ■ ■ ■ ■

The best managers have a knack for motivating people and keeping them focused on their priorities.

■ ■ ■ ■ ■ ■ ■ ■ ■ ■ ■

simply have to be careful in your dealings with the press. As I said before, the press can make you or break you.

During your event you and your press officer should be prepared for the press by making sure there is a specific place for them (with phones, desks, computer hookups, food, and the like). You should be hospitable and cordial. The press love to be coddled and in many cases are used to this. They expect good food, perhaps a gift (some outlets will forbid their staff from accepting gifts), and generally to be treated as VIPs around your event site.

Most important, though, you should be informative. If someone is hurt, let the press know immediately. If something of significance happens—good or bad—inform the press as soon as you can. Give them the information they need to do the job of reporting on your event.

In this regard, it is very helpful to have information on all of the participants, the venue, and any other element that is important to the event available at a moment's notice. Keep in mind that not everyone who covers your event is going to be well versed in the detail of your sport or your project for that matter. I have been at major tennis events at which the person covering for the biggest local paper was assigned because all of the paper's better-known writers were busy. Your sport may not be a subject that the local press covers on a regular basis. As a result, no one at the paper may know much about your sport to begin with.

I realize that when you read a story in the newspaper, it always seems as though the writers understand what they are talking about—even if at times you totally disagree with their assessment—but this is not always the case. You have to be equally prepared for the seasoned veteran and the "stringer" who has little or no experience in covering your sport but was assigned to the story neverthe-

■ ■ ■ ■ ■ ■ ■ ■ ■ ■ ■ ■

Try to visualize what your words will look like in the morning paper (or on television) before you say them.

■ ■ ■ ■ ■ ■ ■ ■ ■ ■ ■ ■

less. If you can make the people on both ends of the press spectrum feel comfortable (and having access to plenty of information is a great place to start), you will have gone a long way toward handling the press well.

As for what you say, if you sugarcoat everything and speak in very bland sound bites, you probably won't read your quotes too often. If you give the press interesting snippets, you likely will see your words in print. Just remember to try to visualize what your words will look like in the morning paper (or on television) *before* you say them. You should do everything possible to turn the press into an ally, knowing all the while that they are not going to pull any punches in their reporting just because they might like you. A press officer who is savvy to the needs of the press can be very helpful in this area.

Working With the Sponsors

In terms of working with sponsors, all I can say is that you need to remember where your bread is buttered. As much as you prepare for the press, make doubly sure that you are prepared for your sponsors. Review all of your contracts to make sure that every detail that you promised is delivered . . . and then some. Carve out time in your schedule to see their displays, booths, ads, or promotions. Check in with them periodically to make sure everything is being taken care of. Be sure that you have assigned someone on the staff to monitor the sponsors' needs and to interface with their representatives. How your sponsors experience your event is going to come down to your ability to manage their expectations and deliver the benefits during the event itself.

Contact With the Players

Don't forget that yours should be a *player-friendly event*. Everyone else is important, but the talent is critical. There is no event without the players, no matter how many sponsors and fans show up. Once the participants arrive on site, your job is to make sure that they get what they need in order to perform at the top level. This is true whether you have world-class athletes or weekend warriors.

During the course of the event make sure you get around to as many of the athletes as possible to talk to them about their experience at the event, make sure they have what they need, thank them for coming, invite them back for the next year, and so on. In short, as it relates to the players, you are the host; they are the guests at your party. You want them to feel comfortable without being doted on. You want them to perform well without feeling that there is any more pressure than the moment dictates. You want them to walk away saying that your event was a nice place to play.

If you have someone on staff who gets along well with the athletes—and this is a talent in and of itself—you will be ahead of the game. Maybe the best person I ever saw at getting along with the athletes was Bob Basche. He has long been a good friend, but he was also the first guy I worked closely with at Colgate-Palmolive. Part of his job was to interact with the tennis players, and he was great at it. He knew when to approach them, what to say, how to cajole, and when to stay away. We look back now at bringing T-shirts to the players at the U.S. Open tennis event when it was at Forest Hills as a means of staying in touch with the players. But the fact is that Colgate as a company had a close relationship with the players because of Bob. It takes a real feel to get along with the athletes, particularly at the professional level. You will have to take a role in this, but make sure that you also have someone who has the "feel" to interface with the athletes.

■ ■ ■ ■ ■ ■ ■ ■ ■ ■ ■ ■

There is no event without the players, no matter how many sponsors and fans show up.

■ ■ ■ ■ ■ ■ ■ ■ ■ ■ ■ ■

Monitoring the Television Production

Keeping in mind that you can't do everything, I urge you to pay close attention to what is going on with regard to your television production. Remember, this takes on a life of its own and can consume you. Assuming that you have a strong producer and/or director, it shouldn't. However, more people who view your event will do so through the eye of television than in person. As a result, it is important to stay in touch with the television crew throughout to be sure that they remain on the same page as you with regard to the look of the show and its contents. If your show is taped and you have ample editing time, you are going to have a chance to shape the show as it is put together. However, you can only edit what gets shot, so make sure that the crew is getting on tape whatever it is that you had agreed to incorporate into the telecast. I suggest regular communication with the director throughout the course of the event so that you are not constantly running back and forth to the television truck, which will be tiring for you and annoying for the TV crew!

Dealing With Problems

One of your major roles during the event will be to troubleshoot. As a result, you are going to have to be on your toes and in the frame of mind to look for solutions, not lay blame (you can do that later), and keep things moving despite what might in some cases be major setbacks. You are the final word when it comes to solving problems, so be prepared.

THE SHOW IS OVER . . . SORT OF

At this point you have probably made it through the event, meaning that the last ball has been hit or the last runner has crossed the finish line; the awards have been presented (keep your speech short!) and the fans have gone home . . . but that does not mean that your work is done. In fact, some of your most important tasks are still to come.

Postevent Party

This is not the most important function, but it is potentially the most fun. Assuming that your event does not turn out to be a disaster, everyone will have worked very hard throughout the period leading up to and during the event. I have always found that a postevent party for the staff, sponsors, any VIPs, and even some of the athletes serves a great purpose. If you throw a nice little party, it allows everyone to relax a bit, trade some stories from the event, and generally let their hair down. While many on your tournament staff will probably be part-time workers or volunteers who won't be involved with you a week after the event ends, it is still a nice touch to give everyone a little time to celebrate. But this does not have to be a big event. In fact, something intimate will be a lot more appreciated than a major bash. Keep it simple but classy, and everyone will leave the site feeling good about themselves, the event, and you.

Tear-Down and Load-Out

I cannot stress enough how important the postevent tear-down and load-out will be. Speed is one factor based on your site agreement. But efficiency in packing, sending the right things to the right places (if you think something is in storage and then can't find it weeks or months later, you will rack your brain in frustration), keeping track of inventory, not losing or breaking anything . . . all of these are critical issues even though the event is over. This is where the saying "It ain't over till it's over" really rings true. You have to make

sure that load-out is a real priority for your event team. They can't let down too soon.

Postevent Reports and Thank-Yous

The event is over, you are on to your next project, and the last thing you want to talk about or hear about is "the event." Regardless of whether you are going to run this event the following year or if it was a one-time event, what you do in the days and weeks immediately following the event can be as important as everything you have done up until now. You may think that you will never forget a single detail from your event, but believe me, you will. So that you repeat the good aspects of the event and improve on the bad ones, I suggest you do the following:

You may think that you will never forget a single detail from your event, but believe me, you will.

- Make notes on every detail.
- Write reports to your key staff about issues that were not handled as you would have liked.
- Have the staff submit detailed reports on whatever aspect of the event they were responsible for.
- Make sure that all of the bills get paid. Some will come late and could get overlooked as a result.
- Make sure that the fees due on all of the invoices you send out are collected.
- Send out gifts of appreciation (these can be T-shirts from the event or photos) to everyone who you think deserves some special acknowledgment.
- Make a notebook that contains everything by subject matter from the event (I use a simple three-ring binder).

All of this is so that when it comes time to start to put together the event for the following year, you are not starting from scratch and going from memory. You have come a long way at this point from having conceived the event and applying for a sanction. You don't want to have to "reinvent the wheel" next year.

Selling Next Year's Event

Don't forget about next year's event! You should start selling your next event during or immediately following the current one (as if you didn't have enough on your mind already!). Nothing will better impress a potential sponsor, television distributor, media partner, or vendor than being there while the event is taking place, particularly if it is someone who passed on the opportunity to sponsor the current event. If you have a full house or just an exciting atmosphere, having someone out to the event that may ultimately want to get involved in the future can only be a plus. You might not think you will have the time for this while the event is going on, but you will. Anyone that you invite to the event won't expect to get much of your time. Even if you say hello and spend five minutes, they will be happy. So, make a list well in advance of the event of the people you would like to have attend and make sure you get your invitations out early. Then, during the event, know who is coming and where they are sitting. Take a moment to drop buy, say hello, take them on a short tour of the site, and so forth. There is no better time or place to sell your event than while it is taking place.

Financials

First of all, make sure that all the money that you are due is paid. In direct correlation to that, make sure that all the money you owe gets paid, or if there is a problem or question about an invoice, that it gets dealt with. No matter how artistically successful or unsuccessful your event has been, this is a business at the end of the day. People should pay you on time, and similarly, you should pay them on time. Review every invoice to make sure that it is correct. If people are slow to pay, give them gentle reminders by phone, e-mail, or fax (you probably won't have to resort to legal action, but it could happen). And pay your bills on time.

Returns

Some people are going to come to the event and not think that they got their money's worth. You should be prepared with a refund policy. Typically, for weather, we say that as long as play begins, the spectator is not entitled to a refund. In a tennis tournament this would mean that as long as one game were played, we consider that the ticket has been used. You should make this judgment and policy *before* the tournament starts and then deal with people who insist on refunds for whatever reason. We have had people ask for (read "demand") refunds without good reasons. We have granted refunds or denied them depending on the situation. If we thought that the goodwill outweighed the potential downsides (once you give one refund, where do you draw the line?), then we give the person some kind of refund. This might be tickets to the event the following year. Anyway, this can be tricky because there is a public relations side to all of this. Give this some careful thought in advance of the event, then draw the line and treat each person as if he or she were the most important and only person who attended the event.

Remember, you are a promoter. In this case, a promoter is a person who begins, secures financing for, and helps to organize a sports event. If you are passionate about your project and want to see it take a permanent place on the social and sporting landscape, your work is never done. If you truly have the internal makeup to follow in the footsteps of Barnum,

> ■ ■ ■ ■ ■ ■ ■ ■ ■ ■ ■
>
> *There is no better time or place to sell your event than while it is taking place.*
>
> ■ ■ ■ ■ ■ ■ ■ ■ ■ ■

Disney, Ringling, Stern, Feld, and others, you will come to love promoting, thrive on the pressures, and live for the excitement.

After all the work, to see a full house and the smiles on the faces of the people of the audience, to hear the thank-yous from the participants, to read the reviews, make the deals, and make a profit . . . well, that is what it is all about. Promoting an event is a roller coaster ride, but it can be an enjoyable and lucrative ride at that.

Good luck. I hope that some of what we have discussed will come in handy and make your event just a little better.

✔ Checklist for Event Week

✔ Make sure your event team is in place.

✔ Hire tournament-week specialists.

✔ Set communications procedures so the staff is fully informed.

✔ Manage your finances and cash closely.

✔ Create a comprehensive time line.

✔ Be sure your insurance is in place.

✔ Manage by walking around the site.

✔ Be prepared to solve problems, not point fingers.

✔ Provide information for the press; think through your comments to the press.

✔ Make contact with the participants; make sure they know you think they are important.

✔ Sell future events during the current one.

✔ Make detailed notes about the good and bad points of this year's event.

✔ Have a refund policy in place.

✔ Have a good time! You have worked hard for it.

Working Model: Tournament List and Time Line

In order to be ready for our event, we will need a time line to guide us. Use the following sample time line to guide you in creating your own.

Two weeks before move-in, be sure you do the following:

- Acquire office supplies: paper, pens, markers, stapler, copying machine, envelopes, stamps
- Confirm television camera positions
- Confirm entry list
- Confirm details for draw party
- Send invitations to all sponsors and other VIPs
- Attend to catering details
- Acquire tents and port-a-johns
- Acquire gift bags

One week before the event, hold a full staff meeting to review all of the details of the event.

Three days before move-in, review all of the details with the full staff.

Move-in (one day before the event)

8:00 A.M.	All staff on site
8:45 A.M.	Deliveries begin
9:30 A.M.	Phones to be set up/office functional
10:00 A.M.	Tents and other construction begins

12:00 noon	Press walk-through of event
1:00 P.M.	Calls to press to confirm their attendance at draw party
2:00 P.M.	Practice courts available
5:00 P.M.	Catering delivered for draw party
6:30 P.M.	Draw party begins
7:00 P.M.	Draw with press in attendance

Day one of event

9:00 A.M.	Staff meeting
10:00 A.M.	Site walk-through
12:00 noon	Referee/umpire meeting
1:30 P.M.	Matches begin
4:00 P.M.	Sponsor promotion on center court
7:30 P.M.	Matches end
8:00 P.M.	Player party

Day two of event

10:00 A.M.	Staff meeting
12:00 noon	Referee/umpire meeting
12:30 P.M.	Lunch with title sponsor
1:30 P.M.	Matches begin
7:00 P.M.	Matches end
8:00 P.M.	Press conference with semifinalists

Day three of event

10:00 A.M.	Staff meeting
11:00 A.M.	Site walk-through
12:00 noon	Television production meeting
1:30 P.M.	Scheduled interviews for television
2:30 P.M.	Matches begin
7:30 P.M.	Matches end

Day four of event

11:00 A.M.	Staff meeting
12:00 noon	Production meeting
1:00 P.M.	First final
3:00 P.M.	Second final
5:00 P.M.	Awards ceremony
6:30 P.M.	Wrap party

Day after event

| 8:00 A.M. | Load-out begins/transportation to airport begins |
| 9:00 A.M. | Staff meeting/clean office out |

SPONSOR THANK-YOU LETTER

Dear _____,

Just a short note to thank you for your participation in last week's XYZ Cup. Your involvement made our first year a reality and paved the way for this to become an annual event that will make it possible for local area youth to pursue their tennis dreams.

As a token of our appreciation, I have enclosed a photo of match point, which captures the essence of this event. As you can see, there are smiles all around from the players to the fans. It was this atmosphere that contributed to the warm feeling that everyone had about this tournament.

Once again, thanks for your support of this inaugural event. We have already begun planning next year's event (August 15–19) and look forward to working with you to make that tournament an even bigger and better event.

Best regards,

Tournament Director

Epilogue

You would think that I am "talked out" after writing this book, but I'm not. In fact, I feel as though I still have a lot to say. Now that Skating Goes Country is "in the books," I thought you might be curious as to how it fared. I also want to share with you some final thoughts on the challenges of another "event," writing this book.

CONCLUSIONS FROM SKATING GOES COUNTRY

First of all, this event was a lot of hard work that in the end was pretty rewarding. We made a lot of good new contacts in Nashville, at TNN, and within the country music community. Everyone who participated was happy with the result. We got a nice thank-you letter from Billy Ray Cyrus, and TNN aired the show several more times than originally planned. I thought the television show looked good, although the set came across a little darker than I had anticipated (which just reinforces the importance of lighting). TNN and the sponsors all seemed very pleased with the show, and Mothers Against Drunk Driving, our charity for this event, received a lot of exposure for their cause. Several categories that deserve special mention are outlined here:

• **Attendance.** We did not sell as many tickets as we anticipated, and in fact, at about 5,000 spectators, we did not come close to the numbers realized by the Tom Collins show that we had visited. Some people felt our ads were a bit confusing and did not explain clearly enough the collaboration between the skaters and the country music acts.

• **Television ratings.** Our ratings were quite good; we received a 1.6 rating in the initial airing, more than double TNN's regular rating for that time slot. This encouraged TNN to air the show a total of *eight* times.

• **Sponsor relations.** This may have been the most successful area of the event. We were able to develop sponsorship packages for Lane Furniture, Opry Mills Mall, Aquatrend, Northwest Airlines, Sportssound, and the Nashville Renaissance Hotel. Everyone seemed very pleased with the results, and we are currently working with several of these same sponsors on a couple of new events.

• **Press coverage.** The press coverage, which was nothing short of outstanding, I must credit to TNN's publicity department. In addition to articles in the local newspapers and coverage on local television stations, we had full-page coverage in *TV Guide* and several country music magazines. In addition, the weekly television guides for several major markets carried stories or reviews of the show in their holiday pullout sections. All of this helped deliver the strong television rating that we received.

• **Financial results.** StarGames is a private company, so we do not publish our financial results. I can tell you that we did not hit our projections, which was primarily because of lackluster ticket sales. We had based all of our budgets on about 7,000 paid spectators. In the final analysis, we had fewer than 5,000. To compound the problem, certain of our costs (shipping, music clearance, stagehands, and overtime) ran over our projections. On the positive side, the majority of our costs stayed in line with our budget, and our domestic and international television revenues were quite a bit higher than anticipated. As a result, the overall financial picture was not as good as we would have liked it to be, but nothing to cry over either.

Looking to the future, I think there is a spot for Skating Goes Country on the skating calendar. However, we are going to take at least a year off to redefine the concept. I would expect that this show will make its way back on our slate of events in 2002 or 2003.

CONCLUSIONS FROM THE AUTHOR

Writing this book has been quite an education for me. I have never written anything even a fraction of this length. I was under the false impression that I could just sit down and bang out a couple of hundred pages with no problem. *Wrong.*

Writing a book is hard work. Having been through this exercise, I have a whole different level of appreciation for authors. How they do this on a daily basis, I will never know.

Nevertheless, with all my complaining, I am really glad that I tackled this. As I said at the outset, I have always wanted to write a book as a means of giving something back to the industry and of helping people trying to get into our business. I hope that I have accomplished part of that through all of these words, examples, charts, and pictures.

I was not always on the event side of our business. For years I represented athletes and negotiated with promoters on their behalf. I was one of the critics when things didn't go well while also pushing the organizers to treat my clients better. At some point, I began wanting to run the events myself. In our business nothing reflects your personality more than an event that you put together. The look, feel, and result are in your hands. After years of

sitting in the stands while my clients performed, it is nice to be the one with everything on the line.

I love what I do now. I have found nothing in our business more satisfying than walking out into the arena and seeing a full house. The creative opportunities offered by the television productions are liberating. Working closely with the event staff is invigorating. All in all, while there are a lot of nervous moments in the course of putting the event together, it is a hell of a lot of fun. I can't think of anything that I would rather be doing at this time.

Also, as I alluded to briefly, as promoters we are part of the fraternity that includes some of the entertainment geniuses of all time. Charlie Chaplin and Walt Disney have long been two of my idols. I think their creative genius is unparalleled, and the chance to use things learned from them and even measure myself against them is equally as exciting. While to date I have not had any productions that are nearly on their scale, I hold them up as the standards and hope someday to have one event and television production that is at least in their league. We'll see.

I hope that you have been somewhat inspired by what I have had to say on these pages. I hope too that some of the examples in this book will transfer over to what you are doing in your event. If you can apply just a few things from this guide to your own efforts, then perhaps I can consider this project a success. It has been fun. It has been a learning experience for me. It has forced me to write down what I do every day out of instinct and habit.

The event business is a hard way to make a living. Yet, with everything that might be stacked against you from the outset, there is always another event, always another year to try it again, always someone that you can hope to entertain with your ideas.

A skating agent told me not long ago that he thinks StarGames creates some of the best new productions in the business. I don't know if he meant it or if he was just trying to butter me up so that I keep hiring his clients. I prefer to take his comment at face value. When we give people some entertaining moments and make some money at the same time, I am very happy.

I hope that producing events can give you as much of a rush as it gives me. Now I will finally shut up and let you get to work. I look forward to seeing how you do!

Appendix A

Official
Site Proposal

T he following is a sample site proposal that we used to solicit a site deal for the Best of the Beach Invitational. You may want to use elements from it when preparing a site deal for your event.

BEST OF THE BEACH SERIES HOST SITE PACKAGE
Tournament Site Guidelines

A. Physical Needs

1. Construction/removal of a one-court stadium, including bleachers, platforms, and court sand, consisting of no more than 2,500 seats in 1999, 3,000 seats in 2000, and 4,000 seats in 2001. There will be the need for a minimum one (1) outside court.

2. Permitting and approval for the on-site sale of event tickets, food and beverages (alcoholic and nonalcoholic), souvenirs, and merchandise.

3. Space necessary for tenting and/or appropriate covered space in locations to be agreed upon for a period of five (5) days prior to the event to include a Box Office, Player Area, Medical Area, Officials Area, Media/Press Area, Volunteer Area, Sponsor Entertainment Area, VIP Sandbox Hospitality Area, and Tournament Office (a space of 275' × 275' will be well suited for all needs).

4. Temporary office space for StarGames to manage the event for a period no less than ninety (90) days prior to the event and fourteen (14) days following the event.

5. Water and electric access utilities for the areas specified in point 3 above; electrical power for the center court (i.e., television production, public address, scoreboard, etc.).

6. Sanitation to include a dumpster, public trash receptacles, and garbage pickup for the event period.

7. Local law enforcement support for the event period.

B. Hotel

    1. Complimentary Rooms

        a) Event Weekend: A total of 125 room nights (room/tax only) to be used for athletes, event staff, media, television executives, officials, etc., during the event period (Thursday–Sunday).

        b) Ten (10) room nights (room/tax only) to be used by StarGames during the contract year. Any room needs above this number would be purchased at an agreed-upon discounted rate as available.

    2. Discount Rates

        a) Beach Party Packages: A total of 50 rooms per night (Thursday, Friday, and Saturday of the event weekend) would be provided to StarGames at a premium discounted price, which may be incorporated into a special hotel/ticket package for fans.

        b) Player Rooms: 32 VIP rooms at no cost to StarGames for player accommodation needs.

C. Entertainment/Food and Beverages

    1. Two (2) press functions (food and beverages included) during the event year.

    2. Food and beverage catering for players and media Friday, Saturday, and Sunday of the event.

D. Host Site Benefits

    1. The host site will become the official host and home of the event for three years (1999–2001).

    2. The host site will receive the public and private food and beverage rights and 80 percent of the revenue.

    3. The host site will receive 20 percent of the net ticket proceeds.

    4. The host site will receive two (2) commercial spots per hour on the national television broadcast(s).

    5. The host site will receive a minimum of 60 seconds of beauty shots of the resort on each television broadcast.

    6. The host site will receive graphic and announcer mentions on the broadcast.

    7. The host site will appear in all advertising and promotional materials.

    8. The host site will receive two (2) full-page, four-color advertisements in the official event program (if produced).

    9. The host site will receive rotational signage, if used, and four (4) banners above the court. If static signage is used, the host site will receive a total of four (4) banners on the court and four (4) above the court.

    10. The host site will receive public address announcements throughout the event.

    11. The host site will receive twenty (20) sandbox and twenty (20) reserved tickets for each session of the event.

    12. The host site will be featured on the corporate sponsor board.

    13. The host site will receive one (1) on-court promotion during each session of the event.

E. Cost

1. In exchange for the above benefits and consideration, the host site will provide the following:

   a) A cash fee of $50,000 per year

   b) All of the site and hotel costs as listed in Physical Needs, Hotel, and Entertainment/ Food and Beverages above

   c) Twenty percent of all net sales for all food and beverages (minus any comp products/ services)

   d) Public relations and promotions assistance to be conducted for a 90-day period prior to the start of the event, including but not limited to the integration of event and sales information in printed materials, signage, and electronic and print media vehicles in materials regularly produced by the site.

Appendix B

Sample Player Agreement

The following is a sample of an agreement we have used to contract athletes to our events. Because this is a multi-year agreement with options, some or all of this may be applicable to your event. For high-profile athletes, I suggest you try to get these agreements signed as far in advance as possible.

Name (of athlete or business representative)
Address (usually care of the athlete's agent)

Re: Player Agreement

Dear Player:

The purpose of this letter Agreement ("Agreement") is to set forth the understanding between (Player's name) ("You/Your") and StarGames, LLC ("StarGames") with respect to Your participation in the Best of the Beach Invitational, a professional beach volleyball event as more specifically described herein below (hereinafter "Event") to be owned, operated, and promoted by StarGames.

The terms and conditions agreed upon by You and StarGames are as follows:

1. **Term.** The term shall commence upon the execution of this Agreement and shall remain in full force and effect through the forty-five- (45-) day period immediately following the Event in 2000, unless sooner terminated or extended in accordance with the terms and conditions set forth herein. "Contract Year" shall be defined as the twelve- (12-) month period beginning upon the execution of this Agreement and shall end forty-five (45) days following the Event. You hereby grant to StarGames an option to renew this Agreement for a period of two (2) additional one- (1-) year periods on the same terms and conditions applicable to the initial Term, except that prize money shall increase in each option year as set forth below. Said option shall be exercisable, if at all, in one- (1-) year increments and by StarGames' delivery to

You of written notice thereof prior to the end of the Term or the applicable option year.

2. **The Event.** The Event, which shall be owned, operated, and promoted by StarGames, shall consist of women professional beach volleyball players ("Player[s]") competing in two-on-two competitions in an individual/round-robin format. The Event shall be known as the "Best of the Beach Invitational" ("BOBI" or "Event") with $100,000 in prize money, with You and 13 professional women's Players competing over a three- (3-) day period. The 2000 BOBI will be held on July 17–19 in Huntington Beach, California.

2001 (if the option is exercised)—Same as in 2000 except that the Event shall have $125,000 in prize money.

2002 (if the option is exercised)—Same as in 2000 except that the Event shall have $135,000 in prize money.

Subject to the FIVB schedule in 2001 and 2002, the BOBI shall be tentatively held on the following weekends (or equivalent weekends) in each Contract Year: June 25–27; July 16–18.

3. **Your Obligations.** In consideration for guaranteeing that the Event takes place as described above, and for StarGames' obligations as set forth in paragraph 4 below, You agree to the following:

a) You will participate in the 2000 BOBI. In addition, You agree to participate in the Event in 2001 (option) and 2002 (option) irrespective of any other event agreements or third party agreements you may have or will enter into if the option is exercised. Your participation shall be subject to You not being injured or excused as set forth herein, and subject to the rules, regulations, and guidelines ("Regulations") of the Event. (*Note:* The Regulations for the Event shall be determined by StarGames in conjunction with the "Player Council" as defined in paragraph 5 below.)

b) Subject to any preexisting professional commitments, you will make up to three (3) non-Event-related personal appearances, if requested by StarGames in each Contract Year and option year of this Agreement to promote the Event. Said appearances could include:
(1) Press or media days
(2) On-court exhibitions
(3) Sponsor meetings or outings, etc.

In the event that You participate in an exhibition, which will consist of a minimum of four (4) teams and two (2) matches on one (1) day, You will be paid One Thousand Dollars ($1,000) for each exhibition plus travel and local expenses. For all other appearances there shall be no fee payable to You; however, Your expenses shall be paid by StarGames. Other than the exhibitions, said appearances shall not exceed two (2) hours in length, excluding travel time.

c) You will make up to one (1) nonplaying appearance in the city where the Event is held, either within thirty (30) days of the start of, or during, the Event weekend, in support of the Event, if so requested. Said appearances shall be scheduled so as not to conflict with the schedule of play. If said appearance is not at the time of the Event (i.e., within two [2] days of the start of the Event or one [1] day following the Event), StarGames shall pay for your expenses in connection with said appearances.

d) You will grant to StarGames Your exclusive marketing rights as part of a group of Players (four or more Players) for purposes of StarGames confirming sponsorship and licensing agreements for the Events(s), so long as the use of said rights does not constitute an individual endorsement of any product or service, nor conflict with any preexisting individual endorsement of which You are a part. You shall have the reasonable right of approval over the use of Your photograph, likeness, and/or endorsement but not the approval over the terms of the agreement itself. In this connection, You acknowledge and agree that StarGames shall have the right to solicit and confirm sponsors and licensees for the Event(s) on a worldwide basis; however, nothing contained herein shall preclude You from entering into individual endorsement agreements, including the right to wear patches, that may be in conflict with Event sponsors and licensees.

e) You will grant to StarGames the right to use your name, likeness, photograph, or facsimile thereof for purposes of promoting and advertising the Events(s), so long as the use of said right does not constitute an individual endorsement of any product or service. You shall have reasonable right of approval over the actual likeness, photograph, or facsimile used.

f) You will not compete or play in an exhibition or tournament in any city or market defined as an area within a 150-mile radius of a city where an Event is scheduled to be held. The above notwithstanding, the parties recognize that each city or market may differ in terms of the exclusivity provision and that StarGames will consider waiving this provision on request by You should you want to compete in an event or exhibition within the 150-mile radius that would not be injurious to the Event.

g) You will serve on a Player Council, if elected, which will function as an advisory body to help determine standards for Player conduct, rules of the game, prize money distribution, etc.

In connection with FIVB events, StarGames agrees to make its best efforts to schedule the Event to avoid any conflicts between the Event(s) and FIVB events. Further, should a conflict develop, StarGames will make its best efforts to change the date of the conflicting Event(s). In the event a conflict exists between a scheduled Event and an FIVB event, You agree that You shall play in the Event unless in StarGames' sole judgment it waives the requirement for playing in the Event and grants an exemption. StarGames agrees to work with the Player Council to develop a policy for granting exemptions should StarGames waive the requirement for playing in an Event. StarGames recognizes that compelling reasons may exist for participation in a conflicting FIVB event; however, You acknowledge and accept the importance of Your participation to the success of each BOBI as set forth herein. Should StarGames waive its rights hereunder in any year of this Agreement, it shall not extend to future years. Further, if StarGames waives its rights in any year, there shall be no obligation to pay You any prize money for the Event.

4. **StarGames' Obligations.** In consideration for Your participation in the Event as outlined above, StarGames agrees to the following:

a) StarGames will produce, promote, and guarantee that the Event(s) takes place as set forth above in a first-class manner, including the payment of all prize money and on-site amenities such as medical staff, Player area, food, media, etc. StarGames agrees that all prize money shall be paid on site at each Event or exhibition.

b) StarGames will provide You with discount hotel accommodations (double occupancy) at a first-class (official Event) hotel throughout each Event. StarGames will make its best efforts to provide You with hotel rooms (double occupancy) at no cost (exclusive of incidentals) to You at each Event so long as You remain in the Event.

c) StarGames will provide you with a point-to-point round-trip airline ticket at no cost to You for each BOBI in which you participate.

5. **Player Council.** The parties agree that the Player Council shall consist of three (3) elected Players. Said members of the Player Council shall be elected by the sixteen (16) top-ranked Players according to the most recent acceptable ranking system.

6. **Olympics.** Should a 2000 Olympic qualifying event or trials be held by the USOC or USA Volleyball in the United States on the same weekend as a scheduled Event, You may play in the qualifying event or trials without being in breach of this Agreement. In the event that such an event takes place on the same weekend as the scheduled Event is to take place, then StarGames may, in its sole discretion, choose not to hold the scheduled Event or reschedule the Event. If the Event is canceled, there shall be no obligation to pay the prize money referred to above.

7. **Men's Beach Volleyball.** Nothing contained herein shall preclude StarGames from owning, operating, and promoting men's professional beach volleyball events separately or in conjunction (same site and date) with the Event.

8. **Physical Condition.** You represent and warrant that You are and shall continue to be, throughout the Term hereof, in top physical condition such that, barring injury, illness, or disability, You shall be able to compete at a first-class, professional, competitive level and that You will maintain appropriate physical conditioning at all times during the Term of this Agreement. In the event You are unable to compete in the Event because of illness or injury, You agree that You will make yourself available for a medical exam by the StarGames medical staff to determine the extent of said illness and/or injury.

9. **Nonperformance/Default**

a) If the Events(s) is prevented or prohibited from occurring as a result of a force majeure occurrence, including any fire, earthquake, blackout, storm, hurricane, and/or other natural disaster, strike, labor controversy, civil tumult, government ordinance, court order, administrative ruling, law, rebellion, or other similar cause beyond the reasonable control of the parties, so as to render it impossible or impractical to conduct such Event on the date(s) scheduled therefor, then StarGames shall have the right, but not the obligation, to reschedule such Event within a reasonable time period. If StarGames elects not to reschedule or if such Event is not rescheduled within a period of twelve (12) months from the original date of the Event, then such Event shall be canceled and both parties shall be relieved of any obligations to each other hereunder with respect to that Event, but not as to any other Events(s).

b) You agree that Your services and the rights granted to StarGames herein are of a special, unique, unusual, and extraordinary character that gives them particular value, the loss of which cannot be reasonably or adequately compensated in any action at law. A failure to perform by You shall entitle StarGames to injunctive and other equitable relief to secure enforcement of this Agreement, provided, however, that StarGames shall, in addition, retain all of its other rights and remedies under law, none of which are waived and all of which are expressly reserved by StarGames.

c) StarGames shall have the right to terminate, or at StarGames' election, suspend, this Agreement if it determines in its reasonable business judgment that You are unable or have failed or refused to perform fully the services required of You, or if You or Your representative indicates that You intend to fail or refuse to perform fully the services required of You. Without limitation, "failure to perform" shall include the following:

(1) Inadequate preparation for or lack of punctuality in attending the Event(s), exhibitions, or appearances as set forth herein;
(2) Intentional or continual activities (whether by commission or omission) contrary to the proper and reasonable instructions of StarGames in consultation with the Player Council. If StarGames terminates this Agreement pursuant to paragraph 9, StarGames shall be released and discharged from all obligations to You.

d) You shall have the right to terminate this Agreement if one or more of the following occurs:

(1) StarGames fails to pay Player prize money within ten (10) days of said money being earned.
(2) StarGames commits any material breach herein.
(3) Other than as already set forth herein, StarGames fails to conduct the Event(s) set forth above during any Contract Year.

10. **Assumption of Risk.**

You understand and agree that injuries may occur in the course of any athletic activity, and You expressly assume the risk of any injury occurring in the course of Your preparation for or during Your participation in any or all Events(s), exhibitions, or appearances. Except to the extent that any injury to You is caused directly by the gross negligence of StarGames, its employees, agents, and/or assigns (collectively "StarGames Parties"), You hereby agree to release and hold harmless the StarGames Parties from and against any and all costs, claims, expenses, demands, judgments of liability, or actions (including attorneys' fees), arising from or relating to any injury incurred by You in connection with the Event(s).

11. **Media/Marketing.** You agree that StarGames shall own all worldwide media and marketing rights in and to the Event(s) (including international television distribution rights), and Your participation therein for no additional compensation except as set forth herein, in perpetuity in all forms of media now known or hereafter developed or discovered.

12. **Representations and Warranties.** The parties herein represent and warrant that they have the right, power, and ability to enter into and fully perform all terms and conditions of this Agreement, and that neither party has made and/or will make during the term of this Agreement any commitments with or to any third party that will or might conflict or interfere with such party's ability to fully comply with this Agreement.

13. **Indemnification.** You agree to defend, indemnify, and hold harmless StarGames, sponsors, and promoters of the Event(s) and their principals, successors, licensees, assigns, agents, and representatives from and against any and all claims, demands, causes of action, obligations, liabilities, losses, damages, costs, and expenses (including reasonable attorneys' fees and court costs) incurred or sustained by reason of or arising out of any breach or alleged breach of any warranties, representations, or agreements herein made by You or from the use and exploitation by StarGames, sponsors, and/or promoters of the Event(s) of any rights granted herein.

StarGames agrees to defend, indemnify, and hold harmless You and Your successors, assigns, agents, and representatives from any and against any and all claims, demands, causes of action, obligations, liabilities, losses, damages, costs, and expenses (including reasonable attorneys' fees and court costs) incurred or sustained by reason of or arising out of any breach or alleged breach of any warranties, representations, or agreements herein made by StarGames or from the use and exploitation by You of any rights granted herein, except for those claims or damages that are a result of Your own negligence or willful misconduct.

All representations, warranties, and covenants and the indemnity rights of the parties hereunder shall survive the date of this Agreement and the termination of this Agreement.

14. **Independent Contractor.** Your relationship with StarGames shall be that of an independent contractor, and nothing contained in this Agreement shall be construed as establishing an employer/employee relationship, partnership, joint venture, or agency relationship between You and StarGames. Accordingly, there shall be no withholding for tax purposes from any compensation paid or owed to You by StarGames, and You will be responsible for paying all taxes, if any. In addi-

tion, You agree that You will be responsible for Your own health, disability, life, and any other personal insurance. In this connection, You hereby warrant that You have or will have sufficient health insurance in place at the time of the Event(s).

15. **Assignability.** You agree that StarGames shall have the right to sell, exchange, assign, sublicense, or transfer its rights and duties under this Agreement, in whole or in part, to any person and/or entity, including, but not limited to, sponsors, promoters, or agents of the Event(s). Notwithstanding any assignment herein, unless mutually agreed upon, StarGames shall remain liable for all of its obligations contained herein.

16. **Governing Law/Arbitration.** This Agreement shall be construed in accordance with the laws of the state of California. All disputes arising under this Agreement shall be submitted to binding arbitration in the state of California in accordance with the then commercial rules of the American Arbitration Association or those of the JMS/End Dispute. Judgment upon the arbitration award may be entered in any court having jurisdiction therein. Should a judgment arise pursuant to this paragraph, the prevailing party shall be entitled to be reimbursed for legal fees and costs in the event that any litigation or arbitration ensues between the parties.

17. **Entire Agreement.** This Agreement contains the entire agreement of the parties with respect to the subject matter contained herein. This Agreement may be amended or modified only by the mutual agreement of the parties hereto. Any such amendments or modification must be in writing and executed by both parties.

18. **Severability.** In the event that any one or more of the provisions of this Agreement or any work, phrase, clause, sentence, or other portion thereof shall be deemed to be unenforceable for any reason, the parties expressly authorize any court of competent jurisdiction to modify any such provision or portion thereof in order that such provision or portion thereof shall be enforceable by such court to the fullest extent permitted by applicable laws.

On behalf of StarGames, we are looking forward to a great event.

Sincerely,

Tournament Director

ACCEPTED AND AGREED

By: _____   Date:_____
    (Athlete)

By: _____   Date:_____
    StarGames

Television Production Budget Line Items

As discussed in chapter 7, outlined below is a full budget for the television production for an event telecast. Some or all of this will apply to the television show produced for your event.

Truck Cost

Rental $_____

Equipment Rental

Beta recorder $_____

Digi recorder $_____

D2 recorder $_____

Hi 8 rental $_____

Wide-angle lens $_____

Lipstick $_____

Crane $_____

Generator

Generator $_____

Operator $_____

Fuel $_____

Talent Fee

On-air hosts/
    color commentators $_____

Travel $_____

Hotel $_____

Food $_____

Tape Cost

Beta 90s $_____

Beta 60s $_____

Beta 30s $_____

1" $_____

Digi Beta 90 $_____

Digi Beta 60 $_____

Postproduction

Features $_____

Interstitials $_____

Online edit $_____

Hal $_____

Linear on line $_____

Animation/graphics $_____

Music laydown	$_____	Cam4	$_____
Voice-over/narration	$_____	Cam5	$_____
Catering	$_____	Cam6	$_____
		Cam7	$_____
Phones	$_____	Utility 1	$_____
Office	$_____	Utility 2	$_____
Site	$_____	Unit manager	$_____
Shipping	$_____	Crane operator	$_____
		Truck driver	$_____
Crew Cost		Stage manager	$_____
Producer	$_____	Photographer	$_____
Director	$_____	Writer	$_____
Associate director	$_____	**_Crew Hotel_**	$_____
Creative director	$_____	**_Per Diem_**	$_____
Production assistant	$_____	**_Travel_**	
Tape producer	$_____	Site survey	$_____
Feature producer	$_____	Show	$_____
ENG crew	$_____	**_Rental Car_**	$_____
TD	$_____	**_Cabs/Miscellaneous_**	$_____
A1	$_____	**_Music Clearance_**	$_____
A2	$_____	**_Location Expenses_**	
A3	$_____	Scaffolding	$_____
Video 1	$_____	Lights	$_____
Video 2	$_____	Security	$_____
Video 3	$_____	**_Executive Producer Fee_**	$_____
Tape OP1	$_____	**_License/Rights Fee_**	$_____
Tape OP2	$_____		
Cam1	$_____	**Total**	$_____
Cam2	$_____		
Cam3	$_____		

Sports Organizations

T Throughout the book, I have referred to various governing bodies, television networks, and agents. What follows is a list of many of these. Hopefully, this will help you get started in your search for information related to your specific event.

NASCAR
1801 West International Speedway Blvd.
Daytona Beach, FL 32114
904-253-0611

CART
755 West Big Beaver Rd.
Suite 800
Troy, MI 48084
248-362-8800

Major League Baseball
Office of the Commissioner
245 Park Ave.
31st Floor
New York, NY 10167
212-931-7800

National Basketball Association
(NBA and WNBA)
Olympic Tower
645 Fifth Ave.
10th Floor
New York, NY 10022
212-826-7000
212-688-WNBA

National Basketball Players Association
(NBPA)
1700 Broadway
Suite 1400
New York, NY 10019
212-655-0880

United States Tennis Association
1212 Avenue of the Americas
New York, NY 10036
914-696-7000

Association of Tennis Professionals
201 ATP Tour Blvd.
Ponte Vedra Beach, FL 32082
904-285-8000

Women's Tennis Association
133 First St., NE
St. Petersburg, FL 33701
727-895-5000

International Tennis Federation
Paliser Rd.
Barons Court
London, W149
England

PGA Tour
Ponte Verde, FL 32082

Ladies' Professional Golf Association
100 International Golf Dr.
Daytona Beach, FL 32124
904-274-6200

United States Figure Skating Association
20 First St.
Colorado Springs, CO 80906
719-635-5200

Federation Internationale de Football Association
Hitziweg 11
P.O. Box 85
8030 Zurich
Switzerland
41-1-384-9595

Major League Soccer
110 E. 42nd St.
10th Floor
New York, NY 10017
212-450-1200

National Hockey League
1251 Avenue of the Americas
New York, NY 10020
212-789-2000

National Hockey League Players Association
777 Bay St.
Suite 2400
Toronto, Ontario
Canada MSG2C8
416-408-4040

National Football League
280 Park Ave.
New York, NY 10017
212-450-2000

NFL Players Association
2021 L St. NW
Washington, DC 20036
202-463-2200

United States Olympic Committee
4615 Foreign Trade Zone Building
Colorado Springs, CO 80925
719-632-5551

USA Volleyball
715 S. Circle Dr.
Colorado Springs, CO 80910
719-228-6800

USA Swimming
One Olympic Plaza
Colorado Springs, CO 80909
719-578-4578

USA Gymnastics
Pan American Plaza
201 S. Capital Ave.
Suite 300
Indianapolis, IN 46225
317-237-5050

Television Networks

Television can be a critical element in your event mix. A strong presentation at the outset will get the networks' attention. When it comes to sports, these are the most important outlets.

NBC
30 Rockefeller Plaza
New York, NY 10112

CBS
51 W. 52nd St.
New York, NY 10018

ABC
77 W. 66th St.
New York, NY 10023

FOX Broadcasting Network
10210 West Pico Blvd.
Los Angeles, CA 90035

ESPN
ESPN Plaza
Bristol, CT 06010

HBO
1100 Avenue of the Americas
New York, NY 10036

FOX Sports Net
1440 South Sepulveda Blvd.
Los Angeles, CA 90025

Nickelodeon Games & Sports
1515 Broadway
New York, NY 10036

Turner Broadcasting
One CNN Center
P.O. Box 105366
Atlanta, GA 30348

Major Agents and Talent Agencies

TVirtually every professional athlete will have someone who represents his or her business affairs . . . and, if they don't, they should. This impacts event organizers in that you will be dealing directly with these business managers or agents. As a long-time representative, I can tell you that agents have a lot of influence, so get to know them. The major agencies are listed below.

International Management Group
IMG is the oldest and biggest of the agent groups. They represent athletes in virtually every sport. They also produce events and television shows and find sponsors. IMG can be a good ally for you.
One Erieview Plaza
Suite 1300
Cleveland, OH
216-522-1200
www.imgworld.com

Octagon
Perhaps the second-biggest sports marketing agency in the world, Octagon is a full-service sports agency that gets involved in everything from athlete representation to event management to sponsor and television solicitation.
1751 Pinnacle Dr.
#1500
McLean, VA
703-905-3300
www.octagon.com

Artist Management Group
One of the newer agencies, AMG is a growing factor which is run by Hollywood power Michael Ovitz. AMG is a full-service agency but, to my knowledge, does not produce their own events.
9465 Wilshire Blvd.
Beverly Hills, CA 90212
310-860-8000

SFX
SFX (also known now as Clear Channel Sports) is an amalgamation of several of the better-known sports marketing companies, including ProServ. SFX is involved in virtually every aspect of the sports business and represents a vast array of athletes.
888 Seventh Ave.
New York, NY 10036
212-728-2000
www.sfx.com

Creative Artists Agency

CAA has long been one of the most powerful agencies in Hollywood. Their involvement in sports has been limited, but when it comes to television, they are among the best.

9830 Wilshire Blvd.
Beverly Hills, CA 90212
310-288-4545
www.caa.com

William Morris Agency

Another Hollywood talent agency, WMA has branched out a bit more aggressively into sports through client representation, with figure skating being their strongest area.

151 El Camino Dr.
Beverly Hills, CA 90212
310-274-7451
www.wma.com

Endeavor

One of the newer Hollywood agencies, Endeavor is more sports-oriented than some of the others.

9701 Wilshire Blvd.
Beverly Hills, CA 90212
310-248-2000

Index

About the Author

Jerry Solomon is president and CEO of StarGames, a sport and entertainment company located outside of Boston, Massachusetts. He is an adjunct professor of sport management at the University of New Hampshire and is the former president of ProServ, Inc.

Mr. Solomon has 20 years of experience in creating, planning, and managing sporting events, including events on the ATP tennis tour, LPGA golf tour, and AVP beach volleyball tour. He has also developed popular properties in swimming, figure skating, and golf. His clients have included tennis stars Ivan Lendl and Michael Chang, swimmer Janet Evans, gymnast Shannon Miller, volleyball icon Karch Kiraly, and figure skater Nancy Kerrigan.

He was named among the 100 Most Influential People in Sports by *The Sporting News* in 1994 and among the 25 Most Powerful People in Figure Skating by *Figure Skating Magazine* in 1997. Mr. Solomon lives in Lynnfield, Massachusetts, and enjoys spending time with his family, going to movies, and playing golf.